SELLING
Principles, Practice and Management

SELLING
Principles, Practice and Management

Simon Cooper
BA, MCIM, FInstSMM, QTS

PITMAN PUBLISHING

London · Hong Kong · Johannesburg · Melbourne · Singapore · Washington DC

To Ricky, Ben and Louise, with all my love

PITMAN PUBLISHING
128 Long Acre, London WC2E 9AN
Tel: +44 (0)171 447 2000
Fax: +44 (0)171 240 5771

A Division of Pearson Professional Limited

First published in Great Britain in 1997

© Pearson Professional Limited, 1997

The right of Simon Cooper to be identified as Author
of this Work has been asserted by him in accordance
with the Copyright, Designs and Patents Act 1988.

ISBN 0273 623 78 8

British Library Cataloguing in Publication Data
A CIP catalogue record for this book can be obtained from the British Library

1 3 5 7 9 10 8 6 4 2

Typeset by Tek-Art, Croydon, Surrey
Transferred to digital print on demand, 2002
Printed and bound by Antony Rowe Ltd, Eastbourne

*The Publishers' policy is to use paper manufactured
from sustainable forests.*

Contents

Contents

Foreword

Jim Blythe
University of Glamorgan,
Business School

The business environment is growing ever more competitive: if there is room in a given market for four companies, there will be five in it struggling for survival. The sales person is at the forefront of such a cut-throat environment, and the bottom line is that the sales person who looks after the customer's interests most thoroughly will be the one whose company succeeds. It is therefore more important than ever that sales people are trained, and that they understand the theoretical background of what they are doing.

This book, unlike many others, looks at selling as an activity in its own right, with the sales person as an adviser, a negotiator, and a problem-solver who knows that the future lies in looking after the customer as never before. Selling is marketing at the personal level, and the modern sales person has to be able to make decisions about price, product, promotion and place in real time, in front of customers, without the chance to check with the market research findings.

Sales people are not born with these skills, any more than dentists are born with the ability to drill teeth; what Simon Cooper has done in writing this book is to produce, in a user-friendly and interesting way, a tool, which will enable sales people to understand better what selling is all about. Whether you are a rookie, a student on a marketing course, or even an experienced sales person, you should read this book – it has much to tell you about surviving and prospering in a tough profession.

Preface

Who is this book for?

A wide number of audiences are served by the content, depth and approach of this book. Primarily, it is an educational text aimed at the following study programmes:

- A range of undergraduate degree courses in marketing, management and business subjects
- The Chartered Institute of Marketing: Certificate in Selling
- The Chartered Institute of Marketing: Advanced Certificate in Sales Management
- The Institute of Sales & Marketing Management: Foundation Certificate in Sales & Marketing
- The Institute of Sales & Marketing Management: Certificate in Sales & Marketing
- The Institute of Sales & Marketing Management: Diploma in Sales Management
- The London Chamber of Commerce & Industry: Level 3 Selling & Sales Management
- Supporting MBA modules.

Additionally, the book will serve the practitioner and may be used:

- for training and continuous professional development
- as a handbook and reference guide
- by managers and marketers to understand the dynamics of sales force operations
- to inspire strategic thought.

How should the book be used?

A comprehensive and straightforward narrative is supported by a range of interesting material in the form of case studies, activities, tips for success and practitioner's tales. These may be read or used selectively in order to support specific learning objectives, the development of skills or general areas of interest (see Part 5 for an analysis of study techniques).

The book is divided into four core parts, each containing a group of chapters in a logical and progressive order. Tutorial and/or practical activities, tips for success and practitioner's tales are included at appropriate points within the narrative and each chapter concludes with an essay question which is relevant to the typical level of study for the topic. Each part concludes with a case study which addresses the core issues of the preceding chapters, reinforcing the learning experience.

Each chapter is individually referenced to encourage students/practitioners to read around the subject, increasing the depth of understanding and level of appreciation. As appropriate, the text is also internally referenced and, accordingly, the full book may be read in chronological order or, alternatively, only appropriate sections or chapters may be used. Similarly, tutors/trainers may use the activities selectively, in relation to their appropriateness to the programme of study and the specific learning objectives/skill developments which are required.

The fifth and final part of the book contains appendices of supporting material, including study guidance, sources of relevant information for practitioners, and a comprehensive set of role play simulation exercises.

For tutors/trainers adopting the book, a comprehensive Tutor's Guide is available. This includes:

- a tutor-to-tutor narrative by the author
- tips for using and debriefing the tutorial and practical activities
- case study solutions
- an outline of typical essay responses
- notes on applying and using the role play simulations
- a full set of overhead transparencies providing figures and bullet point summaries.

Do you have any comments or further enquiries?

The author has been bold in producing a book which uniquely addresses both academic and practical requirements. He has aimed to bring the two environments closer together, advancing the acceptance of selling as a profession and integrating its function with the customer-based business philosophy. Apart from a career which spans both sectors, the author has spent two years specifically researching this book. The research is far reaching and includes a dedicated survey of over 1000 senior sales force managers in the UK.

Looking ahead to the second edition of the book, the author seeks continually to improve its content and quality. In pursuit of these improvements, the author invites feedback from tutors, trainers, students and practitioners. Additionally, the author invites enquiries on training or education issues relating to sales and marketing. The author may be contacted by writing to the following address:

Simon Cooper Consulting
The Exchange
29 Headswell Avenue
Bournemouth
Dorset
BH10 6JX

Acknowledgements

I would like to thank my wife, Sara, for her continued love and support and apologise to my children for the reduction in 'quality time with Dad' throughout this project. I would also like to thank Mike Dawney for his proof-reading efforts, Pradeep Jethi at Pitman Publishing for his support and guidance and Clive Cooke at Bournemouth & Poole College for inspiring me to take on this project. I also owe a debt of gratitude to the following people:

Academic contributions

Stephen Hogan – University of Brighton
Jim Blythe – University of Glamorgan
Ray Brown – Bournemouth University
Alison Atkinson – University of Brighton

Case study contributions

Paul Kaye – EDI Consultant, Kewill-Xetal Systems Ltd.
Martin Guntrip – Sales Director, Dudley Stationery Ltd.
Ian Blunt – Sales Director, St. Austell Brewery Co. Ltd.
Paul Tansey – Sales & Marketing Director, PSSM Ltd.

Professional contributions

Don Hales
David Maddock – Veitchi (Scotland) Ltd.
Mike Fallon – Sales Director, Cussons (UK) Ltd.
Bill Gallagher – Sales Director, Dictaphone Company Ltd.
Paul Tuley – Sales Director, Geo. W. King Ltd.
Alastair Mowat – Chief Executive, Foxberg Ltd.
JWD Campbell – Director Marketing & Sales, Scottish Mutual Assurance PLC
Moira O'Brien – Managing Director, Hilden Manufacturing Co. Ltd.
Allan Bell – General Manager UK Operations, Scott Bader Co. Ltd.
Trevor Hart – Sales Director UK, Weetabix Ltd.
John Mallon – National Sales Manager, Keystone (UK) Ltd.
PA Massey – Sales Director, Potterton Myson Ltd.
Derek Hurst – National Sales Manager, Versatile Fittings Ltd.
Ken Campbell – Sales Director, Playtex Ltd.
Simon Burrows – Sales & Distribution Director, Rothmans (UK) Ltd.
Lesley Boughton – Commercial Training Manager, Yorkshire Post Newspapers Ltd.
Nick Lloyd – Distribution Sales Director, PSION (UK) PLC
MA Standish – Managing Director, Towry Law Financial Planning Ltd.
Liz Robertson – Marketing Manager, Matrix Workstations
Derek Little – National Account Manager, Baron Meats Ltd.
Tony Dunlop – Sales Director, Green Flag National Breakdown
Eddie Stanton – Sales Director, Baxi Heating Ltd.

Brian Reilly – National Sales Manager, General Accident Life
John Seabrook – Sales Director, Moorlite Electrical Ltd.
GR Sharpe – Marketing Manager, Vickers Shipbuilding & Engineering Ltd.
Louis Eperjesi – Director of Sales, Caradon Mira Ltd.
Glyn Owens – Sales Director, E.R.F. Ltd.
Mike Hodgson – Sales Director, St. Ivel Ltd.
Graham Haigh – National Sales Manager, Vibroplant PLC
James Hurst – Sales Director, Project Office Furniture
Tony Pearce – Sales Director, Birds Eye Wall's Ltd.
Vicki Belcher – Service Brand Manager, Birds Eye Wall's Ltd.
David Heeley – Director of Wholesale, Clarks International
Peter Mosley – Agency Director, Abbey Life Assurance Co. Ltd.
Peter Hetherington – Sales Director, Flexiform Business Furniture Ltd.
John Griffin – Sales Director, S.C. Johnson Wax Ltd.
Robert Vale – Managing Director, Office International Ltd.
Floyd Lewis – Partner, Concept Marketing Consultants
John Appleton – Sales Director, Spire Technology Ltd.
Cal Bailey – Sales Manager, Bailey Telecom Ltd.
Martin Adshead – National Sales Manager, Philips Lighting
Richard Lucas – Director of Sales, Westwind Air Bearings Ltd.
Amanda Webster – Marketing Director, Save & Prosper Group Ltd.
Susan Hilland – Corporate Training (UK) Ltd.
Howard Ward – Training and Development Manager, Institute of Sales and Marketing Management

Part I

The selling environment

Chapter 1

The role of selling within the marketing concept

Learning objectives

By the end of this chapter, you should :

- Understand the principle of the marketing concept

- Appreciate the different types of organisational orientation

- Begin to appreciate the special relationship between selling and marketing

- Understand the key differences between selling and marketing.

1.1 Introduction

Before we can consider current selling practice within the UK, we must first consider the environment in which the modern sales person operates. The dynamic development of marketing has completely changed this environment in recent times and, indeed, it is marketing which provides us with our context.

The book begins in this area and progresses to provide a clear view of the UK selling environment.

Tutorial activity A

Prior to progressing with this chapter, consider what you believe marketing is. Discuss these thoughts with your tutor.

1.2 Definition of marketing

The Chartered Institute of Marketing (CIM) defines marketing as:

> *the management process which identifies, anticipates and supplies customer requirements efficiently and profitably.*

Tutorial activity B

Study the CIM definition of marketing and highlight four words which you feel are the most important. Review these conclusions once you have studied the following analysis of the CIM definition.

There are other valid definitions of marketing but, for the purposes of this text, the CIM definition is totally adequate.

Marketing is concerned with looking at the whole business from the customers' point of view. It is from this basis that the business will succeed. In the first instance, this involves analysing who the customers are and what needs and desires they have. From this, the marketer is concerned with planning how best to meet these requirements, given the resources and objectives of the organisation. Marketing plans are then implemented and controlled/managed.

From this, it is clear that marketing is concerned with both strategic (long-term) and operational (short-term) planning and management. The objectives of virtually all commercial organisations will focus primarily on profitability and, further, all organisations should be concerned with operating efficiently. Indeed, lack of efficiency will invariably impair the ability of the organisation to satisfy the requirements of the customer.

In the dynamic business environment of the 1990s, customer requirements are constantly changing. Anticipating these changes and taking the appropriate course of action is essential. Because of this, it is often said that marketing is concerned with *the management of change*. In many respects, this is a natural development of our original definition.

Tip for success

Change is the one constant in life!

Standing still will invariably result in business failure. The successful marketer recognises this and not only manages change but also welcomes it as a potential opportunity.

To regard marketing as a function or department within an organisation is too narrow a view. It is a total management philosophy which runs throughout the organisation. This philosophy must be driven from the very top in that the strategic objectives will recognise that the success of the business will only come from the identification and satisfaction of customer requirements.

The presence of a marketing department in itself does not confirm that an organisation has a marketing philosophy. Such a philosophy can only be facilitated by a marketing function. Indeed, many smaller businesses have a marketing or customer approach without a specific marketing department.

1.3 Evolution of the marketing concept

In business terms, marketing is a relatively new concept. Prior to the development of this concept, business tended to be product based rather than customer based. That is, organisations were concerned with producing products which they perceived as being good and then persuading or encouraging customers to buy them.

Such a product-orientated approach to business has two distinct variations: production-driven and sales-driven. The former is concerned with reducing costs to their lowest possible level on the basis that customers are price sensitive rather than being appreciative of value for money. In competitive markets, it is unlikely that this approach will be successful in the long-term. In order to compete, there is a need for the organisation to persuade customers to buy its product. Sales-driven business activity revolves around aggressive personal selling activity, often supported by equally aggressive promotional campaigns such as advertising and sales promotions or discounting.

The late 1950s/early 1960s saw the introduction and development of a customer-orientated approach to business in the US. This involved producing products which customers, rather than the organisation, perceived as being good. This is referred to as the evolution of the marketing concept. The concept has travelled over the Atlantic to the UK, and indeed throughout the developed world.

A summary of the evolution of the marketing concept is shown in Figure 1.1.

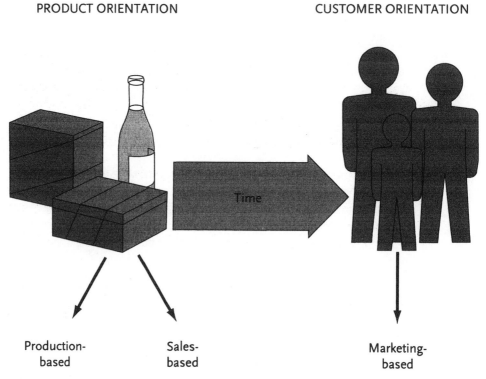

Fig. 1.1 *Evolution of the marketing concept*

From this, it is important to make some further observations. First, if an established organisation is looking to move from a sales-based approach to a marketing one, it will take time to make the transition. Strategically, the organisation will need to review its objectives and this can be accomplished

Tutorial activity C

Identify three organisations which you believe take a customer/marketing approach to business and one organisation which has a product/sales approach. Give reasons for your selections and discuss these conclusions with your tutor.

Extension: Considering the product/sales-orientated organisation selected above, what changes will it need to make if it is to make the transition to customer/marketing orientation? Discuss these conclusions with your tutor.

relatively instantly. However, achieving these objectives will involve a major overhaul of the organisation's operation which can only be accomplished over a period of time. On the other hand, new and developing organisations can adopt a customer approach with greater ease.

No doubt it was easier to identify the marketing-orientated organisations during Tutorial activity C than the sales-orientated one. This is because the majority of larger British businesses are now adopting a customer approach, although some are still in the process of transition. Nonetheless, even given the success of marketing in recent years, some businesses still adopt a sales orientation. This tends to occur where there are very large markets and virtually whole industries remain static in their business orientation, or with some smaller businesses, where the management does not fully appreciate the benefits which can be derived from a customer orientation.

In order to establish the role of selling in either form of business orientation, we can view a basic organisational structure by operational function. This is shown in Figures 1.2 and 1.3. However, it should be noted that these structures are not comprehensive nor are they the only possibilities. They merely provide us with an opportunity to understand the operational nature of the two business orientations and help us to begin to understand the relationship between sales and marketing.

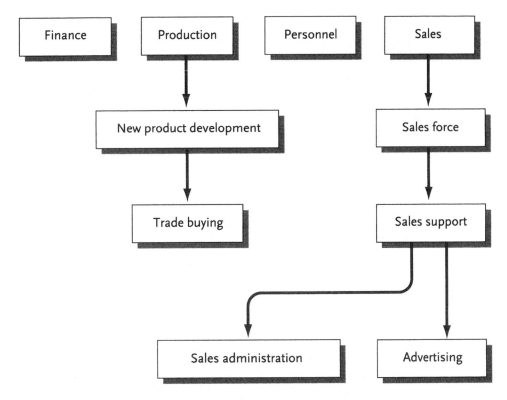

Fig. 1.2 *Organisational structure of sales orientation*

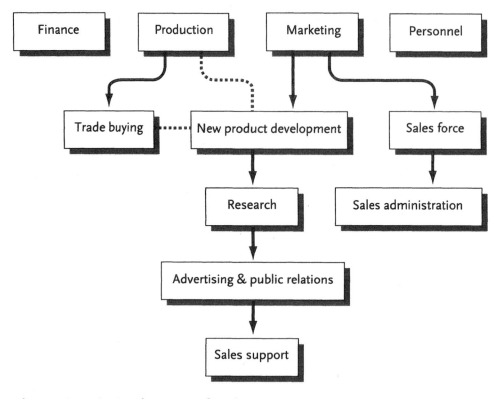

Fig. 1.3 *Organisational structure of marketing orientation*

Further consideration of these structures points towards some major and fundamental differences:

1 The wider marketing operation needs to control all promotional activities. This enables a co-ordinated approach with increased efficiency being the net effect, often involving a degree of interdependency.
2 Sales support is controlled by the marketing operation as opposed to the sales function. In fact, sales support is not necessarily the term which would be used in practice as it takes on a much wider role. This may include an involvement in co-ordinating the promotional activities, customer service, point-of-sale promotional considerations, secondary data application and possibly an involvement in direct marketing activities.
3 Research becomes a key function, providing the foundation for all marketing activity.
4 New product development is controlled by the marketing operation. However, there is a shared responsibility with production for this function, as that is where the technical expertise will be. The key to this relationship is that the marketing operation will make the final decision as to whether or not a new product is added to the organisation's range. Further consideration is given to this aspect in the next chapter.

1.4 Definition of selling

In its purest form, selling can be described as:

> *a personal exchange between a host organisation and a potential purchaser of its product/service which results in a business transaction.*

However, this is too simplistic a viewpoint. As we shall see later in this book, a sales person achieves their goal of completing a business transaction through first understanding the needs, desires or problems of the potential buyer and then demonstrating how their product/service can be matched to these, providing satisfaction by benefit or solution. In this, the product/service is accorded value in the eyes of the buyer for which they are prepared to pay a fiscal sum. Further, the term 'selling' as used in this text refers to personal selling which intimates a transaction between two people.

Therefore, perhaps selling can be more accurately described as:

> *a function which is concerned with identifying the specific needs, desires and problems of individual customers and providing satisfaction of these through benefit or solution in order to facilitate profitable business transactions.*

Tutorial activity D

Compare the above description of selling with the CIM definition of marketing discussed earlier in this chapter. What are the similarities? What are the differences? Discuss these conclusions with your tutor.

1.5 The relationship between selling and marketing

Sales orientation is a management approach to business, whereas personal selling is a function within the organisation. As we have seen, the personal selling function can be used in both sales- and marketing-orientated businesses. Although many aspects of selling covered in this book apply independently, the author's intention is to consider selling within the context of marketing orientation. Therefore, it is imperative to analyse the relationship between the two.

Marketing holds a strategic management role whilst also being concerned with a range of operational functions. Selling is just one of these functions. Indeed, it is a singular aspect of a range of promotional tools available to the marketer. The decision to use selling as a promotional tool is a strategic one on behalf of the marketer. However, once selected, selling has a vital role to play in the application of an organisation's promotional activities.

The employment of a sales force can represent a substantial investment on behalf of the organisation. It is therefore essential to ensure efficient use of it and profitable return from it. This involves clearly identifying objectives and managing the selling function in conjunction with other promotional activities to ensure maximum effect.

However, to regard selling as solely another promotional tool is insufficient. In many respects selling and marketing share the same goals. They are both concerned with identifying and satisfying customer needs on a profitable basis. The difference lies in the scale. Marketing is concerned with a wide range of customers and selling with the individual customer. Necessarily, the identification and satisfaction of customers and their needs on a mass scale must take on a strategic role as the implications are far reaching and affect many, if not all, areas of the organisation.

Additionally, there is an operational side of marketing and, in this respect, the sales person can be regarded as a micro-marketer. By understanding and applying marketing principles on an operational level, the sales person is able to extend the marketing effort to the 'front line' by identifying and interacting with customers on a personal basis. For this to be effective in practice, there must be mutual appreciation and communication between the two.

A practitioner's tale

"Marketing is about the whole war. It is run by the Commander-in-Chief, who must consider all forces at his disposal: army, air force and navy. A complete strategy must be formulated to win the war. In implementing the strategy, all operational forces will be employed. Ultimately battles are won by the front line foot soldiers – the Sales Force. They cannot do it alone and will not win the war by themselves, but few battles can be won without them.

The chain of command dictates that the Foot Soldier may never meet the Commander-in-Chief but neither will be effective without the other and both must appreciate the interdependency which they share."

The relationship between selling and marketing, as discussed in this chapter, varies from a traditional and widely accepted view of the relationship as put forward by Levitt[1]. He generally did not make the distinction between personal selling and sales orientation; indeed he predicted that, through marketing, selling would become obsolete. This has not been the case and selling performs a major and, in some cases, primary role within the wider application of marketing. This said, it is important for sales people to appreciate the concept of marketing, as it provides the context for modern day practice.

1.6 Summary

In order to study modern day selling it is important to appreciate the environment in which sales people work. Increasingly, the context of this environment relates to the marketing principle which is being adopted by many organisations. However, it is also important to appreciate that some organisations still adopt a sales orientation.

Many aspects covered in this book are applicable to the selling function, regardless of organisational orientation. Where appropriate, the text assumes the selling function to be operating under the wider umbrella of marketing.

This chapter has defined both selling and marketing, and has introduced the special nature of their relationship. This special relationship is continuously examined throughout the text. The following chapter considers the basics of marketing, and the sales environment is then more specifically explored in the remainder of this first part.

Essay question

Many people believe that sales and marketing are essentially the same thing. In your own words, discuss this belief in terms of the similarities and differences, drawing an appropriate conclusion.

Reference

1 Levitt T. (1960), *Marketing Myopia*, Harvard Business Review.

Further reading

Adcock, D., Bradfield, R., Halborg, A. and Ross, C. (1995), *Marketing: Principles and Practice* (2nd edn), Pitman Publishing, Chapters 1 & 2.

Lancaster, G. and Jobber, D. (1964), *Selling and Sales Management* (3rd edn), Pitman Publishing, Chapter 1.

Chapter 2   # Tools of marketing

Learning objectives

By the end of this chapter, you should :

- Be aware of the key tools and scope of marketing within the customer-orientated organisation

- Have an appreciation for market segmentation and targeting

- Appreciate the broad area of marketing research and the role of sales research within it

- Be aware of the components of the marketing mix and appreciate their combined function

- Understand the additional considerations required for marketing a service

- Appreciate the extended area of customer care

- Have an understanding of the relationship between customer care and service marketing

- Have a critical understanding of the roles which selling and sales management fulfil within the marketing-driven organisation.

2.1 Introduction

Within some organisations, the selling function operates as the so-called 'marketing' arm of the organisation. In fact, the true marketing-driven firm, which is focused totally on managing and developing its business through satisfying the needs of its customers, incorporates much more in its marketing operation than solely selling the product.

This principle was established in the preceding chapter when we looked at both the *evolution of the marketing concept* and the *relationship between selling and marketing*. In this chapter, the overriding principle established previously will be further reinforced. It is only by fully appreciating the role and scope of marketing that one will develop a critical understanding of the roles which selling and sales management have to fulfil.

The space given in this book to the practice of marketing is necessarily limited. As such, the coverage of the subject in this chapter should only be regarded as an outline. For the student studying selling and sales management as part of a wider marketing course, a more detailed text will be required. However, for the practitioner or student purely concerned with the selling and sales management specialisations, this chapter will provide a comprehensive overview of the marketing operation, enabling the sales environment to be considered in context.

So, what are the *tools of marketing?*

Traditionally, the tools of marketing have been considered to be: *marketing research, market segmentation and targeting,* and *management of the marketing mix* (the 4 Ps). More recently, the marketing mix has been extended to cover the additional requirements of marketing a *service* (the 7 Ps). Further, there has been the relatively modern approach towards total quality management (TQM), including the introduction of *customer care* programmes. Indeed, the successful impact of these programmes has been consistent with the rapid movement towards a marketing (or customer) orientation from an increasing number of British companies.

Each of the key tools of marketing will now be considered.

2.2 Market segmentation and targeting

Virtually no commercial organisation can regard the whole population as its *market*. Therefore, it is necessary for the marketer to understand precisely which people or businesses are in its market. This involves breaking the whole population down into manageable *market segments*. This principle is shown in Figure 2.1.

In order for a particular segment of the market to be manageable (or valid) in marketing terms, there must be a positive response to each of these three questions:

1 Can the chosen segment be identified and accessed?
2 Can information about the segment be obtained cost-effectively?
3 Is the segment of the right size to be considered, in relation to our resources and objectives?

Assuming a chosen segment is valid, the segmentation process can be regarded as:

Identify a market segment
Research the segment
Adjust its parameters
Target the segment for marketing purposes.

Before we consider specific segmentation systems, it is useful to clarify two terms frequently used during market segmentation:

- **Niche market:** a small or narrow market segment (see Figure 2.1)
- **Mass market:** a very large market segment or a wide collection of smaller segments (see Figure 2.1).

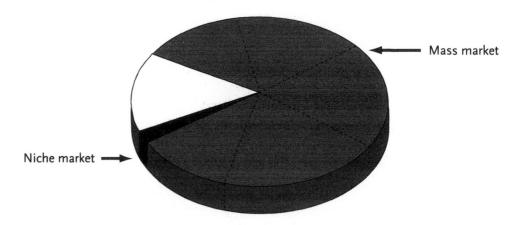

Fig. 2.1 *Segmenting a market*

Having considered market segmentation in general terms, we can now look specifically at the common methods of segmentation. To do this, domestic and commercial markets need to be regarded separately:

Domestic markets

There are two types of data which can be collected: *quantitative data* and *qualitative data*. Commonly, they can be collected demographically and psychographically, respectively.

Demographics involves studying the population and trends in terms of age, income, size, geographic distribution, ethnicity, sex, family make-up, social breakdown, educational breakdown and economic breakdown. There are various public and private sources for gathering demographic data and these are considered in more detail in Part V of this book.

Psychographics involves a more detailed consideration of small samples of the population in relation to lifestyles, opinions, motives and culture. Although demographic data is commonly obtained 'second hand', accurate psychographic data is much harder to obtain in this way. As a result, collection of this data usually entails 'first hand' detailed surveys of small samples of the population, the findings of which can then be combined with demographic data, analysed and applied to wider market segments to provide us with *market information*. This is summarised in Figure 2.2.

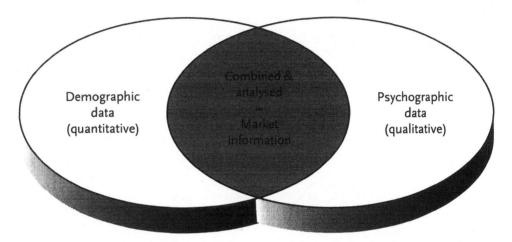

Fig. 2.2 *The relationship between data and market information*

Commercial markets

In many respects, segmenting a commercial market is more straightforward than segmenting domestic markets. There is a large amount of specific data available on many organisations and this is again considered in more detail in Part V of this book. Additionally, there are specific parameters which can be applied to commercial organisations. The most commonly applied parameters are:

- location
- size (e.g. turnover, number of employees)
- usage rates (e.g. raw materials, components)
- industry type/classification.

Given that commercial markets can be more effectively segmented, it follows that targeting these markets will be more accurate. This has specific implications for the sales person, as effective segmentation and targeting will increase the efficiency of the selling function.

Consequently, it is true that commercial selling is often 'less of a numbers game' than selling into domestic markets. In fairness, some organisations have developed very effective segmentation systems for domestic markets but this must be considered in perspective, as a much larger number of organisations are effective in segmenting commercial markets. Indeed, for the sales person working without the benefit of a wider marketing operation, commercial organisations will be far easier to identify and target than the private individual.

2.3 Marketing research

Tutorial activity A

What is the overriding purpose of marketing research? As you read through this section, consider this question. Compare your conclusions with the *Debrief* at the end of the section.

Marketing research can be broken down into a number of component parts, as shown in Figure 2.3.

Fig. 2.3 *The composition of marketing research*

Tutorial activity B

Using the summary of marketing research composition in Figure 2.3, build a list of possible research objectives under each of the component headings. Amend your list as you read through the following narrative and discuss the final conclusions with your tutor.

Market research

Not to be confused with the wider term of marketing research, market research is, quite simply, research which looks into the market place itself. It will include factors such as:

- estimates of market size and potential
- identification of key market characteristics and segments
- forecasting of market trends
- gathering information on customers (and potential customers)
- gathering information on competitors.

As we shall see, market research does cross over with other aspects of marketing research and because of this the terms are often confused. For example, gathering information on customers may include questions such as Where do they buy our product? (place), How much will they pay for our product? (price), in addition to more general considerations such as Who are they? What are their lifestyles? What motivates them? – which are all part of market research.

Pricing research

Here, we are primarily concerned with the relationship between the price of the product and customer demand. This relates to both new products and existing products. The key is to establish the right price for the product(s) in relation to the other marketing mix elements in the context of the overall marketing objective, that is the optimum price.

In order to arrive at an optimum price we need to establish, firstly how many customers are prepared to pay price X, price Y, and so on. Additionally, we need to be aware of the estimated costs at various levels of production and distribution together with the communication costs of achieving various levels of sales. These may be the sales force costs and/or advertising costs and so on. Finally, we can draw on our market research to establish the prices being charged by competitors.

Product research and development (R&D)

For many organisations, the main thrust of their research is developing 'good products'. In marketing-orientated organisations, the emphasis is on developing the right products in relation to customer requirements and the other aspects of the marketing mix. Therefore, we are not purely concerned with product R&D alone but rather in combination with the other components of marketing research. Although sometimes considered as a separate item in its own right, packaging research can also be included in product R&D.

Specifically, product research and development will involve:

- The generation of new ideas or concepts
- Testing these ideas in relation to production capability, resources and the market

- Developing a prototype or sample of the product
- Testing the product prototype/sample
- Test marketing the product
- Making product adjustments before launching the product on a mass scale.

Distribution research

Here, we are concerned with three main areas:

1 **Warehouse research:** How much warehousing space is required? Where should warehouses be located in terms of customer location and transportation logistics?

2 **Transportation research:** What is the most efficient way to transport our products to our customers? This has become more and more important with the growth of global marketing, and this area of research will also be used to support strategic decisions to develop overseas production capability.

3 **Retail outlet research:** This is particularly relevant when considering consumer marketing and will include factors such as the location of competitors, a profile of the neighbourhood, pedestrianisation, and so on.

Communications research

Here we are concerned with four main areas:

1 **Effectiveness research:** This involves predicting and measuring the effectiveness of the various aspects of the promotional mix. For example, with advertising we may test name awareness or buying intentions prior to the campaign and then again after the campaign. Predicting the effectiveness of a campaign becomes more difficult when there is no previous experience of a particular type of promotion.

2 **Media selection research:** Past experience may provide much useful information in this respect. Additionally, the marketer will be able to collect media distribution information (usually directly from the media source) such as how many copies are sold, shelf life of the publication, typically how many people read each copy sold and the target audience(s) of the publication. This is often how advertising agencies will provide additional benefit as they will constantly update this information and be aware of the appropriate media source for achieving a particular promotional objective.

3 **Copy testing:** This involves researching the creative and presentational aspects of marketing communications. For example, a pilot TV advertisement may be shown to a selected audience prior to final approval.

4 **Sales force effectiveness:** As opposed to the general consideration of effectiveness research discussed above, we are concerned here specifically with the sales force of an organisation. Whereas an organisation may have specific advertising campaigns, public relations campaigns or promotional campaigns using various incentives, the sales force of an organisation is a

constant factor. The use of a sales force by an organisation represents a substantial financial investment and, therefore, it makes sense to ensure it operates at optimum efficiency. This can include territory planning by geographical location, product type or customer type; profiling sales personnel in relation to customer and product considerations; and performance analysis.

Sales research

This area is double sided. First, it involves research conducted by or specifically on behalf of the sales force, with the overriding objective of achieving efficient performance (i.e. an increase in profitable sales). Second, the sales force can provide a valuable input into the marketing research process by gathering 'first hand' or primary feedback from customers and potential customers. Given this, it is imperative that an effective communication channel is established between the sales force and the personnel involved with marketing research.

A practitioner's tale

"In my experience, the lack of an effective communication channel between the 'front line' and 'HQ' is a common failing within industry. Many market researchers rely primarily on remote contact with customers, such as mailed questionnaires, and pay too little attention to the potential information which is held by the sales force. In fairness to market researchers, the problem does not lie solely with them. Feedback from the sales force is likely to be subjective or, at the very least, selective. Therefore, this source of information cannot be totally reliable. However, combined with other data and information, it can be very valuable.

How many Commanders-in-Chief can make good decisions without knowing exactly what is going on at the battle front?"

Having looked at the various components of marketing research, there remain a number of important additional considerations.

Marketing research planning

When conducting research within the marketing function, it is important that the research is properly focused in order that results can be optimised. This is achieved through planning. A simple formula for remembering the planning process in marketing research comes from the mnemonic OPIR:

Objective: Set a clear *objective* for the research.
Plan: Develop a *plan* or method which will achieve the objective(s).
Implement: The plan needs to be put into action or *implemented*.
Report: Finally, the data collected needs to be analysed, interpreted and *reported*.

Primary (field) and secondary (desk) research

There are many methods of conducting marketing research. The various methods can be broken down into two main categories:

1 **Primary Research:** This is data collected first hand specifically for the research purpose. It is sometimes referred to as field research, being an active exercise. Primary research will take the form of surveys (both remote and personal interviews), observation and experimentation. If carried out objectively, the information gathered through primary research can be very valuable, but against this it can also be very costly.

Tip for success

Talk to the people!

One aspect of marketing research which is rarely considered in marketing text books, with the notable exception of Tom Peters', is perhaps the most significant of all. It involves senior managers, such as the marketing director or the chief executive, going out into the field themselves. This may involve meeting with members of the sales force, the company's customers or even trialing a new product personally. Such an exercise is non-scientific in nature with many potential pitfalls and flaws. However, the practice is widespread among large organisations in the US and it can provide a remote decision maker with valuable first-hand feedback. Given the overriding objective of any marketing research, this method can be very useful with the additional benefit of being very inexpensive.

2 **Secondary research:** This involves collecting data available from other or existing sources and analysing it in such a way as to produce useful information. It is sometimes referred to as desk research, being a more passive exercise of gathering and analysing second-hand data. The data can come from either:

- *Internal sources* such as sales force statistics, financial statistics and customer databases, or
- *External sources* including government statistics, data available from specialist marketing research organisations, specialist departments within, say, advertising agencies; or secondary data held by other organisations such as trade associations and trade directories.

Data and information

The distinction is often made when considering marketing research between the terms 'data' and 'information'. Marketing decisions are based on information. The more reliable the information, the greater the aid to decision making. From the marketer's perspective, we have seen how data can be collected from a number of sources. However, it is only when this data is sorted and analysed that it provides the marketer with information. It could be said that *data collection and analysis is the process through which information is obtained.*

In-house versus consultancies

Lancaster and Massingham[2] state that:

> Research should be conducted only when it is expected that the value of information to be obtained will be greater than the cost of obtaining it

This is a very important point because one of the greatest barriers to marketing research is cost. That is, the cost-effectiveness of conducting marketing research needs to be justified. Smaller organisations will rarely have the luxury of their own marketing research department.

Larger organisations will have more choice and it is common for an organisation to have both its own department and the option to use an external consultancy on occasion. For example, few organisations would be able to justify employing a permanent team of field researchers, and so they may elect to use an external consultancy for conducting a one-off field research project. On the other hand, a small team of desk researchers can produce an ongoing stream of valuable information by collecting, sorting and analysing secondary data. Some of this data may be collected from external consultancies and sources, and some from internal sources, but sorted and analysed by the in-house team.

The macro-environment

Marketing research objectives will specifically relate to the market place, elements of the marketing mix or, more often, a combination of these. Additionally, the marketer will need to be aware of issues and changes in the wider environment. These will include Social, Legal, Economic, Political and Technological considerations, summarised by the mnemonic **SLEPT**. The focus of the marketing research function should be sufficiently broad to encompass relative aspects of this macro-environment.

Information technology

We now live in the age of information technology. It is no coincidence that the advancement of information technology has been accompanied by the dynamic development of the marketing function. The principles of marketing remain unchanged but the implementation of these principles is greatly enhanced by the use of information technology. Nowhere is this more true than in the implementation of marketing research. There is now a vast bank of data held by various organisations on computer. Sophisticated databases enable this data to be both analysed and interfaced with data from other sources. Additionally, internal data, such as customer records, can now be stored and analysed in a very efficient and beneficial way. Future advances in technology and its application are likely to continue to enhance the marketing research function in the provision of reliable information.

Debrief

The overriding objective of marketing research is to aid management decision-making. It achieves this by producing reliable information. The cost of obtaining reliable information must be balanced against the benefit which will be derived from it. Effective research will be carefully planned and skilfully implemented to achieve specific objectives, based on the decision(s) which need to be made.

2.4 The marketing mix

The principle of the marketing mix is one of the most fundamental in modern day marketing. It consists of the so-called 4 Ps: *Price, Product, Place* and *Promotion*. Collectively, these four elements form a 'mix of ingredients'. Each element is interdependent and the marketer is concerned with combining and managing them effectively.

In order successfully to combine and manage the marketing mix elements, decisions will need to be based around the characteristics of targeted segments and accurate marketing research information. As we have seen, much, if not all, of marketing research is focused on aiding these decisions.

There is a great deal for the marketer to consider when making decisions relating to the marketing mix, as each element has a number of component parts and, therefore, a wide number of possible combinations. Ultimately, the marketing mix must be managed with a specific view to achieving corporate objectives. Inevitably, this will reduce the number of alternatives, and yet the skill of successfully blending the marketing mix elements and, within this, successfully mixing their components, is one which the marketer continually strives to perfect.

Figure 2.4 summarises the key components of each marketing mix element. These components are then considered in more detail.

Tip for success

Achieve the optimum price!

A number of inputs are required in order to ascertain the optimum price of a product. Cost is only one of these factors, in that it confirms the minimum price which can be charged. It may be possible to achieve a higher price by considering market and competitive factors or, alternatively, these additional inputs to the pricing decision may question the feasibility of the product.

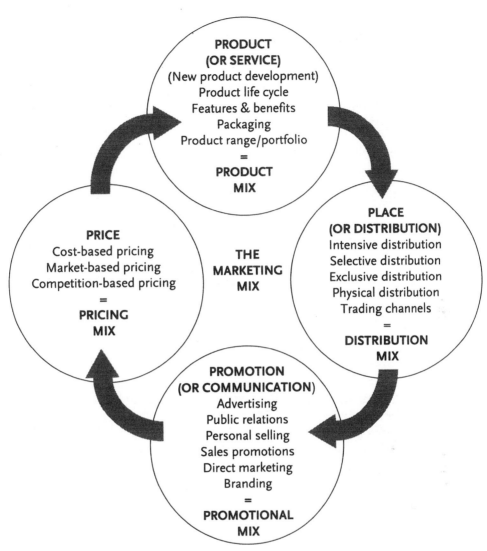

Fig. 2.4 *Summary of the marketing mix components*

Price

As Figure 2.4 shows, there are three main areas to consider when pricing a product or, more likely, a product line: the costs, the market and the competition.

1 **Cost-based pricing:** There are several methods of cost-based pricing, consideration of which goes beyond the scope of this text. Whatever method is used, the principle remains that costs must be considered when pricing a product. This is nothing new. Any accountant, if not common sense, will confirm the point. Where marketing differs from traditional business practice is that costs are only one of three key areas which need to be addressed.

2 **Market-based pricing:** In its purest form, market-based pricing dictates that a product is worth whatever someone is prepared to pay for it. This is certainly the case when a unique item is sold by auction. However, most organisations are concerned with selling their products in volume. Here, the marketer is not interested in what the highest bidder will pay but rather, how many people will buy at various prices. The most common methods of market-based pricing are:

- *Market penetration:* low price (and profit) per unit, high sales volume (i.e. mass market)
- *Market skimming:* high price (and profit) per unit, low sales volume (i.e. exclusive or niche market)
- *Differential pricing:* a different price for different customers, usually by market segments.

3 **Competition-based pricing:** One of the greatest influences on pricing decisions is concerned with competitor activity. When a number of organisations are competing for a share of the same market segment, setting a competitive price is imperative. This does not mean that the price should be set at the lowest in the market. Indeed, only one organisation can have the cheapest product, the rest must compete on the basis of *value.* It is by being aware of competitor products and prices that the marketer can arrive at a price which offers good value to its customers. At the other end of the spectrum, where there are few or no competitors, the marketer can achieve a higher price but must still offer customers good value if new or existing competitors are to be prevented from 'stealing' a share of the market.

Product

There are many issues which concern the marketer with regard to the product or product range of the organisation. Some of the most important decisions which need to be made revolve around the product. The key areas of consideration are outlined below:

(New) product development

The needs of customers are constantly changing. To meet these changing needs, new and existing products need to be continually developed. This area was discussed in more detail in the previous section.

Features and benefits

Product features and their related benefits are a fundamental marketing consideration. In Chapter 6, we will look at this area in more detail. However, there are differences between how a marketer and a sales person should handle features and benefits.

Every product has a variety of features. For example, a car may have an ashtray and a seven-year corrosion warranty. Both of these are features of the product.

However, they will only be of benefit if the customer needs them. If they do not smoke, they are unlikely to have a need for the ashtray. If they are only planning on keeping the car for one or two years, they will have little need for the corrosion warranty.

In a personal selling situation, needs can be specifically identified, e.g. 'Do you smoke?', 'For how long are you planning to keep the car?' The sales person can then *match* features to the needs of the customer and demonstrate how the specific feature(s) will benefit the customer. Those features which are of little or no interest to the customer can be disregarded.

The marketer does not have this luxury of being able to identify specific needs of individual customers. The marketeer is concerned with *satisfying the general needs of a large number of customers* in any targeted market segment. For example, if an organisation were targeting the early and newly retired market for its range of cars, then offering a seven-year corrosion warranty is likely to be of general benefit to a substantial number of customers in that segment.

Packaging

On occasion, packaging has been referred to as the fifth P of the marketing mix. Although not commonly used in current marketing theory, this reference certainly highlights packaging as a key ingredient of the marketing mix. It can be a product feature, affect its cost, be used as a promotional aid and be vital with regard to transportation and storage of the product.

Branding

The branding of a product or range of products is a major area of modern marketing promotion. Clustering products together under a single brand name enables different products in a range to benefit from the success of the others. Additionally, similar products can be branded separately to appeal to different segments of the market. For example, how many brands of washing powder are available in our shops? Our TV screens show a constant stream of washing powder advertisements and yet virtually all of the well-known brands are produced by just two companies.

Product life cycle (PLC)

Just as with humans, every product has a life cycle. It will be 'born' and it will 'die'. The marketer will want to predict and influence the life cycle of their product. There are four main stages of the PLC: *introduction* (birth), *growth, maturity* and *decline*. The 'death' of the product is uncertain. Hopefully it will die at the end of its life when it is in deep decline. (This latter (fifth) stage of the PLC is sometimes referred to as *senility*.) However, some products die earlier than this, potentially at any stage of the PLC, but with the product introduction stage being the most vulnerable, followed by growth and then maturity. There is a further embryonic stage of the PLC, that of *development*. If considered part of the PLC, this is the most vulnerable stage of all, as many ideas never reach the stage of being introduced to the market.

Marketing texts refer to a generic PLC which is shown in Figure 2.5. This perhaps is the ideal shape for a PLC 'curve' and one which many marketers will strive to achieve for their products. A healthy introduction, followed by a period of rapid growth, a long period of (profitable) maturity and, finally, a period of gradual decline before being withdrawn from the market. In reality, there are a wide number of variations of this generic PLC model, some of which arise as a result of *proactive* marketing and others which cause the marketer to *react* to external and market influences.

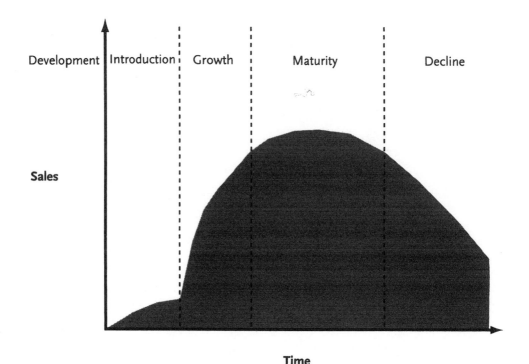

Fig. 2.5 *The generic product life cycle (PLC) curve*

Place (or distribution)

The third aspect of the marketing mix is commonly referred to as *place*. However, this word is a little narrow in description. In fact, *distribution* is a more appropriate term, as we are concerned with having:

THE RIGHT PRODUCT, IN
THE RIGHT PLACE, AT
THE RIGHT TIME, IN
THE RIGHT QUANTITY.

This is achieved through *channels of distribution*, which can also be referred to as *trading channels* or *marketing channels*. The basic channels are summarised in Figure 2.6.

CONSUMER MARKET

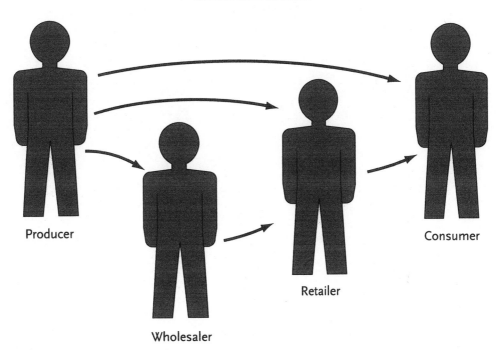

INDUSTRIAL MARKETS

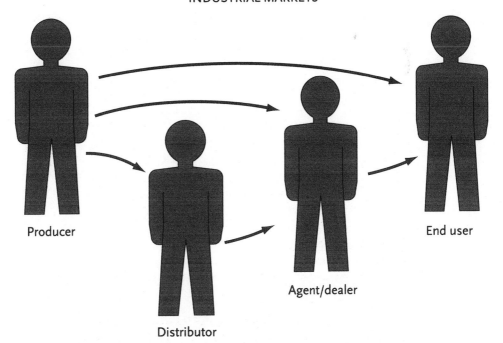

Fig. 2.6 *The basic trading channels*

It must be stressed that these are only the basic trading channels. In the following chapter, there is a much wider consideration of this area, including some important variations.

Tutorial activity C

What influences an organisation in its choice of trading channel?

Consider this question and compare your answers with the author's conclusions in Chapter 3.

At this juncture, it is appropriate to consider one of the influences on an organisation, namely the intensity with which the product needs to be distributed. Or rather, how convenient does it need to be for the customer to purchase the product?

1 **Intensive distribution:** This occurs where an organisation identifies that it needs to distribute its product via a large number of outlets. Primarily, this occurs with Fast Moving Consumer Goods (FMCG). For example, if a consumer goes to a newsagent intending to buy chocolate bar X and the newsagent does not have any, it is unlikely that the consumer will travel to an alternative outlet to find chocolate bar X. They will either buy an alternative chocolate bar or make no purchase at all. The organisation which produces chocolate bar X would want to avoid this situation and, therefore, will try to ensure that as many outlets as possible stock chocolate bar X, i.e. intensive distribution.

2 **Selective distribution:** This occurs where an organisation requires certain criteria of an outlet. For example, a manufacturer of satellite TV systems may require that outlets supplying its product employ engineers who can install and maintain the system. Not all outlets could meet this criterion, and therefore we have selective distribution.

3 **Exclusive distribution:** In this situation, an organisation decides that the needs of the final customers are best supplied by having a sole outlet for its products. The chosen outlet will have an *exclusive territory* for selling the product, which is invariably a contractual arrangement. An example of this occurs with BMW cars.

Tutorial activity D

For each of these three types of distribution, there are varying degrees of interrelationship between the intermediary and producer/manufacturer, as perceived by the final customer. Consider or research this issue and refer your findings to your tutor.

4 **Physical distribution**: Clearly, the physical product needs to be distribut‿ to the customer. In the past, this would have been a warehousing and transportation function and little attention would have been applied to it in a marketing text.

For years sales people have been concerned with the problems of deliveries not being made on time, resulting in lost sales. The evolution of organisations towards a customer orientation has brought this area into a new domain. We now see organisations integrating this aspect of their business into the total marketing effort, if not under the direct control of the marketing department, certainly influenced by it. Adopting this integrated approach to physical distribution of the product is known as *marketing logistics*.

Managing marketing logistics effectively can provide an organisation with substantial cost savings. Perhaps more importantly, it can also give the organisation a competitive advantage. This is particularly true within the industrial market place, where delivery times and service will often influence present and future buying decisions. In recent years, this has been highlighted with the emergence of just-in-time (JIT) purchasing which commands and depends on efficient physical distribution.

Promotion (communication)

The fourth and final aspect of the marketing mix is promotion. This is sometimes known as *marketing communications*, although this term implies that the marketer is concerned only with communicating outwards towards the customer. However, effective marketing operation involves communicating with the customer in two directions: transmitting and receiving. *Receiving information* represents a substantial component of marketing research as we have already seen in this chapter. It is the former *transmitting of information* which we are concerned with when looking at promotion.

Promotion itself can be subdivided into two main categories: *above the line* and *below the line*. Above the line promotion is where an organisation pays to *advertise* itself or its products in the public media, such as TV, newspapers and magazines. Below the line promotion encompasses a wider range of promotional methods such as *public relations, direct mail, sales promotions, branding* and *personal selling*. Brief consideration is now be given to each of these.

Advertising

This is a specialist area of marketing. It requires a range of creative talents, from thinking of original advertising slogans to designing advertisements which appeal to the targeted audience. Many smaller firms will handle all their advertising internally. That is, they will place advertisements directly with the advertising media. However, larger firms with larger advertising budgets will usually 'contract-out' much of their advertising work to specialist advertising agencies. Such agencies will have specialist knowledge of advertising media combined with a wide range of creative skills.

The most common forms of advertising include television, radio, national newspapers, local newspapers, magazines, cinema and posters. Within the constraints of an advertising budget, the marketer will use either one or a combination of these to reach the optimum number of people within the targeted market, in relation to the distribution and production capabilities of the firm.

Public relations

Public relations (PR) involves communicating both internally and externally. The *internal* 'publics' (or stakeholders) of an organisation will include management and employees. Extending from this are the *connected* stakeholders such as shareholders, customers, suppliers and financiers. Finally, there are the purely *external* 'publics', such as the local community, government, and pressure or interest groups.

There are many methods of communicating with these various stakeholders, including newsletters, exhibitions and trade fairs, sponsorship, press releases, press conferences, product launch events, product evaluations, speeches, public information and access days. Ideally, PR will be *proactive,* that is, carefully planned and implemented in a manner which is consistent with corporate objectives, thus building a *corporate identity* or 'personality' as described by Lancaster and Jobber[3]. Inevitably, unpredictable circumstances will dictate that PR also has to be *reactive,* sometimes seen as troubleshooting or damage limitation exercises.

As with most aspects of the promotional mix, PR is a specialist field. It requires a range of skills including creative written and verbal communication, diplomacy, operational and strategic management. Although it will virtually never be used as a 'stand alone' promotional tool, PR is an important component of the promotional mix and it can be used either to support or lead the other components.

Direct mail

This is fast becoming a specialist field. The increasing sophistication of segmentation and marketing information systems, largely due to continuing advances in technology, has facilitated enormous growth in this area of marketing communications. Audiences can be efficiently targeted for direct mail approaches. Some organisations use direct mail as their sole promotional tool, but for most firms, it will either support an advertising campaign or lead a sales campaign.

Sales promotion

Sales promotions will invariably be used in conjunction with other components of the promotional mix. They may be used to boost sales during quiet periods, to support a product launch, in support of an advertising campaign or even to test the effectiveness of an advertising campaign. Sales promotions may include discounts, money-off coupons, special offers, competitions, product endorsements and special credit terms. Merchandising can play an important role in successful sales promotions, particularly when supporting an advertising initiative (e.g. 'as seen on TV').

Personal selling

Many pages in this book are devoted to the role and technique of personal selling. However, it is important to look at its position within the promotional mix. Many organisations use personal selling as their main promotional tool; others use it more selectively, in conjunction with other promotional mix components, most notably advertising and direct mail. Unlike other aspects of the promotional mix, there is a personal or human element to selling. Further, the role of the sales person extends to that of a mini-marketer as they are able to *receive* as well as *transmit information* when communicating with customers and potential customers. Although rightly placed as a component of the promotional mix, the wider scope of selling within the overall marketing function should not be overlooked.

Tutorial activity **E**

Consider the strategic and operational nature of each component of the promotional mix. Discuss these conclusions with your tutor.

2.5 Service marketing

In this chapter so far, we have referred to an organisation's 'product'. Everything that has been said can be applied equally to both products and services. However, the nature of a service dictates that it requires additional attention beyond the basic 4 Ps of the marketing mix.

Tutorial activity **F**

To be clear of what is meant by the term 'service', think of five types of service with which you are familiar. Check these with your tutor to confirm your understanding.

Extension: As you work through this section, see how you can relate the provision of these services to the framework being presented. Discuss these considerations with your tutor.

Generally, a service will have five key characteristics:

- *Intangibility:* It cannot be seen or touched.
- *Inseparability:* It is produced and consumed at the same time.
- *Heterogeneity:* Provision of a service relies heavily on people. As a result, there is likely to be a lack of consistency from one service delivery to another.

- *Perishability:* We have seen how a service is produced and consumed simultaneously. Once provided, the service cannot be regained. For example, a passenger may buy a ticket for a train journey. If they do not embark, the train will leave without them. Although they may be able to board another train, the service which was provided by the original train will have perished.
- *Ownership:* Unlike a product, a service has no title. Although the service provider may be contractually obliged to deliver the service, it cannot be owned.

In order to address these characteristics, the marketer needs to apply an additional 3 Ps to form what is known as the 7 Ps of the service marketing mix, first suggested by Booms and Bitner[4]. These are:

1 **People:** Virtually all services rely heavily on people. The service organisation must ensure that its staff are well trained and motivated to provide a high level of service. This cannot be achieved by the marketing department alone, and successful delivery will depend on a cross-company approach, driven by the senior management team and implemented throughout the organisation.

2 **Processes:** Here, we refer to the management or business processes which need to be applied to ensure that services are provided efficiently. The combined application of these processes should relate to high quality service levels, based on customer satisfaction. In recent years, many organisations have recognised the need for efficient business processes in pursuit of customer satisfaction. This has led to the emergence of Business Process Re-engineering (BPR), where all operational procedures are overhauled to refocus on the needs of the customer.

3 **Physical evidence:** Customers need to see evidence of the service and its likely quality. This can be provided by the physical service environment, testimonial evidence, guarantees, corporate image and name awareness.

2.6 Customer care

By being marketing orientated an organisation is, by nature, customer orientated. Therefore, customer care is an integral part of marketing orientation. However, some organisations may overlook customer care in pursuit of broader objectives. Essentially, customer care is the provision of a service to the customers and, therefore, shares many of the same characteristics as service marketing.

In order for it to be effective, customer care must be *total*, that is, it must occur throughout the organisation. Recently, we have seen the emergence and development of Total Quality Management (TQM) which focuses on the satisfaction of customer needs in combination with the achievement of organisational objectives. TQM covers the following vital areas:

- quality
- availability
- service
- support
- reliability
- value for money.

In order to develop an effective customer care programme, the following key factors need to be considered and applied:

1 **The customer:** Customer needs should be identified initially, followed by the monitoring of customer response. Apart from being the foundation of the customer care programme, this customer feedback provides the organisation with a measurement of the effectiveness of the programme. This function becomes another aspect of marketing research, which in turn forms the basis of implementation.

2 **Corporate planning:** In order for customer care to become truly integrated, it needs to be an objective in its own right, within the strategic plan of the organisation.

3 **Management:** The customer care objective needs to be communicated throughout the organisation, and management processes and controls need to be put in place to deliver the *service*. Further, systems need to be put in place which track and measure the internal achievement of the customer care objective.

4 **Personnel:** The staff within the organisation must be trained, committed and motivated in the organisation's pursuit of its customer care objectives.

5 **Physical evidence:** If an organisation is marketing a tangible product, it is easy to overlook this aspect. The product itself provides physical evidence of its existence. However, customer care as a service is separate to the product and, therefore, if the organisation wishes to market customer care as a valuable benefit to the customer, it must provide physical evidence of its existence in the same way as any other service. Commonly, this is achieved with *image association* through advertising initially and in time with the development of a corporate image. However, the *customer contact environment* and *testimonial evidence* can also be used to provide proof of the service.

Marketing orientation dictates that success is achieved through customer satisfaction. Essentially, this dictates that TQM and customer care programmes are prerequisites. If one accepts this fundamental ideology, then it would be true to say that virtually every marketing-orientated organisation should be providing a service and, therefore, the 7 Ps of service marketing can be applied in most, if not all, cases. This principle is summarised in Figure 2.7.

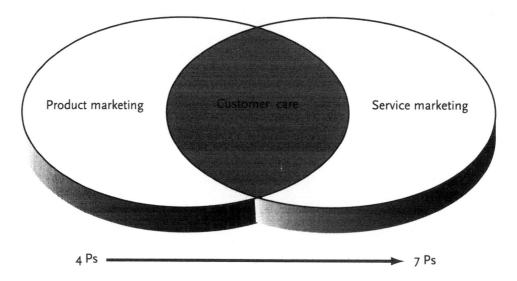

Fig. 2.7 *Customer care as a link between product marketing and service marketing*

2.7 Summary

In this chapter, much ground has been covered. This includes the basic tools of marketing; market segmentation and targeting; marketing research; the marketing mix together with more recent developments; service marketing and customer care. Additionally, it has been suggested that, for marketing-orientated organisations, customer care dictates the application of a service, essentially extending the basic 4 Ps of the marketing mix to the wider 7 Ps.

Although these topics have been covered only in outline, an extensive overview has been provided. Additionally, the text has been presented so as to provoke deeper thought and prompt wider reading. Throughout the chapter, there have been hints made towards the implications and considerations for the selling function within the wider marketing operation.

This final aspect can now be considered in more detail by responding to the essay question which concludes this chapter.

Essay question

By considering the tools of marketing put forward in this chapter, discuss the roles which both the sales person and sales manager are likely to play within a marketing-driven organisation. This should include a detailed consideration of the interaction between the two functions, both operationally and strategically.

References

1 Peters, T. (1988), *Thriving on Chaos*, Macmillan.

2 Lancaster, G. and Massingham, L. (1994), *Essentials of Marketing* (2nd edn), McGraw-Hill.

3 Lancaster, G. and Jobber, D. (1994), *Selling and Sales Management* (3rd edn), Pitman Publishing.

4 Booms, B.H. and Bitner, M.J. (1981), *Marketing Strategies and Organisation Structures for Service Firms* in Donnelly, J.H. and George, W.R. (eds.) (1981), *'Marketing of Services'*, American Marketing Association.

Further reading

Adcock, D., Bradfield, R., Halborg, A. and Ross, C. (1995), *Marketing: Principles and Practice* (2nd edn), Pitman Publishing, Chapters 7, 8, 11, 13, 14, 15, 16, 17, 20 & 21.

Borden, N. (1964), 'The concept of the marketing mix', *Journal of Advertising Research*.

Jobber, D. (1995), *Principles and Practice of Marketing*, McGraw-Hill, Chapters 6–13.

Lancaster, G., and Massingham, L. (1994), *Essentials of Marketing* (2nd edn), McGraw-Hill, Chapters 5–13.

Milner, D. (1995), *Success in Advertising and Promotion*. Murray, Chapters 8, 9, 14, 15, 16, 18, 19 & 20.

Chapter 3

Channels of distribution

By the end of this chapter, you should :

- Appreciate the key factors which influence an organisation in its choice of distribution channel

- Understand how a channel structure is developed

- Understand the relationship between principal and intermediary

- Be aware of the different types of intermediary and their roles

- Appreciate the strategic considerations of reducing channel length and the growth of direct marketing

- Have an understanding of vertical integration and its strategic significance.

3.1 Introduction

In the preceding chapter, the basic trading channels through which an organisation can distribute its products were considered. In this chapter, we shall see how the selection of a channel of distribution is a vital consideration for the organisation. Generally, it represents a long-term commitment to the development of the channel and, as a result, key decisions in this area tend to have strategic implications.

There are many factors which will influence these decisions and detailed consideration must be given to them. Additionally, there are many varieties of channel structure of which an overview is provided in this chapter. In recent times, two variations in particular have been popularly exposed as growth areas, namely *vertical integration* and *direct marketing*. These exciting areas are considered in some depth.

This aside, traditional channel structures involving a range of intermediaries remain important. The most common types of intermediary are considered and also the varying relationships between principal and intermediary in the context of channel lengths.

3.2 Selecting a distribution channel

Debrief

In the preceding chapter, you were asked to consider the factors which may influence an organisation in its choice of distribution channel. Compare your conclusions with the comments made by the author in this section.

The customer

One important factor affecting the choice of trading channel revolves around the needs and requirements of the customers. For example:

- What level of after-sales service do they require?
- How much technical information do they require to make a buying decision?
- How accessible does the product need to be?
- What delivery times do they require?
- What are their installation needs?

Customer requirements will vary enormously according to the type of product. Clearly, the needs of the customer will vary between buying a loaf of bread and a new car (consumer market) or between buying stationery items and a new computer system (industrial markets). It is vital to take into account the needs of the customer when choosing a trading channel. This is consistent with the *definition of marketing*, introduced in the first chapter.

Competitor activity

Most decisions regarding trading channels will take account of those which are adopted by competitors. That is not to say that an organisation should choose the same trading channels as its competitors, although it may do so. Indeed, a competitive advantage may be gained by choosing a different channel structure.

Size and resources

The size of the organisation and the resources it has available will be an important influence in the choice of trading channel. In some cases an organisation will be restricted in its choice purely because of these factors, but for a larger organisation the choices are greater. They will often be able to choose whether to trade directly with the customer or whether to conduct this trade via intermediaries. So, for smaller organisations, this factor will often be the main, or sole, influencer on their choice of trading channel; for the larger organisations their size and the resources they have available provide them with a greater choice. Therefore, the other factors become greater influencers.

Channel power

In every trading situation there is a balance of power. By balance of power, we are really saying 'Who needs this trading arrangement most, the buyer or the seller?' As a result, one or the other will have the most influence within the channel. Often the large manufacturer will have the most influence; for example, Canon will have the main influence over its trading arrangements with a photocopier dealer supplying Canon photocopiers. However, this is not always the case. Sainsbury's is a large supermarket chain and it will have the main influence over its trading arrangements with its suppliers, to the extent that many suppliers are prepared to brand their products as 'Sainsbury's own brand'. When an organisation is choosing its trading channel, it must first ask the question 'How much influence do we need within a trading channel?' and then it must go on to ask 'What channel structure can we adopt which gives us this level of influence?'

Promotional strategy

This factor can both influence the choice of trading channel in the first instance and, conversely, be affected by the activities within the adopted trading channel.

Essentially, a *pull strategy* is where the organisation aims to pull the customer into the trading channel. This can be achieved through activities such as advertising and public relations; that is, the organisation creates a demand for the product and this demand can be supplied by the trading channel. Against this, an organisation can adopt a *push strategy* where the product is pushed through the trading channel, with the last link in the channel selling the product to the customer. This can be achieved by a variety of activities such as offering trade discounts to channel members and promotional incentives. In practice, most organisations use a combination of push and pull techniques or tactics but the overriding emphasis will be on one or the other. Whichever has the greater emphasis over the long-term, can be said to be the organisation's *strategy*.

The channel structure adopted by the organisation must be consistent with its promotional strategy and, in turn, its promotional tactics must take into account the channel structure which it has in place.

The choice of distribution channel and the development of its structure has strategic implications. Channel structures take time to develop and time to close down.

- Relationships need to be cultivated.
- Loyalty and trust need to be built.
- Systems and procedures need to be put in place.
- Employees need to be recruited and trained.

In addition, we can consider that orders may be in the pipeline, stock may be in transit and cashflow may be in the system. Decisions relating to channels of distribution must take a long-term view and be consistent with corporate objectives.

Tutorial activity A

Considering the strategic nature of developing channel structures, address the following questions:

- How will this impact on decisions relating to the sales force?
- What role does the sales force have in the development of the structure?

Discuss your conclusions with your tutor.

3.3 The relationship between principal and intermediary

The relationship which a producer, manufacturer or service provider has with the intermediaries within its channels of distribution requires some detailed consideration.

First, the intermediaries must be identified, an agreement reached, and from this a mutually beneficial relationship can evolve. The personal interface between the two organisations commonly involves a trade sales person representing the principal and a trade buyer representing the intermediary. The number of intermediaries with which the principal establishes trading links will be consistent with its corporate objectives and resources. In turn, this will dictate the size of sales force employed by the organisation.

Over the long-term the sales force can increase the volume of sales through a combination of cultivating relationships with existing intermediaries and steadily increasing the number of intermediaries within the channel structure. However, this growth cannot be purely dependent on the efforts of the sales force.

The sales force must be supported by the whole of the marketing effort. This will include considerations such as pricing, volume discounts, product/service promotions, end-user advertising and publicity, product quality, efficient physical distribution, dealer support, customer care and many other areas.

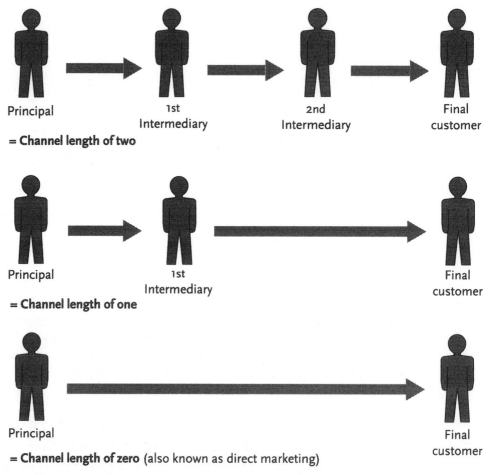

Fig. 3.1 *Channel lengths*

Against this, the value of the sales force in establishing a distribution network must not be underestimated. The vast majority of intermediaries need to be procured and cultivated by personal selling.

So far, in this section, we have considered the relationship between principal and intermediary for the *first line of distribution*. If appropriate, these intermediaries will, in turn, develop relationships with other intermediaries before the product is made available to the final customer in the chain. The number of intermediaries involved between the principal and the final customer is known as the *channel length*. This is shown in Figure 3.1.

In most situations, the principal organisation will only have direct contact with the first line intermediary. These first line intermediaries will be responsible for developing the *second line of distribution* and so on, through to the final customer. The role of the principal changes as it becomes more removed from the *final line of distribution*. Its sales people will have little or no contact further down the channel as each line of distribution becomes a remote extension of its own sales force.

When a longer channel structure is adopted, the role of the principal shifts to that of supporting the intermediaries within the channel. Production capability and efficiency, product quality, distribution capability and efficiency, final customer promotional activity and competitive pricing are all factors which are likely to be considered.

Tutorial activity B

Why would an organisation adopt a longer distribution channel? To answer this question, compare the advantages and disadvantages of using intermediaries against those of marketing directly to the final customer. Present these conclusions as a series of bullet points to your tutor.

3.4 Types of intermediary

There are a wide number of terms applied to intermediaries. In some cases, the terminology relates to distinctly different types of intermediary and in other cases it can vary in significance from one industry to another, often because of some historical perspective. The range of terminology and the general position each intermediary would take in the channel structure is shown in Figure 3.2. It

Tutorial activity C

What is meant by channel width?

Research this question and discuss your findings with your tutor.

is highly unlikely that the full range of intermediary terms will ever be used within one industry, although some organisations will necessarily adopt a wide range of structures, perhaps of varying lengths, in order to reach a mass audience.

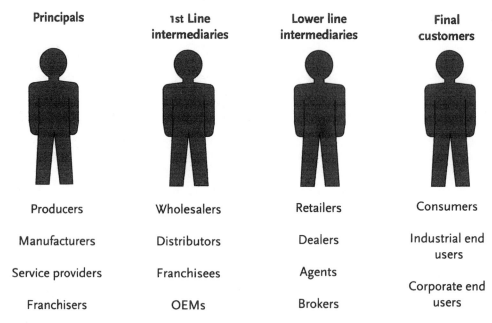

Principals	1st Line intermediaries	Lower line intermediaries	Final customers
Producers	Wholesalers	Retailers	Consumers
Manufacturers	Distributors	Dealers	Industrial end users
Service providers	Franchisees	Agents	Corporate end users
Franchisers	OEMs	Brokers	

Fig. 3.2 *Terminology used to describe intermediaries in channels of distribution*

The first and lower line intermediaries can now be considered. However, in doing so, it should be remembered that their position in the channel is not fixed. For example, it is possible for a dealer to be a first line intermediary in a short channel. Similarly, a distributor may be a second line intermediary when an original equipment manufacturer (OEM) is the first line intermediary.

Wholesaler

This term is usually used in retail markets when considering fast-moving consumer goods (FMCG). FMCGs need to be moved through the channel quickly and retailers' stocks replenished frequently. Wholesalers will buy from the producer in similar quantities to the large retail chains and receive similar discounts. They then distribute the product to smaller retailers. Within this category there may also be further divisions such as main wholesalers and sub-wholesalers. In recent years the wholesaler has been threatened by vertical integration, an increasing number of retail chains, a reducing number of independent retailers and the formation of buying co-operatives by independent retailers.

Distributor

Distributors operate on a similar principal to wholesalers. They buy the product from a range of manufacturers in bulk quantities and distribute the product to the market place either directly or via lower line intermediaries, or even a combination of the two. The term 'distributor' tends to be used for both commercial and domestic products, other than fast-moving consumer goods. The computer hardware industry provides a good example of this type of intermediary.

Franchisee

The relationship between franchisee and principal (franchiser) is a special one. An increasing number of organisations are preferring to distribute their products through franchising. In many respects this is a form of exclusive distribution, as discussed in the preceding chapter. The principal appoints a franchisee to run a distribution outlet as their own business. The franchisee owns the business but must run it in the image of the franchiser's business and with certain contractual obligations. For example, they must buy the franchiser's product, send their staff on the franchiser's training courses and so on. Common examples of franchise operations include The Body Shop, McDonald's and Prontaprint, although there are a large number of smaller, less well known franchises at the other end of the spectrum.

Tutorial activity D

Select a famous franchise, such as one mentioned in the narrative, and a smaller, less well-known one.

What is the level of initial capital investment required of each franchisee in both cases?

What reasons can you think of to explain these differences? Discuss these conclusions with your tutor.

Original equipment manufacturer (OEM)

This is perhaps one of the more confusing terms used to describe an intermediary. It occurs where the actual product manufacturer tends not to market its products in its own name. Instead, it trades through an OEM who places its own 'badge' on the product before distributing it to the market place. It is common for a number of manufacturers to trade through an OEM who, in turn, is able to add 'value' to the product by offering the market place an established brand name. Texas Instruments is a good example of an OEM.

Retailer

A term with which we are all familiar. The retail outlet distributes products to the consumer. More significantly, the size of the retailing organisation will tend to dictate from where it buys its stock. Many larger chains with multiple outlets will buy directly from the principal organisation, whereas the smaller retailers will tend to buy from a first or second line intermediary.

Dealer

Dealers are similar to retailers in that they are the last link in a distribution chain before the product reaches the final customer. This term is often applied to trade in the capital goods market. Some dealers, such as those in the new car market, sell to domestic consumers, although dealers are particularly common in industrial markets. As with retailing, larger dealers will often buy directly from the manufacturer, compared to smaller dealers who necessarily purchase in lower volumes from a higher level intermediary.

Agent

Agents are similar to dealers and retailers in that they sell to the final customer, but there the similarity ends. Agents act on behalf of one or several principals. They do not take ownership of the product but receive a 'commission' for sales made. In these situations, the principal will often deliver directly to the final customer. Agents will tend to be smaller organisations, private individuals, service industry intermediaries or businesses in a related but non-competitive industry, such as cars and mobile phones.

Broker

A broker is a special form of agent. Brokers receive a commission from the principal for selling the product or service. However, brokers tend to trade on behalf of the final customer rather than the principal. As a result, brokers will often have trading arrangements with a large number of principal organisations.

3.5 Direct marketing

An increasing number of organisations are moving towards direct marketing as the primary method of distribution. That is, they are finding it more efficient and more profitable to distribute directly. This growth trend has been facilitated by:

Tutorial activity E

Find an example of direct marketing, taking the form of each of the following:

- mail order catalogues
- direct response advertising
- direct mail
- personal selling.

Discuss these with your tutor to confirm your understanding.

Extension: Consider how personal selling can be combined independently with direct response advertising and direct mail to form a direct marketing promotion and distribution strategy. Find actual examples to support your conclusions and discuss these with your tutor.

- increasingly sophisticated marketing techniques
- more efficient information systems through developments in information technology
- increasing consumer awareness
- advancements in communication capability.

Commonly, direct marketing will take the form of mail order catalogues, direct response advertising, direct mail, personal selling and ownership of retail outlets. This latter consideration often occurs through vertical integration, which is discussed in the following section.

3.6 Vertical integration

Although this has existed for some years, it has become increasingly common since the recession of the early 1990s. It occurs where an organisation aligns itself in a different position within the trading channel. For example, a producer which trades through a retailer may also set up its own chain of retail outlets, either from a start-up situation or, more likely, by acquiring an existing chain of outlets. It will either do this to replace its existing trading channel or use it in addition to its existing trading channel. In the latter case, it would effectively put itself into competition with its existing trading channel, the implications of which must be considered carefully.

A producer aligning itself further down the trading channel is an example of *vertical integration downline* and is the most common form of vertical integration. However, it is also possible for an organisation to align itself further up the trading channel, that is *vertical integration upline*. For example, a large retailer may decide to produce some of its own products, again either from a start-up situation or, more likely, by acquiring an existing producer.

Tutorial activity F

There has been a growing trend of vertical integration through and beyond the recession of the early 1990s. Consider why this has been the case in terms of both strategy and operations. Compare your conclusions with the author's comments in the *Debrief* at the end of this chapter.

3.7 Summary

Channels of distribution and the structures which are formed are of crucial significance to the selling environment. Indeed, they dictate the broad environment within which the sales person operates.

The role of personal selling is relevant to many different types of channel structure. The long-term nature of distribution channels and the development of an appropriate sales force are of strategic importance. In many respects, major decisions relating to these two main areas are among the most important decisions an organisation will make in marketing its products.

Necessarily, channels of distribution have been given extended coverage in this text. It is only through understanding these channels and their relationship with personal selling that we can progress to consider the many different types of selling which abound and attempt to categorise them. This area is covered in depth in Chapter 5, after we have considered the closely related area of buyer behaviour in the following chapter.

Debrief

Given the impact of the 1990s recession, we can consider why there has been an increasing amount of vertical integration. First, firms have used vertical integration as a method of recapturing lost product sales (*operations*). Perhaps more importantly, larger organisations have seen an opportunity to increase their market share and/or improve their efficiency with the objective of strengthening their position in the market place (*strategy*). If we refer back we can see how this relates to the evolution of the marketing concept and the increasing number of marketing-orientated organisations, as the decision to integrate vertically is very much either a marketing-driven or marketing-influenced decision.

Essay question

The financial services/life assurance industry has seen some dramatic changes in its distribution strategies in the past decade. These have been due to legislative changes, greater national and international competition and increased consumer awareness.

Select a major principal organisation within this industry. Research its range of distribution structures in terms of both width and length. Present these structures in diagrammatic form and discuss the role, purpose and responsibilities of each type of sales person within the structure.

Extension: For the selected organisation, research the distribution structures which were in place around 1980. Contrast them with the current structures to highlight the changes which have taken place. Analyse the reasons for these changes, including legislative, competitive and consumer considerations.

Further reading

Adcock, D., Bradfield, R., Halborg, A. and Ross, C. (1995), *Marketing: Principles and Practice* (2nd edn), Pitman Publishing, Chapter 12.

Bucklin (ed.) (1970), *Vertical Marketing Systems*, Scott, Foresman, Glenview.

Jobber, D. (1995), *Principles and Practice of Marketing*, McGraw-Hill, Chapter 14.

Lancaster, G. and Massingham, L. (1994), *Essentials of Marketing* (2nd edn), McGraw-Hill, Chapter 10.

Stern, L.W. and El-Ansany, A.I. (1988), *Marketing Channels*, Prentice-Hall.

Chapter 4   # Buyer behaviour

Learning objectives

By the end of this chapter, you should :

- Be aware of the key motivation theories applied to buying behaviour

- Be aware of the new product adoption process and consider a process for repeat purchasing

- Understand the main principles of decision-making units and processes

- Be able to identify the basic types of buyer

- Appreciate the key factors which influence buying decisions for each type of buyer

- Understand the importance of buyer behaviour in the context of the selling environment

4.1 Introduction

It is vital for the sales person to understand the behaviour of buyers and potential buyers. An intimate understanding of such behaviour in the sales person's specific environment provides a foundation upon which successful sales can be built.

In organisations aspiring to achieve a customer-orientated approach to business, the whole of the marketing operation will be devoted to understanding buyers' behaviour in relation to identifying and satisfying their needs. Regardless of this, the sales person must go a stage further and be fully aware of the fluctuating needs and key buying motivators, not only within their market place but specific to each individual customer and potential customer.

Given the specificity of buying motivation from one customer to another, the sales person can only enter each selling situation aware of the broad behavioural and motivational considerations of their particular environments. This chapter aims to provide an overview of these broad considerations.

General aspects which may apply to all buyers are considered: motivational theories, decision-making units and processes and the new product adoption process. There is then a specific consideration of the three main buying categories: domestic, commercial and trade buyers, focusing on the special factors and influences which apply to each.

First, it is important to be clear of the terminology which is applied to these three buying categories:

1 **Domestic consumers:** This is a massive category, consisting of virtually the whole population. All of us, at some point, will make a decision to purchase. This ranges from a child deciding to buy a packet of sweets with their pocket money to major adult decisions, such as a home purchase, buying a new car, retirement planning, home improvements and so on. Identifying the domestic consumer is straightforward. It involves the use of personal funds to make a private purchasing decision for the benefit of oneself or other individual person(s).

2 **Commercial buyers:** Commercial buyers are people who make a buying decision with a view to benefiting the business entity which they represent. The word 'benefit', suggests that the purchase should in some way enhance the business. Indeed, this is the overriding principle behind commercial buying. For example, this could involve the purchase of a new computer system to increase efficiency, setting up a company pension scheme to enhance employee relations, motivation and loyalty, or any number of other purchases. Not included in this category is the purchase of stock for resale, including items such as component parts. Therefore, it follows that commercial transactions usually occur between organisations in unrelated industries, such as a computer dealer selling a computer system to, say, a food wholesaler.

3 **Trade buyers:** As the name suggests, trade buyers make purchasing decisions based on the trade value of the item(s) to the business entity which they represent. This would include stock which is being purchased for resale by a retailer, or component parts being purchased by a manufacturer. Trade transactions invariably involve purchasing items in volume and frequently, on a repeat basis. The nature of these transactions usually dictates a mutually intimate knowledge of the other party on behalf of both buyer and seller.

Tutorial activity A

Identify a recent purchase which

- you made as a domestic consumer
- a commercial organisation with which you are familiar made to enhance its business operation.

In both cases, consider what benefit the buyer hoped to achieve from the purchase and what you think were the key factors which encouraged them to buy from the chosen source rather than a competitive product or service. Discuss these conclusions with your tutor.

4.2 Motivational theories

There are a number of motivational theories which can be applied to the behaviour and motives of people making purchasing decisions. In this section we shall consider Maslow's Hierarchy of Needs[1], the Black Box Theory, McClelland's Theory of Need Achievement[2] and Vroom's Expectancy Theory[3]. There are other theories which one can explore but the key to their practical application in selling is that of understanding what will motivate an individual customer or potential customer to buy. Motivational theories merely provide an outline and background of the context in which sales people find themselves each day. At an individual level (selling), it is the sales person's perception of each customer's needs and personal motivations which are required, whereas, when considering a large group of customers (marketing), it is the marketer's general awareness and understanding of the group's motivational influences which is more appropriate.

Maslow's Hierarchy of Needs

Abraham Maslow is widely regarded as the pioneer of modern day behavioural and motivational psychology. He concluded that all people are motivated by needs and, further, that there is a hierarchical structure through which we seek to satisfy these needs. The six levels of need put forward by Maslow are shown in Figure 4.1. The argument behind these is that we must satisfy the lower level or

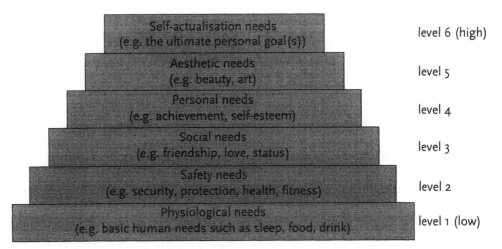

Self-actualisation needs (e.g. the ultimate personal goal(s))	level 6 (high)
Aesthetic needs (e.g. beauty, art)	level 5
Personal needs (e.g. achievement, self-esteem)	level 4
Social needs (e.g. friendship, love, status)	level 3
Safety needs (e.g. security, protection, health, fitness)	level 2
Physiological needs (e.g. basic human needs such as sleep, food, drink)	level 1 (low)

Fig. 4.1 *Maslow's Hierarchy of Needs*

basic needs before progressing to the next level. The highest level of self-actualisation is one which many of us strive for but few achieve.

Maslow argued that higher level needs are more powerful but cannot be addressed until lower level needs have been satisfied. For example, one may have a desire to change appearance, say through plastic surgery (a level five need) but most of us would not embark on satisfying this need at the expense of losing our home (a level two need). Although Maslow's theories have been criticised, updated and improved, it is a testament to his vision that we are still referring to his work over fifty years after it was first written.

Group tutorial activity B

Consider how Maslow's hierarchy of needs theory can be applied by

- a marketer
- a sales person
- a manager.

Think of an example which emphasises the point in each instance and discuss these examples in your tutor or seminar group.

The Black Box Theory

This theory is commonly adopted in the application of marketing, perhaps most notably in advertising. However, it can also be applied in personal selling situations. The theory is summarised in Figure 4.2. The 'black box' is the human brain. Various stimuli or messages are sent or input to the black box. These are then processed to produce an appropriate behavioural response or output. Although we cannot know for sure what is going on within the black box, hence the terminology, we can analyse how a stimulus produces a response. Again,

Input/stimuli → BLACK BOX → Output/responses

Fig. 4.2 *The Black Box Theory*

marketing is concerned with predicting the likely response of a group of people to any given stimulus, whereas selling is concerned with the specific response of an individual. Good sales people and, indeed, good managers, are able to judge accurately this response in order to persuade and motivate.

McClelland's Theory of Need Achievement

McClelland argued that there were three main need categories:

- *Affiliation:* the need to belong and to be part of a social group
- *Power:* the need to have control over both other people and one's own environment
- *Achievement:* the need to achieve personal goals and, often, to be seen to be achieving them.

This provides an alternative perspective to Maslow's Hierarchy of Needs. In relation to the sales person, one can consider how the identification of an individual's specific personal needs can provide an insight into the motivational influences which will provoke positive buying behaviour.

Vroom's Expectancy Theory

This provides a framework for measuring the motivation of buyers in terms of the value which they perceive will be gained from making the purchase. The expectation of a certain outcome from buying is combined with the preference or desire which an individual has for that outcome. Students wishing to gain a more comprehensive understanding of this theory are referred to Phipps and Simmons[4] where a worked example is provided. In terms of practical application in the field of selling, one can consider the identification and prioritisation of needs together with applied benefits and unique selling points, discussed in Chapter 6 of this book.

4.3 Decision-making units and processes

There are many roles involved in the decision to purchase a product/service. For example, there may be *the financier* (Who is going to make provision to pay for it?); *the user* (Who is going to use it and potentially benefit from it?); *the influencer* (Who is concerned with the benefit and/or consequences of purchase?), *the buyer* (Who is going to negotiate and make the transaction?). It is unusual for one person to take on all of these roles in any buying situation.

Tutorial activity C

1 Consider the purchase of a child's toy in the context of a family decision-making unit. Who may take on the role of:

- the financier
- the user
- the influencer
- the buyer?

2 Consider the purchase of a personal computer in a small business decision-making unit. Who may take on the role of

- the financier
- the user
- the influencer
- the buyer?

Discuss these conclusions with your tutor to confirm your understanding.

In larger organisations, one can consider extended roles within the decision-making unit, such as *the initiator* (the person who begins the purchase process), *the decider* (the person who authorises the decision to purchase), and *the gatekeeper* (the person who controls the flow and distribution of incoming information).

The decision-making process involves the stages which the decision-making unit will go through in making a purchasing decision. A worked example follows for the purchase of a family car:

1 **Identification of need:** Our car is becoming unreliable and needs to be replaced.
2 **Finance:** How much capital do we have available? Are we prepared to borrow money? What monthly repayments can we afford?
3 **Evaluation of alternatives:** What cars are within our price range? What preferences and requirements do we have?
4 **Trial:** Test drive the vehicle(s) which seem most appropriate.
5 **Negotiate:** What discount can we obtain? How much will we be offered for our vehicle in part exchange?
6 **Purchase:** Conduct the transaction.
7 **Evaluate the purchase**: Did we make the right decision? Are we happy with our purchase?

The need for an understanding of the decision-making unit (DMU) and the roles which are being adopted, combined with an appreciation for the stages involved in the decision-making process (DMP), should not be underestimated by the sales person. It is the understanding of both the DMU and the DMP in every individual situation which will enable the sales person to handle the sale successfully. For example, with whom should one negotiate the financial arrangements? at whom should the product benefits be directed? when should this occur? at what point should the sale be closed?, and so on.

Tutorial activity D

Choose an organisation with which you are familiar, and consider a purchase which was recently made. Identify the members of the DMU and the roles which they fulfilled. What was the DMP for this purchase?

Discuss these conclusions with your tutor to confirm your understanding.

4.4 The adoption process

This is an extension of the decision-making process, providing a generic framework for first-time purchasing. Although commonly applied to fast-moving consumer markets, the adoption process can apply to all types of buying, to varying degrees. The basic adoption process for first-time purchasing is summarised by Figure 4.3.

The buyer first becomes aware of and then interested in the product. Following this, some form of evaluation is made, usually focused on considering the advantages of the product against other buying opportunities. The product is then tested, usually through an initial purchase. If successful, the product will be adopted for regular use.

Post-adoption confirmation is perhaps the most overlooked aspect of

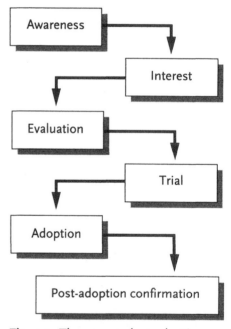

Fig. 4.3 *The new product adoption process*

Tutorial activity E

The mnemonic AIDA is often applied as a promotional approach. Research its meaning and consider how it can be applied to the adoption process. Discuss these conclusions with your tutor.

Extension: In Chapter 6 of this book, a component of *The Selling Process* is referred to as the 'follow-up'. How can this be applied to the adoption process?

this process in the practical environment. This occurs as the buyer, often subconsciously, seeks confirmation that they have made the right decision. There are many methods of achieving this, such as advertising, after-sales service and customer care.

Advanced tutorial activity F

In direct comparison with the adoption process, develop a buying process for repeat purchases. Write a critical evaluation of this process for your tutor.

4.5 Domestic buyers

Frequency

There will be different influences on domestic buyers, dependent on the frequency with which a decision is made by an individual. For example, a frequent visitor to a supermarket may be particularly sensitive to a small price increase; indeed, it may cause them to switch brands. On the other hand, such sensitivity is unlikely to arise for a person buying fireworks once a year.

Importance

How major or minor a purchase is will be relative to the wealth and purchasing habits of each individual. The level of importance placed on a particular purchase by the individual will influence the decision. For example, a well-paid professional person who purchases a new car every year will be influenced by different factors (e.g. status, speed, acceleration) than, say, a person who is retiring and buying their first and probably only brand new car (e.g. reliability, rust protection, economic fuel consumption).

Socio-economic category

For many years, consumers have been categorised by social and economic class. The view taken is that what an individual buys and how they buy it will be influenced by which category they belong to. The classic socio-economic categorisation is as follows:

A   Upper middle class: senior managers and professionals (e.g. barristers)

B   Middle class: middle managers and professionals (e.g. university lecturers, high street solicitors)

C1   Lower middle class: junior managers, professionals (e.g. social workers) and administrators

C2   Upper working class: skilled manual workers

D   Working class: semi-skilled and unskilled manual workers

E   Sub working class: those people at the lowest level of subsistence (e.g. people dependent on state benefits, casual or low grade workers, state pensioners).

For example, selling by party plan (until recently) was aimed at people in C1, C2 and D categories. Recently, this approach has been extended to include people in the B category and yet the promotional focus to this new category remains different (i.e. 'up market' product, high quality brochures etc.).

In recent years, it has been thought by many that these classic socio-economic categories are inadequate as methods of classifying consumers. Whilst this may be true, the principle of categorising consumers into social and/or economic groups as a method for understanding their general buying behaviour remains valid.

Tutorial activity **G**

Consider other ways in which consumers can be categorised. Discuss these conclusions with your tutor.

Extension: Choose one method of categorisation from those identified above. In what ways will buying habits vary between categories? Present your tutor with a summary of your conclusions.

Logic and emotion

In every purchasing decision there is a mixture of logic and emotion. How much logic and how much emotion will vary according to some of the factors already considered and, perhaps, a further factor will be the personality of the buyer. However, in general, it is fair to say that domestic buying situations involve a greater degree of emotion in arriving at a decision, whereas in commercial buying situations the reverse applies. As a result, domestic consumers are more prone to impulse purchasing and buying from people they like, compared to those purchasing for a commercial purpose.

A practitioner's tale

"I had the good fortune of entertaining a delegate on one of my courses who was a high level professional buyer. I say good fortune because it gave me the opportunity to provide first-hand demonstrations to the group of many aspects of my lecture. However, the most potent example I drew from this individual was how he completely removed emotion from his professional buying decisions. He would never make a decision in front of the sales person; he would either insist on 'sleeping on it' or make some other excuse to give himself thinking time. His decision would be based purely on the facts; that is they were logical decisions. What followed was even more revealing. This most prudent professional purchaser then admitted that when he was buying domestically, his decisions would contain a high level of emotional influence, indeed many minor decisions would be purely impulsive. It was only for his most major personal purchasing decisions that he would employ some of his professional skills and use a greater degree of logic."

Third party influences

In the domestic situation, there may be more than one influencer in the decision-making process. For example, a child may like a toy they see advertised (pure emotion) and they will try to influence their parents. The decision of the parents will be based on a combination of emotion (trying to please the child) and logic (can we afford it?). It is not only the close family unit which will influence the decision-making process. Good and bad experiences will be widely recounted from one person to another. For example:

'Don't buy that make of car. I had one of those and it was forever going wrong.'

'That's the third time in a fortnight that I've bought bad meat from that supermarket.'

'I think party plans are a good idea. I went to one last year and it was really good fun.'

Tip for success

Spread good words!

If someone has something bad to say about a product or service, they will tell more people than if they have something good to say. For this reason alone, it is imperative that the sales person and the organisation maintain excellent customer relations. Further research on this topic is considered by Engel *et al*[5].

Buying environment

This is the last but perhaps the most important consideration in looking at buyer behaviour for the domestic consumer. In Britain at least, any good sales person will tell you that most of their time is spent creating an environment in which people can buy rather than one in which they think they are being sold to. If you don't believe this statement on face value, consider these two questions:

- How many times have you walked into a shop, the assistant has approached and asked 'Can I help you?' and you have replied 'No, I'm just looking thanks.'?
- How many times have you been approached by telephone or at your doorstep, the sales person/canvasser has launched into a sales presentation about double glazing or insurance or a similar product and, without really listening or without letting them finish, you have said 'NO!' and ended the conversation?

In both cases, what you are really saying is 'I don't want you to sell me anything'. When considering the domestic consumer market in the UK, the sales person must consider this attitude and act accordingly, as it is applicable to the majority of people.

4.6 Commercial buyers

We have already seen how there is far less emotion involved in commercial buying situations and how decisions are based far more on logic. That is not to say that there is no emotion involved, but it is reduced to a minimum. As a result, commercial buyers are happy to be sold to, unlike domestic consumers, as they are confident in their ability to make the right decision, based on logic, good business practice and good buying skills. Therefore, it follows that there is a different set of factors which influence the commercial buyer:

Instigation

Who instigates the exchange is an important factor in commercial buying. Has the organisation decided that they need to buy XYZ and they are looking for the right deal, or has the organisation been approached by a sales person who is trying to convince them that they need ABC? If it is the former, then some of the other factors we shall consider will be important in influencing the buying decision. However, if it is the latter, then the psychology of the buying decision takes on a different perspective. The buyer must first be convinced of the concept – that is, a need for the product or service based on the general benefit which will be derived – before other factors enter the equation.

Competition

The commercial buyer will be keen to use competitive factors to their advantage. The number of potential suppliers will be an important factor. If there is a large number of potential suppliers, then the advantage is with the buyer, as they can use competitive factors to obtain a good deal (e.g. better price, favourable payment terms, bespoke changes). However, if there is only one or a small number of potential suppliers then the advantage shifts to the sales person.

Quantity

Commercial buyers will expect to receive a discounted price for buying in large quantities. For example, they may only need 5000 envelopes for the current month, yet may choose to purchase 10 000 if they receive sufficient discount.

Value

Commercial buyers have a greater appreciation of value than does the domestic consumer. They may be prepared to pay a higher price, if they can be convinced they are obtaining better value. For example, a buyer negotiating for a fleet of vehicles may be prepared to pay a slightly higher price if the contract includes the use of courtesy cars during times of service or maintenance. In this instance, the extra value to the buyer may be that the organisation can keep its entire sales force on the road all year round, thus resulting in an increased sales turnover.

Quality

Every commercial buyer will expect a minimum standard of quality. This will become a prerequisite in the purchasing process. However, they may also be convinced of increased quality providing increased value. They may also see higher quality as a decisive feature when all other factors are equal among competitive sellers. Later, when considering trade buying, we shall also see how quality has become an important feature of 'just-in-time' purchasing. Incidentally, the application of the word 'quality' is not merely a reference to the pure product quality in terms of reliability, performance etc. It also refers to the quality of service which is provided in terms of sales support, technical backup, delivery time and so on.

Repeat business

A commercial buyer may often see repeat business as a negotiating tool in the purchasing process. For example, a competitive one-off deal may be negotiated on the basis that a large contract will follow if the organisation is satisfied with the purchase. The sales person must identify the importance and validity of this factor in each situation where it arises.

Price

Although we have considered a whole range of influencers in the commercial buying environment, price remains of crucial importance. If a buyer chooses not to buy from the most competitively priced supplier, they must justify their decision. It is here that the skill of the sales person is tested. Only one supplier will have the best price. Invariably, having the best price has a downside. It is the role of the competitive sales person to highlight the downside of best price by emphasising the strengths of their own product; that is, to promote value rather than price.

4.7 Trade buyers

As we saw earlier in this chapter, a trade purchase will either be *upline* (e.g. a component supplier selling upline to the main manufacturer) or *downline* (e.g. a manufacturer or producer selling to an intermediary). From this, it is easy to see that the selling organisation may be larger than the buying organisation or it may be smaller. The selling organisation may be a major or key supplier to the trade buyer or it may be one of a large number of suppliers or even only an occasional supplier.

Although some of the factors which influence a trade buyer are the same as those we have looked at with a commercial buyer, there are differences and, perhaps more significantly, there is a difference in emphasis.

Price

Whereas with a commercial buyer price is important, we have seen how a skilled sales person can highlight *value factors* in order to overcome price uncompetitiveness. In a trade situation, price becomes a far more important influencing factor. Why?

In both upline and downline trade situations, the buyer will be very conscious of the price at which they will need to sell their product. In the case of, say, a manufacturer buying components, the cost of producing its product will impact on the price at which it can sell the final product. Therefore, if a buyer buys at the wrong price, it may mean that the final product is sold at an uncompetitive price. This will clearly have far-reaching implications for the buyer's organisation. Similarly, a retailer buying from a producer will need to be aware of the price at which it will be able to sell the product and whether this price will be a profitable one based on the buying price. Often, in trade situations, the margins involved in these decisions are very tight and a difference of only a few pence per unit can make a very large difference to the buyer.

So, trade buyers are far more sensitive to the price they are paying for their purchases than is the case with many commercial buyers. As a result, any organisation selling a trade product will need to be aware of this sensitivity for its particular market and be able to compete on price. However, the sales person should be aware that they will not be competing on price alone and other factors can be incorporated into the negotiation of a sale.

Bulk purchase

One of the biggest factors involved in negotiating the price at which a buyer can buy is the quantity they are intending to purchase. This is what is known as *purchasing power*. Purchasing power does not only affect price; for example, a buyer may be able to specify product changes if they are buying in sufficient quantities, but it is reduced price which is the main benefit of bulk purchasing. It is in this way that a supermarket can buy at significantly better prices than the local convenience store, providing them with a competitive advantage in dealing with the mass market.

Quality

Again, this refers to both the quality of product and the quality of service which will be demanded by the trade buyer. As we have seen, purchasing power will affect the quality the buyer can command. However, all trade buyers will expect to negotiate a price, consistent with their purchasing power, which will take into account the quality of product they are buying and will also specify the quality of service they expect to receive (e.g. delivery times, procedure for return and replacement of faulty goods).

Repeat business

It is rare for a trade purchase to be a one-off purchase. Invariably, both buyer and sales person are seeking to set up an agreement which will involve a series of consecutive automatic purchases. Often, an annual agreement will be set up which will include a price per unit and payment and delivery terms for the whole year, also including a minimum number of units to be purchased during that year. Negotiating skills in such situations are often tested to the maximum as both sales person and buyer learn and develop them in their respective specialisms. However, the overriding factor in repeat business negotiations is developing a relationship which provides mutual and long-term benefit to both parties.

Payment terms

Cashflow is important to virtually all commercial organisations. For a small organisation it can mean the difference between success and failure, but it is also important to the large organisation. A trade buyer will be keen to negotiate competitive payment terms which benefit their organisation. However, it is rarely the decisive factor, and most trade buyers will be fair and reasonable when negotiating this aspect. For example, typically they would rather pay a competitive price and have prompt delivery, even if it means paying on 30 day terms rather than 45 days.

Just-in-time (JIT)

This is becoming an increasingly common aspect of trade buying. Many organisations have discovered the benefits of not holding large quantities of stock, such as reduced wastage or reduced warehousing. As a result, they will set up purchasing agreements with suppliers which involve stock being ordered and supplied at short notice. Lancaster and Jobber[6] quote the example of the Nissan car plant in Sunderland. The carpets for the cars are ordered 42 minutes before they are fitted. This is an extreme example of JIT in action, known as synchronous supply, but it emphasises the point. In order for JIT to be effective, the quality of supply is a crucial factor. The delivery time must be right and the quality of the product supplied must be high. Therefore, a trade buyer negotiating a JIT agreement is more likely to be concerned with the quality of supply than perhaps the price they are paying. That is not to say price is unimportant, but it becomes less important.

4.8 Summary

This chapter has provided an overview of buyer behaviour; that is, what influences and motivates people to buy. In this text, we are concerned specifically with how knowledge of buyer behaviour can be applied in the selling environment. The marketer is concerned with the general behaviour of buyers in their chosen market segment(s). For the sales person working within an effective marketing function, this will result in products carefully targeted to meet the needs of customers and potential customers, thus satisfying their broad buying motivations. However, this in itself is not sufficient for the sales person to be successful.

The sales person must further appreciate the key individual factors which will motivate the buyers and potential buyers they are dealing with. That is, their understanding of buyer behaviour and motivation needs to be specific to each individual sales negotiation. This is a finite skill which can only be acquired by practical field experience. The key factors outlined in general terms in this chapter provide an indication of the most common considerations.

The successful sales person will need to develop a specific understanding of customers and potential customers in their market place and in relation to their product. This understanding then needs to be extended to interpret and anticipate the buying motivation in each individual situation.

The sales person who truly understands the factors which will motivate a buyer to buy is half way to successfully concluding a sale.

A practitioner's tale

"I have the very simple idea that human beings have two inherent traits which can display themselves in any number of guises, but are there as the motivation for all actions and decisions. These basic traits are *selfishness* and *laziness*.

How does this impact on a sales person? First, one must discover the selfish motivation and appeal to it during the selling process, as it will be the driving force behind any buying decision which is taken. When considering laziness, one must make it as easy as possible for people to make a buying decision. This requires that the right environment is created and positive action is prompted (at the right time).

I have no scientific proof to support my theory but it is one which has served me well throughout my sales career and I have yet to be proven wrong."

Essay question

For an organisation of your choice, identify a trade purchase which it makes regularly. Discuss the three factors which you feel will be most important to the organisation when making a buying decision and give your reasons for them.

Imagine you were a sales person for a competitive supplier. Explain how you might persuade the organisation to buy your product.

References

1 Maslow, A.H. (1943), 'A theory of human motivation', *Psychological Review*, July.

2 McClelland in Phipps and Simmons (1995), *Understanding Customers*, Butterworth-Heinemann.

3 Vroom, V.H. in Phipps and Simmons (1995), *Understanding Customers*, Butterworth-Heinemann.

4 Phipps and Simmons (1995), *Understanding Customers*, Butterworth-Heinemann, P. 207–8.

5 Engel, J.F., Blackwell, R.D. and Miniard, P.W. (1990), *Consumer Behavior*, Dryden Press, P. 276–278.

6 Lancaster, G. and Jobber, D. (1994), *Selling and Sales Management* (3rd edn), Pitman Publishing, P. 51–2.

Further reading

Adcock, D., Bradfield, R., Halborg, A. and Ross, C. (1995), *Marketing: Principles and Practice* (2nd edn), Pitman Publishing, Chapters 5 & 6.

Allen, P. (1993), *Selling: Management and Practice* (4th edn), Pitman Publishing, Chapters 5, 6, 10 & 14.

Drew-Morgan, S. (1993), *Sales on the Line*, Metamorphous Press, Chapters 2, 3 & 4.

Foxall, G. (1993), *Consumer Psychology in Behavioural Perspective*, Routledge.

Jobber, D. (1995), *Principles and Practice of Marketing*, McGraw-Hill, Chapters 3 & 4.

Maslow, A.H. (1954), *Motivation and Personality*, Harper & Row.

Milner, D. (1995), *Success in Advertising and Promotion*, J. Murray, Chapter 7.

Chapter 5

Types of selling and the role of the sales person

Learning objectives

By the end of this chapter, you should :

- Understand the different types of selling in relation to industry structures

- Understand the differences between selling in push and pull environments

- Appreciate the differences between new business and repeat selling

- Appreciate the main issues involved in considering face-to-face and telephone selling situations

- Fully understand the direct strategic relationship between selling and both promotional and distribution strategies

- Begin to consider the wider strategic issues indirectly associated with selling.

5.1 Introduction

Personal selling takes many different forms in the practical environment. Throughout the following chapters, the practice of selling will be discussed in very general terms. The framework and skills which are covered need to be adapted and applied to individual situations. The major key in achieving this, is an appreciation of the type of selling involved.

Understanding the different types of selling is not aided by the range of job titles and jargon used by organisations to describe their sales people and their role. In the previous chapter, it was noted that the nature of UK domestic consumers was one of resistance against being sold to. This has led to organisations using a variety of terms, such as adviser, consultant, estimator, to describe their sales people.

Further, job advertisements will often seem to be written in code to the lay observer, with expressions such as FMCG selling, industrial selling, commercial selling, account management selling, new business development, lead driven environment, direct selling, retail selling, business-to-business experience, telesales, capital goods selling, pioneering opportunity, development opportunity, expansion opportunities. You may have a good idea of what they all mean but they are frequently used differently from one organisation to another.

When considering types of selling, it is most important to understand clearly the role of the sales person in relation to the environment within which they are working. This can be achieved by gaining an awareness of the factors which shape and influence the role and the environment.

In this chapter, the key factors are considered as distribution structures, promotional strategy, selling to new and existing customers, and the method of communication. The use of personal selling as a promotional tool represents a major investment by the organisation and consequently has much wider implications. We have already seen how the decision to employ a sales force is a strategic one, but we must also consider the type of selling which is appropriate in relation to other corporate objectives. These wider strategic issues are considered at the end of the chapter.

Tutorial activity A

Collect job advertisements for a variety of selling positions. The most likely sources are local and national newspapers and specialist or trade magazines.

As you work through this chapter, apply the positions advertised to each of the four areas discussed in sections 5.2, 5.3, 5.4 and 5.5. Discuss these interpretations with your tutor at the end of this chapter.

5.2 Selling in the context of industry and corporate distribution structures

In Chapter 3, we considered the channels of distribution which may be available to an organisation and how a channel structure is developed. The channel structures adopted will vary from industry to industry and between organisations in the same industry.

The type of selling involved in the whole channel structure will vary depending on the role of the organisation within it. The number and type of sales people will vary according to the distribution capacity and requirements of the organisation in developing its channel structure. This latter point is an important one. Channel structures are always developing. Relationships are cultivated, markets contract and expand, and market needs are constantly changing.

In this section, the types of selling will be considered with reference to a generic zero-, one- and two-level distribution channel as shown in Figure 5.1.

1 **Retail selling:** This can be found in all three channel structures and will apply to the last link in the chain which sells to the domestic end user or consumer. In the zero-level structure, it involves the principal organisation owning its own retail outlets; the one-level structure is likely to relate to major retail chains, and the two-level structure will tend to be small retail chains and independent outlets.

2 **Direct selling:** Again, this can be found in all three channel structures but can be applied to the last link in the chain which sells to either domestic or industrial end users. In the zero-level channel structure, it will either involve a large sales force or occur with high value capital products and service provision. The one-level structure will often be an extension of this, with the principal trading through a number of agents or a sales force of varying size employed to sell to dealers and distributors. This latter situation is usually found in industrial markets. The two-level model would tend to relate to smaller dealers in industrial markets. Direct selling to industrial end users may also be referred to as *industrial selling, commercial selling, business-to-business selling, end user selling, concept selling* or *corporate selling*, depending on the appropriateness to the organisation and the industry.

3 **Trade selling:** This does not occur with zero-level channel length but arises further up the chain where either the principal sells to an intermediary, or a higher level intermediary sells to another. It can also be applied to a component supplier selling up the channel to a principal manufacturer or producer. Where there is a domestic end user at the end of the chain, the terms *fast moving consumer goods (FMCG)* and *capital consumer goods (CCG)* may be applied. Additionally, other terms may be applied to a variety of situations within trade selling environments, such as *distribution selling, wholesale selling, merchant selling, industrial trade selling, parts and components selling*.

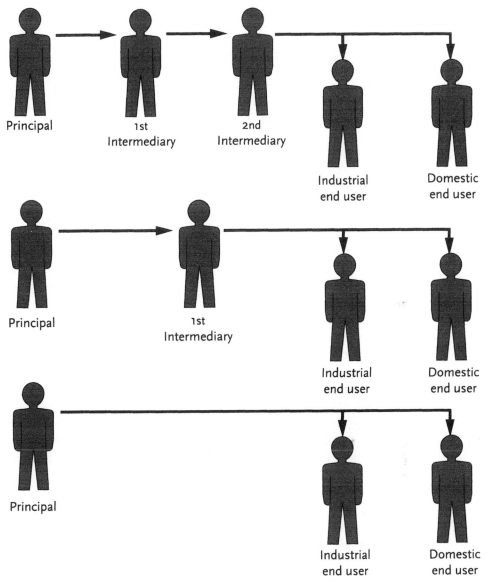

Fig. 5.1 *Generic two-, one- and zero-level channel structures*

Tutorial activity B

Think of an example for each of the three types of selling considered in this section. What terms do the organisations use to describe the role of their sales people?

Extension: Compare and contrast organisations at different levels in each of the selling categories covered in this section. Write summative notes to your tutor to confirm your understanding.

5.3 Promotional strategy and promotional mix considerations

Although the basic forms of selling are dictated by channel distribution structures, there are a number of other factors which further affect the type of selling environment. The first area which we shall consider is the promotional strategy of the organisation and the interaction of personal selling in relation to other elements of the promotional mix.

Pull strategy

This results in the end user being pulled or drawn into the distribution channel. It is most common in retailing situations where the consumer is drawn into the retail outlet by factors such as the store's location, advertising and other promotional activity by the principal and retail intermediary, either independently or co-operatively. Additionally, it can be used in direct and trade selling environments through persuasive end user advertising, general promotional activity, such as exhibitions, and also through the practice of *back selling*. This occurs where a principal or higher intermediary uses its own sales force to sell further down the trading channel with a view to passing orders on to lower level intermediaries. As with all pull techniques, the generation of demand encourages channel intermediaries and enables the sales person to establish and cultivate trading links.

Tip for success

Every retailer knows – if a product is advertised on terrestrial television it makes sense to stock it!

This principle applies wherever there is demand or interest generated for a product. When a pull strategy is used, the role of the sales person becomes more straightforward as a facilitator of purchasing. This is not to detract from the skill required of the sales person. Enquiries still need to be converted into orders but, in general terms, this is easier than sourcing the customers in the first instance and then selling to them.

Push strategy

Diametrically opposed to a pull strategy is the push strategy. Here, the product is pushed or sold through the channel. This can be achieved through persuasive selling techniques and a variety of trade and end user purchasing incentives, such as discounting and competitions. To sell in a total push environment can be very demanding and it is usual for some pull techniques to be used in a supporting role, such as corporate advertising aimed at increasing name awareness.

With the exception of retailing and some trade selling situations, most sales people will find themselves in an environment where some leads are provided but additional business is expected from self-generated activity. In situations where the sales person is given no lead or enquiry support, it is unlikely that they will be working in a marketing-orientated environment.

Missionary selling/third party endorsements

In many respects, this is an extension of a pull strategy but it can be so fundamental to an organisation's promotional strategy, and in particular the way that it utilises its sales force, that it warrants individual consideration. It is especially prevalent in the pharmaceutical and construction industries and involves convincing a third party, such as a doctor or an architect, of the value and benefits of the product. In turn, they then recommend the product to their clients.

In the examples quoted, this would manifest itself as a GP prescribing a drug for their patients or an architect specifying the use of a particular product or material on a construction project.

A practitioner's tale

"It has been suggested to me that selling is a numbers game. The more people a sales person speaks with, the more sales they will make. I cannot dispute the mathematical truth of this statement but I can crunch the numbers for my sales people and make them more efficient. I can achieve this in three ways. First, I can improve their skills through training, but also I can present them with people who are at least interested in talking to them and give them a range of products which have appropriate appeal.

The first mentor I had in selling taught me his three golden rules:

1 Meet the people
2 Meet the people, and
3 Meet the people.

These are no longer golden rules which I apply to my sales people. Instead, I tell them:

1 Meet the right people
2 Establish their requirements
3 Sell them the right product."

Having considered the general *push versus pull promotional strategies*, it is now appropriate to look at the various elements of the promotional mix and how they can interact with personal selling:

Advertising

Advertising can have two relationships with personal selling. In the first scenario, it plays a leading role, and in the second, a supporting role.

In its leading role, persuasive advertising is a demand generator. As part of a pull strategy, it makes people *aware* of the product/service, generates *interest* in it and builds a *desire* to buy it. It results in them taking *action* to buy the product by drawing them in to the distribution channel. This process can be summarised by the mnemonic AIDA.

Awareness
Interest
Desire
Action

In its supporting role, informative and corporate advertising underpins the selling process. It can generate general enquiries, as opposed to creating a demand for the product/service, and can reassure the customer with general name awareness and a particular corporate image. In most cases, this approach will form part of a push strategy and can also be used in conjunction with sales promotions and direct mail campaigns.

Public relations (PR)

PR and publicity tend to support the sales effort in a similar way to informative and corporate advertising. A long-term and planned approach develops an organisation's identity or rather the way in which customers identify with the organisation. This acts to reassure the customer and enhances the credibility of the sales person.

Sales promotions

Sales promotions tend to form part of an organisation's push strategy, providing incentives for the customer to buy. Generally, promotions are an aid to the sales person, but it should be noted that the successful impact and use of sales promotions are optimised when they are used for a limited period. In this way, they provide a short-term boost to the sales effort, perhaps in times of reduced demand or increasing competitive activity.

Direct mail

We have already seen how direct mail can be used to good effect in the implementation of a direct marketing distribution strategy. Sometimes considered as an extension to advertising, direct mail can also be applied as a promotional activity in its own right. As an enquiry generator, it can be used to enhance the efficiency of the sales person.

When considering the role of the sales person, we can view it in the context of the full promotional strategy of the organisation. Key questions which will affect the role of the sales person are:

(a) How can leads/enquiries be generated?
(b) What approach can be taken to increase name awareness, corporate image and corporate identity?
(c) What promotional incentives can be used to encourage customers to buy?
(d) How can the customer be reassured after purchasing the product/service?

5.4 New business development and repeat selling

Perhaps the most distinctive difference in the type of selling and role of the sales person lies in this area. Selling to a new customer for the first time has many different characteristics from selling to existing customers. In some instances, different sales people are used for each discrete function, but in many cases the functions are integrated, with the sales person taking a split responsibility for both the maintenance of existing customer accounts and the cultivation of new customers.

New business development

The role of sourcing and converting new customers can be both arduous and highly skilful. The level of rejection can be high and the ability to withstand such rejection is implicit within the role of the sales person. However, a combination of skilfully-applied sales techniques and an integrated marketing effort can greatly improve the efficiency of sourcing efforts and the conversion ratio from prospective customers to actual customers. Although certain skills can be acquired and developed through training and experience, the sales person working in this environment must possess some special qualities as a prerequisite to the role. The range of skills is discussed and implied throughout the text and the special qualities required for a new business development role are covered in Chapter 8.

The objectives in developing new business tend to revolve around profitable selling in relation to sales force activity, promotional support and efficient conversion ratios.

Repeat selling/account management

Successfully cultivating a customer is a highly skilful exercise requiring commitment and enthusiasm from the sales person. The objectives of account management are to retain and maintain existing customers in the first instance, to build customer loyalty over the longer term and to increase profitability through sales volume.

The increasing trend towards integrating selling with the total marketing effort has identified this area of selling as having enormous growth potential. In the past, many organisations have seen account management as a maintenance or consolidation strategy. The growth of an organisation has often been achieved through increasing the number of customers. This philosophy has been turned upside down by the concept of relationship marketing.

Relationship marketing is discussed in more detail in Chapter 16 but, in short, it revolves around the simple principle of increasing profitability through sales volume rather than the number of customers. That is, if an existing customer can be encouraged to increase their purchase volume steadily, it is more profitable than adding several new customers with smaller purchase volumes.

In the latter scenario of adding new customers as the primary method of achieving growth, there is a danger of neglecting existing customers and effectively losing ground in the effort to grow. However, the danger with the relationship marketing concept is that it carries an increased risk if a customer is lost. In some cases, this could seriously damage an organisation if the lost account were sufficiently large. Therefore, it is important to ensure that the base of customers is sufficiently broad and, at the same time, effectively managed in order to limit the risk and reduce the potential impact if a loss occurs.

Clearly, sales people involved in managing customer accounts need to be skilful. This skill level increases with the importance of the account. Common job titles are key, major and national account managers, and usually require extensive sales experience and a successful track record. Although these roles have existed for a number of years, the extension towards a relationship marketing concept involves an integrated marketing effort with the sales person spearheading it.

Tutorial activity D

- What qualities would a sales person require to be effective in the role of new business development?
- What qualities would a sales person require to be effective in the role of account management?

List your answers to these questions and compare them with the author's comments in chapter eight.

5.5 Face-to-face and telephone selling

The medium to be used when communicating with customers is an important consideration. Personal selling requires personal communication. Although written and electronic modes may play a part, most personal selling situations involve either (or both) face-to-face and telephone communication.

Face-to-face selling

One should be careful not to think of this only as *field selling,* as it incorporates, most notably, *retail selling.* Personal meetings between customer and sales person enable the full range of personal communication tools to be used. Many of these are discussed in Chapter 7 but, additionally, we should consider the ability the customer has to see the physical product and possibly to be able to observe or participate in a demonstration. Further, face-to-face communication can play an important part in the cultivation of customer relationships. With specific regard to field selling, the limitations are the prohibitive factors of cost against customer contacts. Ideally, face-to-face communications will be managed to optimum effect, utilising the telephone and other modes of communication as supporting tools.

Telephone selling

As we have seen, the telephone can be used as a support tool to field selling. This may take the form of *telemarketing* for lead generation and customer qualification, or *telephone sales support* for after-sales service matters such as order processing or customer follow-up calls. However, the telephone can also be used as a medium for actually selling the product. This is most likely to be effective in repeat selling situations, although it can be used for new business selling in some situations. The key to a true *teleselling* role is where the sale is concluded over the telephone. There has been a growth in recent years in teleselling within industrial markets, particularly with account management situations. This has been driven by the need to increase efficiency and reduce costs. However, this method does have its restrictions in cultivation of customer relationships and is unlikely to be used in isolation for the organisation's larger customers, particularly when considering growth through relationship marketing.

5.6 Wider strategic considerations

The decision whether or not to use a sales force is a strategic one. If in the affirmative, how to use the sales force to its optimum effect becomes a further strategic decision. This involves an integrated promotional strategy and, further, impacts on and is influenced by the distribution strategy. Indeed, promotion and distribution strategies are directly related to the personal selling function and, in particular, affect the type of selling and the role of the sales person.

However, the sales force of an organisation becomes an intrinsic part of it. As a result, there is an indirect relationship between personal selling and many other functions within the organisation. It both affects and is affected by other functions within the organisation, and, therefore, must be considered in a number of strategic decisions.

Extended tutorial activity E

For an organisation with which you are familiar, consider which functions within the organisation share an indirect relationship with selling. How will these relate to strategic issues?

Report on these considerations to your tutor.

5.7 Summary

In this chapter, we have seen how personal selling has a direct relationship with the promotional and distribution strategies of an organisation. It can also play an important part in the general growth strategy of an organisation. Some students will have researched and considered the wider implications of this.

Specifically, we have seen how the type of selling and the role of the sales person can be considered in relation to distribution structures and the promotional mix which is utilised by the organisation. Further, a distinction has been made between new business and repeat selling, with the additional consideration of the communication medium, namely face-to-face and telephone selling.

These considerations are vital if the student is fully to understand the sales environment, or rather the variety of sales environments, within which the sales person may operate.

Essay question

List and discuss ways in which an integrated marketing effort can positively impact on the role of the sales person.

Further reading

Allen, P. (1993), *Selling: Management and Practice* (4th edn), Pitman Publishing, Chapters 1, 4, 11 & 14

Gillam, A. (1982), *Principles and Practice of Selling*, Butterworth-Heinemann, Chapter 8.

Lancaster, G. and Jobber, D. (1994), *Selling and Sales Management*, Pitman Publishing, Chapter 6.

Stafford, J. and Grant, C. (1986), *Effective Sales Management*, Butterworth-Heinemann, Chapter 11.

Case study: Friendly Investments Ltd.

Friendly Investments is a wholly-owned subsidiary of the Bonds' merchant banking group. It is the financial services arm of the group involved in a mixture of corporate and domestic business. The long-term subtitle to their name is 'The Investment House' which became synonymous with their public image during a sustained TV advertising campaign in the early 1980s.

Friendly Investments' portfolio consists of a full range of life assurance, pensions and investment products. Although selling to a generally wide base of customers, their core business is with middle to upper income groups, corporate accounts and the middle class retired population. The company has three main distribution channels:

- selling through specialist brokers
- direct selling through a sales force of around 450 in size
- an in-house direct marketing team of around 25 in size.

Friendly Investments' most successful products are their core investment ones, including a range of personal equity plans and unit trusts. Also, it has an established reputation for providing corporate and small business pension schemes.

Strict regulation of the industry from the mid-1980s led to a major change in the broker market place. No longer could broker business be developed through skilful account management by the broker sales people. Independent brokers became obliged to consider the products of all insurance and investment providers when advising their clients on a principle of 'best advice'. The result was that each provider could only compete with their very best products in terms of customer benefits, such as investment performance and return, flexibility of contract, low management charges and so on.

Some of Friendly Investments' investment products remained attractive to this market place, along with their corporate and small business pension schemes. However, they had to have direct trading channels if their full range of products was to be marketed and further developed. The direct sales force provided a steady return of business, but the regulatory changes increased the expenditure on the development of the sales force in terms of management processes, controls and training considerations. Although the sales force was able to sell the full range of products, the organisation needed an increased level of the more profitable life assurance contracts to be sold.

Increasing consumer awareness made this a difficult area in which the sales force could succeed. Despite providing a high quality range of life assurance products, Friendly Investments were perceived as expensive. Additionally, innovative competitor contracts, such as those offering critical illness benefits, limited the success of the sales force in this area. The sales force tended to remain successful in the sale of the company's investment and pension products, but, by the early 1990s, it was a loss-making division of the company.

Against this, the direct marketing division, which was set up in the mid-1980s to help meet the changes brought on by the regulation of the industry, proved to be a great strategic success. Employing around twenty-five people, it brought in business initially through direct response national newspaper advertising and then, through skilful database management, continued to develop customer accounts on a direct mail basis, with telephone support. The products sold were almost entirely from the investment range, as life assurance and pension products generally require detailed advice on a personal basis.

By the early 1990s, the direct marketing division was producing nearly as much business volume as the sales force but on a far more profitable basis. The three divisions of the organisation retained discrete customer records, with virtually no exchange between them. The broker division necessarily had to retain confidentiality as this is a prerequisite of broker relationships. The sales force argued against sharing its customer base with direct marketing on the basis that its customers were being personally serviced and that direct marketing would represent a duplication and confusion of effort. Similarly, the direct marketing division argued against sharing its customer base as it compromised people who generally preferred not to have a sales person calling and were proven to be responsive to direct advertising.

The validity of this was disputed at a meeting of field sales managers, as one commented, 'My team spends an enormous amount of time prospecting and I would like to see them spending more of that time in front of customers. It's all very well saying these people buy from advertising and direct mail but what about all the missed opportunities? the things they should buy but don't. Okay, so some of them don't want to see sales people, but how many of our customers do want to see our sales people when they first make contact? And how many people are glad they did see them even though they didn't necessarily want to? The direct marketing division claims that customers with an investment profile are not the same as those with a life assurance or pension profile. We should all know that is not the way to view it. For example, people with investment profiles tend to have an inheritance tax liability which gives us vast potential. We can solve their inheritance tax problems, through rearrangement of their portfolios, trust provision and life assurance contracts. Further, it provides an excellent opportunity for us to meet their adult children who will have their own life assurance and pension needs and, in time, will need advice about how to invest their inheritance. We have got to work closer with direct marketing. They are good at bringing the customers in and we are good at developing them.'

One thing was for sure: things had to change. The sales force was duplicating the efforts of the direct marketing division in respect of investment products, and the broker sales division in respect of pension and investment products. Moreover, it was substantially more expensive in doing so. The only way for the sales force to remain viable was for it to produce more life assurance business. First, this business was more profitable and would remove the burden of the direct losses incurred by the sales force. Additionally, Friendly Investments needed more life assurance business in order to be able to develop its products, and remain competitive in terms of costs and benefits.

Task 1

The sales manager referred to in this case study called for an integrated approach between direct marketing efforts and personal selling efforts. In a general context, discuss the validity of his perspective, and suggest ways in which a sales force may become more efficient and profitable through direct marketing efforts.

Note: For those sales people/students with personal experience of the financial services industry, this task should be completed with specific reference to the context provided in the case study.

Task 2

Strategically, the marketing director should control both the sales force and direct marketing functions. In this way, the two areas can be integrated for maximum impact in terms of customer satisfaction and organisational profitability.

Discuss the validity of this statement.

Note: For those sales people/students with personal experience of the financial services industry, this task should be completed with specific reference to the context provided in the case study.

Task 3

In the scenario presented in the case study, what strategic options are open to Friendly Investments with regard to its sales force? Place yourself in the role of marketing director for the organisation; what would you do?

Part II

The practice of selling

Chapter 6

The sales cycle/process

Learning objectives

By the end of this chapter, you should :

- Understand the process involved in the complete sales cycle

- Be able to apply this process to various types of selling

- Understand how efficiency can increase the performance and effectiveness of the sales person

- Appreciate the overall role of marketing in the selling process

- Have an awareness of the skills which need to be acquired and applied by the practitioner.

6.1 Introduction

The *sales cycle* is a complete *process* which can be applied in the selling environment. For some types of selling it will be used in its entirety and in other situations only some aspects of the cycle will be relevant. Regardless of whether some or all of the full cycle is appropriate, it provides a framework for the sales person to work within.

Tutorial activity A

As you work through this chapter, consider which aspects of the sales cycle are appropriate to the various types of selling which were introduced in the preceding chapter. Discuss these conclusions with your tutor.

In practical terms, an awareness of the framework which the sales cycle provides is insufficient. Its successful application is dependent upon the sales person acquiring a wide range of skills. The receptability of the sales person to develop these skills is dependent upon them having certain personal qualities. Many of these skills and qualities will be discussed in this and the following three chapters. However, the range of these, when placed in context of the various types of selling, is immense. Therefore, many skills and qualities which are required of a sales person remain implicit within the text.

Tutorial activity B

Consider the selling environment of your own organisation or one with which you are familiar:

- What aspects of the sales cycle apply?
- What skills are required of the sales person in applying these aspects of the cycle?
- What qualities do they need to have if they are to be receptive to the development of these skills?

Then consider (if appropriate):

- Are your qualities appropriate to the selling environment?
- What additional skills do you need to acquire and develop?
- How are you going to achieve this?

6.2 The sales cycle: a ten-point plan

There are ten key stages in the full sales cycle (Figure 6.1). In the purest and often toughest forms of selling, the whole cycle will be applied by one employee, the sales person. In most cases where this occurs, it is evidence of a sales-orientated organisation. As we have seen earlier in this book, many organisations have a more marketing-orientated approach. In such an environment, much of the sales cycle is either simplified or subsumed by other functions within the overall marketing operation.

Tutorial activity C

Identify a marketing-orientated organisation. Consider which aspects of the sales cycle are either simplified or subsumed by other functions within the marketing operation. Discuss these conclusions with your tutor.

Extension: Can you think of ways in which the role of the sales person can be further simplified?

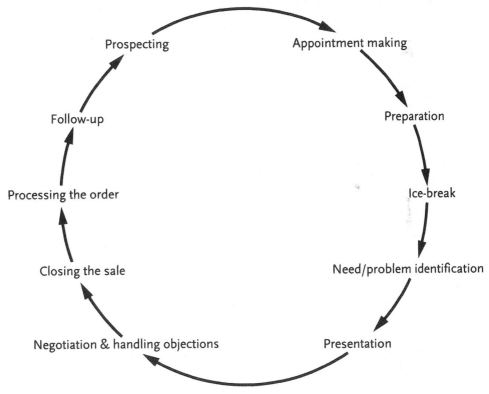

Fig. 6.1 *The sales cycle*

6.3 Prospecting

Prospecting is sourcing information which will enable the sales person to identify potential buyers of their product/service. There are a wide number of methods which can be used to source information. Many are identified in Part V of this book, but other methods would include local and national newspapers, trade journals and personally acquired information.

For the sales person working within the scope of a fully functioning marketing department, the appropriate markets would have already been segmented and targeted. Indeed, many research and supplementary promotional activities will provide the sales person with accurate information and/or customer enquiries.

However, many sales people do not work within such an environment and will have to devise their own 'micro' segmentation and targeting systems. Such a 'micro'-system is unlikely to display the sophistication of the full marketing system. It is likely to involve:

- *Lateral thought:* who has a need for my product/service?
- *Sourcing:* where can I find information about these people/organisations?
- *Filtering:* now I have analysed this information, are my initial thoughts confirmed?
- *Targeting:* if my initial thoughts are confirmed they will be added to my *prospect list* and if it appears they are unlikely to have a need for my product/service they will be added to my *suspect list*.

Apart from the most fortunate and few sales people who work in a completely lead-driven environment, most sales people will have a *prospect list*, that is, a list of people/organisations who are likely to have a need for their product/service. For those sales people involved in repeat selling, a large part of their prospect list

Tip for success

Always keep a suspect list!

You have spent hours of your valuable time collecting and analysing information. It makes sense to gain maximum value from this time. What if your company brings out a new product/service? What if you move to a new company to sell a different product/service?

A practitioner's tale

"When I was selling computer software to industry, I organised a lunch club. This club consisted entirely of sales people and every member worked in a different industry, so there were no conflicts of interest. Apart from the obvious motivational aspects of meeting with a peer group, such as status, ego, competition and the pooling of ideas, we also developed an excellent system for sharing information. Essentially, we would compare and share information from our suspect lists. Information on one suspect list would be added to another person's prospect list and so on. In this way, our monthly lunches provided valuable benefit, increasing our efficiency and performance."

will be made up of existing clients: that is, a *client list*. Where many sales people miss an opportunity is they fail to build a *suspect list*; that is, a list of people with whom they suspect they cannot do business at the present time. This is understandable, what is the point of keeping a list of people/organisations with whom they cannot do business?

In this time of information technology, collecting, recording and utilising client, prospect and suspect information has never been more efficient. A simple database can be used or one can invest in a specialist sales/customer software application. This can be an investment either by the organisation or by the individual. The sales person must not see the use of a customer database as an administrative burden, but rather a valuable tool which can reduce time spent on prospecting and increase customer contact time. This area is explored further in Chapter 17.

6.4 Appointment making

First, one needs to establish with whom to make the appointment. In Chapter 4, the decision-making process within an organisation was considered. There was the actual *decision-making unit* which could be made up of one or more people; additionally there were the *gatekeeper*, which some sales people refer to as the screener, *influencers* and *users*. This can be seen in Figure 6.2. In most cases, the sales person will want to make an appointment to see the decision maker or a member of the decision-making unit, although they may meet in the first instance with an influencer, particularly relevant in the case of products with specialist applications. With whomever they are planning to meet, they must first pass the gatekeeper. This is in itself an acquired skill which will be considered shortly.

In a domestic situation, the identification of the decision maker is less complex. In the vast majority of cases it will be either the husband and/or wife and, if one is not a decision maker, they are likely to be an influencer. Therefore, most domestic sales people will try to make an appointment to meet with both partners.

Having identified with whom they wish to meet, the sales person must then make contact In a domestic situation this will purely mean calling at the right time. However, in the commercial situation, this will involve a more skilful

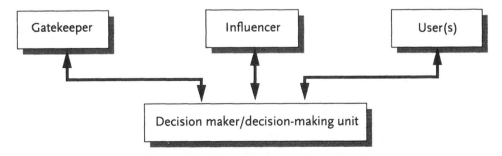

Fig. 6.2 *The decision-making process*

approach. Many sales people have found success by calling outside normal working hours. Using this approach has two main benefits: first they connect directly with the decision maker and, second, their prospects are often more receptive outside of their busiest periods. There are also some additional benefits, for example it is a good way to utilise time which would otherwise be unproductive and avoid the frustration of constantly being 'screened out'.

There are a number of alternative approaches, such as preceding the call with a letter of introduction, building a rapport with the gatekeeper, or any number of other innovative methods.

Tip for success

Be innovative!

If you do not speak with the prospect, you cannot succeed. Success in this area will often depend on finding an innovative method, consistent with the type of market in which you operate.

A practitioner's tale

"If the decision maker is unavailable, I always leave a message for them to call me back about 'a matter of mutual interest'. They nearly always return my call. I have their attention, a psychological advantage and it saves on telephone."

When connected with the decision maker, two things have to happen. First, the sales person needs to qualify them: that is, are they the decision maker and do they have a broad need for the product/service? How this is achieved will vary according to the type of product/service, but in general terms it will involve a series of carefully worded questions.

Second, the sales person will need to give the decision maker a reason for sparing the time for a meeting. This is usually achieved through an overriding *benefit statement*. For example, 'My existing clients have found that their fuel costs can be reduced by as much as 30 per cent', or '90 per cent of the people I meet find that I can reduce their tax bill'. The benefit statement must be true and it should also be general in nature. The sales person should treat any attempt by the decision maker to gain more information, such as 'How much can you save me?', as a reason for making the appointment: 'At this stage I have no idea; that is precisely why I would like to meet with you'.

At this point it is then appropriate to make the appointment. A general question such as 'When would be best for you?' may be appropriate if the response has been very warm. However, many sales people opt for the assumptive approach, using an alternative close, for example, 'I can make next Tuesday afternoon or Thursday morning. Which is best for you?'

Tip for success

Don't talk yourself out of the appointment!

A real danger with sales people making appointments is that they have a tendency to overtalk the situation. The objectives of the call are to qualify the prospect, provide them with a reason, and make the appointment. Once these objectives have been achieved, the sales person should bring the call to a swift conclusion.

Once an appointment has been made, it is good practice for the sales person to confirm the appointment in writing. This avoids confusion and enhances the commitment on behalf of the prospect to keep the appointment.

6.5 Preparation

Having made an appointment with a prospective client, the sales person must next prepare for that meeting. In the busy schedule of a sales person, this aspect can often be overlooked. A simple approach to preparation is outlined as follows:

1 **Route planning:** At the very least, the sales person should know where they are going, how they are going to get there, how long it will take and possibly where to park on arrival. This could have been achieved by asking at the time of making the appointment, calling through to reception to ask for directions, using a map, asking a colleague or local knowledge.

2 **Diary planning:** Many sales people are so keen to make appointments that they fail to organise their diaries properly. They find themselves driving from one end of their territory to another and doing the same thing the next day. They allow insufficient time between appointments, finishing one in a rush and arriving late for the next. As a result they lose sales, gain driving convictions and increase their stress levels. A well-planned diary improves the efficiency of the sales person.

3 **Research:** It is often appropriate for the sales person to conduct some specific additional research on the company or person they are going to meet. This is particularly true when dealing with large order values and low volumes but can also be appropriate lower down the scale. Research could be as simple as ascertaining the number of employees, the profitability or, in more specific terms, what equipment they currently use, who they buy from at the present time, and so on.

4 **Frame of mind:** It is important to enter a selling appointment in the right frame of mind. How this is achieved will vary according to the type of selling environment and individual preference.

A practitioner's tale

"My three top sales people all prepare for appointments differently. One listens to heavy rock music as he claims it gets him 'pumped up', another listens to motivational and sales technique tapes, and the other listens to the local radio station to collect titbits of useful information. The important thing is that they all go into their appointments in a positive frame of mind, totally focused on achieving their objectives."

6.6 Ice-break

This is the point at which the sales person first meets their prospect.

Tip for success

You only have one chance to make a first impression!

Appearance should be consistent with the general expectations of the prospect, although the specific nature of this will vary according to the type of selling environment. Eye contact is important, together with a welcoming smile and a firm handshake. It is also appropriate to present the prospect with a business card early on.

Having made the first impression, the purpose of the ice-break is to put both the prospect and the sales person at their ease. This is achieved by building rapport, which is considered in more detail in the following chapter. At this point, suffice it to say that rapport will come from asking general open questions with a view to establishing some common ground between two people. The common ground should be non-business specific, as its purpose is to provide a foundation for the meeting to progress. In domestic situations this ice-breaking process may take ten to fifteen minutes, but in commercial situations the sales person should be aware that their prospect is likely to view time as a key factor and the ice-break should take no longer than five minutes.

The skilled sales person will be able to link the ice-break to the next stage of the sales cycle without the prospect noticing. Indeed, the ability to progress from asking non-business, rapport-building questions to asking business-related questions in a smooth transition is often the hallmark of a top quality sales professional.

6.7 Need/problem identification

This is the single most important aspect of any selling situation.

During this stage, the sales person must find out what the prospect needs and wants. These two considerations are often at conflict with each other when the sales person first meets their prospect. That is, the prospect will perceive that they want one thing (or sometimes nothing at all) and the sales person can see that they do in fact have an unidentified need. The sales person must help the prospect to identify that they have a need(s), often developing this in the form of a problem, for example, showing them that they are paying too much tax or that their business expenditure is higher than it could be for producing the same or higher revenue.

Having developed the problem in the eyes of the prospect, the sales person must clearly identify the needs of the prospect and seek their agreement to these needs. At this stage, the sales person must seek to clarify the specific buying criteria and also discover what, specifically, will motivate the prospect to buy.

The skill factor at this stage on behalf of the sales person is very high, as most prospects are not forthcoming with all of this information. The techniques to be employed during this stage can be broken down as follows:

Questions

The sales person must ask a series of questions to elicit information from the prospect. Many textbooks and many practitioners will recite a list of the various types of question at the sales person's disposal, such as leading questions, sharp angle questions, inclusion questions, and so on. Although it is true and valid that questions can be analysed to such an extent, the real skill of the sales person comes from creating an environment in which information is encouraged to flow freely from the prospect. This can be achieved by considering two types of questioning:

1 **Open and closed questions:** A closed question is one which requires a 'yes' or 'no' answer and is diametrically opposed to an open question, which can be answered by anything but a 'yes' or 'no' response. Typically, open questions will start with what? why? when? who? how? where? and are used to 'open up' the prospect. The sales person uses these questions to control the conversation. For example, an open question such as 'What effect did the recession have on your organisation?' may engage the prospect in a protracted answer. When the sales person believes they have gathered enough information, they may confirm key points with a closed question, such as 'So if I have understood you correctly, the recession initially had a negative impact but, by streamlining the organisation, the end result has been a positive one and the company is now in a strong position. Is that how you see it?' By linking questions together, the sales person is able to achieve a number of key positive outcomes: they can confirm their understanding, highlight key areas, gather and define information, move the conversation in whatever direction suits them; and all this is accomplished in what the prospect will perceive as a natural discussion, and yet the sales person has hardly discussed anything, merely given the prospect the opportunity to talk.

2 **Soft and hard fact questions:** In combination with open and closed questions, it is also appropriate to define questions further into soft and hard facts. A hard fact question elicits the indisputable, for example, 'How

many people do you employ?'. Hard facts are important because they provide real, factual information. On the other hand, soft facts are powerful. They enable the sales person to establish the attitudes and opinions of the prospect. Typically, questions will be phrased as 'How do you feel about that?', 'Is that important to you?' or 'Why?' These soft facts enable the sales person to discover what the prospect is thinking or feeling. As a result, they are able to uncover key motivators which can be used powerfully in the next stage of the sales cycle.

Listening

For questioning techniques to work effectively, the sales person must listen carefully to the response of the prospect. This may seem obvious, but in reality it is a difficult skill to acquire. It is not to be confused with hearing, where we hear words and noise. Listening is analysing those words and making sense of them. Again, this skill is considered in more depth in the following chapter. For now, suffice it to say that the sales person must listen to the response of the prospect in order to ask effectively a series of linked questions which uncover all of the information relevant to making a successful sale.

Tip for success

The 80/20 rule of communication!

This is a rough guide for the conduct of this stage of the sales cycle in that the sales person should spend 80 per cent of their time listening and 20 per cent talking and asking questions. Information should never be assumed; it should be asked for. Further, when the sales person asks a powerful question, the prospect may hesitate in their answer, creating a brief silence. For the sales person, silence is golden. The prospect should be allowed to consider their response uninterrupted.

Define buying criteria

By using the questioning and listening techniques outlined above, the objective of the sales person is to elicit the buying criteria of the prospect. As we have seen in Chapter 2, the objective of the marketer is to understand the general needs and wants of customers in their chosen market segment(s). In the selling environment this process becomes more specific and the sales person needs to discover the specific needs and desires of individuals.

Prioritisation

Having defined the buying criteria, it is often a good idea for the sales person to ask the prospect to sort the criteria into an order of priority. This is mainly important if the product/service being offered by the sales person will not satisfy all of the criteria. It could be that there is no single product or service available which will satisfy all of the criteria. In this situation, it may be possible for a sale to be concluded if the sales person's product/service satisfies the most important criteria. Even if the sales person is not going to ask the prospect to prioritise all the criteria, it is often useful to have them specify their *most important need (MIN)*.

Summarisation

In many selling situations it is often appropriate for the sales person to check back with the prospect to confirm that *all* of their needs and desires have been covered and understood. This is particularly important if there is a substantial number of criteria or the sale is to be conducted over more than one appointment. If the sale is to be conducted over two appointments, as is often the case, then this point is usually the link between the two appointments. The first meeting will be concluded by summarising the buying criteria and the second meeting will begin with a recap or summary of how the previous meeting was concluded.

6.8 Presentation

This stage of the sales cycle is intrinsically linked with the previous stage. Having identified the needs and desires of the prospect, the sales person now needs to demonstrate how their product/service satisfies them by providing a solution. This is achieved by using a system of *features* and *benefits*. Every product/service has a number of features. Each feature has a *potential benefit* to the customer; that is, it satisfies a potential need which the prospect may have. A feature is only of *real benefit* to the prospect if it satisfies a specified need or desire.

Tutorial activity D

Select a product/service with which you are familiar. Identify three features and state a potential benefit which each may provide. Discuss this with your tutor to confirm your understanding.

It is important for the sales person not merely to state the feature which satisfies a need but to follow it up with a statement of *how* it will satisfy a need; that is, how it will benefit the prospect. Further, the sales person must only state the features and benefits which satisfy specified needs and desires. To list additional features which are irrelevant to the prospect would be oversell; it will 'switch them off', demonstrate that the sales person has not listened to their requirements, and it will also highlight the fact that they are paying for features that they do not need.

At the end of each *feature/benefit statement* the sales person should gain the agreement of the prospect that the specified need has been satisfied. The sales person should never assume this as the prospect may have a query or may not have understood how their need has been satisfied. Failure to gain an agreement at this point is likely to lead to an objection later on. It is much better to draw any potential objection from the prospect at this stage.

Most products/services have a *unique selling point (USP)* – a feature or features which no other competitive product/service has. This could be as simple as the personal service which will be provided by the sales person or it could be a complex technical capability. If a need specified by the prospect can be satisfied by the USP then special emphasis should be placed on it during the presentation. For example, 'This is X (*feature*), which means to you Y (*benefit*). Do you agree? (*gaining agreement*), and to the best of my knowledge no other product/service on the market can do this for you.' The ultimate situation for a sales person is to find that their USP can satisfy the prospect's MIN.

Having demonstrated how their product/service satisfies all of the prospect's needs, the sales person should summarise. This will involve briefly running over the needs and recapping the appropriate features/ benefits. The sales person can then gain an overall agreement from the prospect to ensure that nothing has been missed.

Tip for success

The process for need/problem identification and satisfying these needs by presenting a full solution can be summarised by the mnemonic **NASA**:

Needs
Acceptance
Solution
Acceptance.

6.9 Negotiation and handling objections

By following the process as stated in this chapter, any objection that is going to arise should have been raised before this point. For example, there may have been an objection when the sales person tried to make the appointment, or objections may have arisen during the presentation stage of the cycle. In theory, no further objections should arise at this point. However, the nature of making a buying decision often means that there will be at least a token gesture of resistance from the prospect before the sale can proceed.

Some managers and trainers in the selling profession advise their sales people to view an objection as a buying signal; that is, a request for more information or clarification before a buying decision is made. From a psychological and motivational point of view this is not a bad approach, but generally objections will fall into two categories:

1 **The smoke screen:** This can be one of two things. Either the prospect is raising an artificial objection because they feel there is a need for some

breathing space before they decide to proceed, or they are raising a false objection to shield the real reason for not going ahead.

2 **The genuine objection:** This is where the prospect has a genuine reason for not proceeding, which usually means that either not all of their needs have been satisfied or they require clarification or more information. This type of objection may be as a result of an error during the presentation stage of the sales cycle, such as the prospect misunderstanding the benefits of the product/ service or, alternatively, they may seek to improve the offer being made by the sales person, if they are to make a positive buying decision.

Whatever the type of objection, it needs to be handled and the process in each case is broadly similar. First, the sales person needs to employ a questioning technique aimed at establishing the importance of the objection and shaping it into a form where it can be handled; that is, turn the objection into a new or revised need/desire. The objection is then handled by restating one or more benefits to demonstrate how the revised need/desire has been satisfied or introducing a new feature/benefit statement if appropriate. This procedure will certainly handle most objections, including the most common – price.

Tip for success

Increase the value of your offer!

When a price objection arises, the prospect is really saying, 'You have not made your product/service valuable enough to justify the price'. Value is achieved through highlighting and enhancing benefits, or rather the prospect's perception of those benefits. It is only when the value perceived by the prospect is greater than the price, that price ceases to be a barrier to the successful conclusion of a sale. This is shown in Figure 6.3.

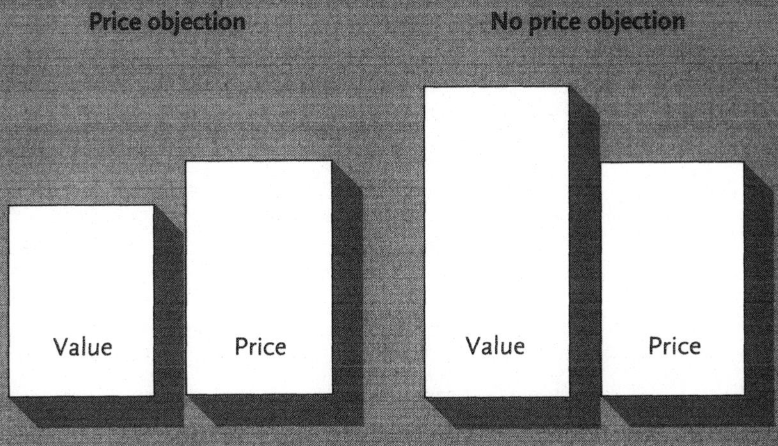

Price objection   No price objection

Value   Price   Value   Price

Fig. 6.3 *The relationship between value and price*

Assuming that the prospect has the means to pay (a fact which should have been established far earlier in the sales cycle) the sales person will need to respond to a price objection if a sale is to be made. Restating benefits and introducing new ones may well be appropriate and powerful. However, prospects, particularly in commercial and trade selling environments, are often looking to negotiate a better deal, i.e. they are seeking extra value.

The sales person must be careful not to treat price negotiation as a requirement to reduce their price. If the proposition offered by the sales person offers genuine value, every attempt must be made to emphasise this, thus testing the resolve of the prospect to gain a price reduction. If price continues to be a barrier, the sales person (assuming they have the authority) should seek to adjust any possible variables. This may mean modifying the product or, more likely, the service, in order to justify a price reduction. Alternatively, the sales person may seek to gain additional value themselves in order to balance any reduction in price. For example, there may be an opportunity to enter into some form of reciprocal trading arrangement, such as taking the prospect's product/service in part payment, gaining agreement to use the prospect for endorsement/ testimonial evidence or the prospect offering to become an introductory source.

Not all objections can be handled. It could be that the sales person needs to go away and liaise with technicians to make changes to the product/service, or perhaps the prospect genuinely wants some time to think before making a decision. If the sales person feels that they have genuinely satisfied all the needs/desires of the prospect, it is often better to back off and give them the thinking time they need.

If, at this stage of the sales meeting, the prospect is clearly not ready to proceed, the sales person should not try to close the sale. Instead, they should seek to gain a commitment from the prospect which keeps the sale alive. For example, 'If I call you after the weekend, would that give you enough time to think things through?' or 'I need a few days to sort these changes out with our technical people; let's make an appointment now for, say, next Thursday and I can show you what they have come up with.'

6.10 Closing the sale

Many sales texts go into great detail of the many clever closing techniques at the sales person's disposal. If the sales person follows the process laid down in this chapter, then the close becomes something of a formality. The needs/desires have been identified and satisfied, this has been agreed by the prospect, and their queries/objections have been handled; the close is simply a matter of asking for the business. Some examples of closing questions are:

- *Alternative close:* 'Would you like the red one or the blue one?'
- *Direct close:* 'Are you ready to place an order?'
- *Cautious close:* 'Is there anything else you would like me to cover before we complete the paperwork?'

- *Assumptive close:* 'I've completed all the paperwork, all you need to do is read through it and sign here. Do you have a pen handy or would you like to use mine?'

Clearly, the sales person will need to decide which closing question to use based on the mood of the meeting and its appropriateness to the situation. There are a variety of other questions which can be used, too numerous for the requirements of this text. The two golden rules for closing the sale can be considered as:

- Ask for the business, using an appropriate question.
- Ask at the right time, i.e. at this stage of the sales cycle.

6.11 Processing the order

The sales person returns to the office with an order, invariably feeling very pleased. Yet, the sales cycle is by no means complete. Once in the office, the sales person needs to consider seriously two things:

1 **Self-evaluation:** This may seem a strange item to place under the heading of 'processing the order' but this is probably the best time for a sales person to evaluate their own performance. As they are going over the paperwork, it is good practice mentally to run through the sales meeting. This can be achieved by answering two questions:

- What did I do really well?
- What could I have done better?

Of course, sales people should also conduct this exercise after an unsuccessful sales meeting.

2 **Accurate administration:** As a rule, most sales people are poor administrators. The personality and qualities of a good sales person are not consistent with the personality and qualities of a good administrator. However, there is nothing worse for a sales person than to conduct a brilliant sales appointment and close a big deal only to lose a customer because they did not process the order properly. Administrative procedures should be followed precisely and, where possible, the sales person should track the processing of the order through to delivery.

Tip for success

Keep it simple!

Managers need to appreciate the nature of a sales person. When developing or reviewing internal processes and procedures, care should be taken to minimise and simplify the input required by the sales person. Skilful sales administrators with procedural responsibility can also improve efficiency in this area.

6.12 Follow-up

This aspect of the sales cycle is often overlooked by sales people and organisations alike. A follow-up call should be made to a customer shortly after they have received delivery of the product/service. Are they completely happy? Are there any problems? First, the sales person's reputation will be enhanced because they are showing that they genuinely care about their customer. Of course, they may have to sort out the odd problem but this should not be seen as a waste of time. Consider this:

Satisfied customers lead to repeat business and referrals/recommendations.

1 **Repeat business:** If a customer is satisfied, next time they are ready to buy, they will buy again from the same source. The sales cycle will be streamlined and the sale will be concluded in an environment of trust, loyalty and mutual respect. In the vast majority of cases this will leave the competition excluded.

2 **Referrals/recommendations:** If a customer is satisfied they will be more than willing to refer or recommend the sales person to other potential customers.

Therefore, the outcome of the follow-up, is that it makes the sales person more efficient. Yes, they will spend time on the follow-up, but they will also substantially reduce their prospecting time, and it is no coincidence that this is precisely where the sales cycle began.

6.13 Summary

At the beginning of this chapter, the point was made that the sales cycle provided an effective framework for successful selling. However, the transition from understanding the theory of the sales cycle and applying it in practical selling situations is dependent on the sales person acquiring certain skills. These skills are wide ranging and it is very difficult to acquire and apply all the skills. Although simulated situations, such as role plays, can help a sales person to acquire some of the basic skills, the only real way to develop them is through experience in the field. Many sales people spend their whole careers in pursuit of perfecting these skills.

This said, the integration of the selling function into the overall marketing operation can make the role of the sales person more efficient. Indeed, it should actually reduce the number and range of skills which need to be acquired by the sales person. However, for many organisations, the role of the sales person remains a vital one. Some aspects of the sales cycle and its successful application will always be under the primary control of the sales person.

Extended tutorial activity E

Throughout this chapter you were asked to consider ways in which the wider role of marketing operations could improve the efficiency of the sales person. However, the selling function itself can actually contribute to the efficiency of the marketing operation.

Consider practical ways in which this may be achieved and discuss these conclusions with your tutor.

Essay question

Draw a summary diagram of the sales cycle. For each stage of the sales cycle discuss:

- if and how the role of the wider marketing function can improve the efficiency of the sales person
- the typical skills which a sales person will need to acquire/develop and apply.

Further reading

Allen, P. (1993), *Selling: Management and Practice* (4th edn),Pitman Publishing, Chapters 8, 9 & 10.

Calero, H. (1979), *Winning the Negotiation*, Hawthorn.

Fisher, R. and Ury, W. (1989), *Getting to Yes: Negotiating Agreement Without Giving In*, Business Books.

Gillam, A. (1982), *The Principles and Practice of Selling*, Heinemann, Chapters 3, 4 & 6.

Lancaster, G. and Jobber, D. (1994), *Selling and Sales Management* (3rd edn), Pitman Publishing, Chapters 4 & 5.

Pease, A.V. (1976), *The Hot Button Selling System*, Elvic & Co.

Chapter 7

The art of personal communication

Learning objectives

By the end of this chapter, you should :

- Understand the principles of personal communication

- Appreciate the transmission and feedback tools of personal communication and the model of active listening

- Appreciate the adapted transmission and feedback tools for telephone and group selling situations

- Appreciate the power of rapport and accept the responsibility which this carries

- Appreciate the skills which need to be developed by the sales person.

7.1 Introduction

In the marketing arena, communication is of vital importance. It involves transmitting a message to the customer and ensuring that it is received accurately by them. Further, it has a reverse element, whereby the marketer will encourage the customer to provide feedback which must be received accurately by the marketer. This principle is shown in Figure 7.1

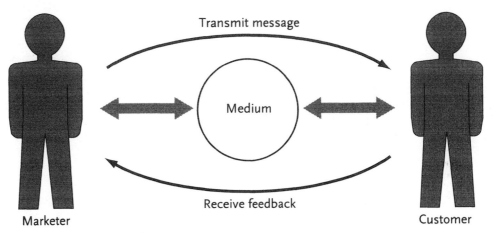

Fig. 7.1 *The principle of marketing communication*

Generally, the marketer is concerned with communicating with a collective number of customers and prospective customers. This is usually achieved through activities such as advertising, public relations and market research. However, it also involves personal selling activities. The sales person differs from the marketer in that they are able to transmit messages and receive feedback on an individual level.

The framework for the sales person is provided by the sales cycle, which was discussed in the preceding chapter. The successful implementation of the cycle requires that the sales person is able to communicate effectively on a personal level with a wide range of individuals. This chapter considers the issues involved in personal communication. It also provides a number of exercises which can be used to develop the basic skills. The advancement of these skills and their practical application occurs with experience in the field.

The development of good habits dictates that first one must appreciate the principles before looking to apply them in the practical environment. Misguided appreciation may result in the development of bad habits and these are far more difficult to change.

Selling myth

Good sales people have a 'silver tongue' or the 'gift of the gab'!

99

A practitioner's tale

"I am a keen and competent skier. I never went to ski school, instead I taught myself by learning from my own mistakes. The result is that I can ski down a piste but without the finesse of others. I cope and manage but my technique is definitely lacking. It lacks so much that I can only ski on pistes. As soon as I try to go off piste, I can no longer manage. I've had to go back to ski school and learn the proper technique before I can progress and extend myself.

Selling is exactly the same. If you learn the wrong or only some of the skills, you develop bad habits. The technique and method may serve you adequately in the short-term but as soon as you try to progress or move up a level, you will fall down. Far better to learn the right habits in the first place and continuously develop them to facilitate success over the long-term."

7.2 The power of rapport

The objective of the sales person in personal communication situations is to reach a state of rapport with the prospect/customer. Essentially, this involves empathy rather than sympathy. Unlike sympathy, empathy is not about agreeing with the other person's point of view but, rather, it concerns understanding their perspective and demonstrating this throughout the communication exchange.

Sometimes, a state of rapport is achieved naturally between two people. When this occurs, it could be said that they are on the same wavelength. However, it is also possible for one party to facilitate a state of rapport with another. This is achieved by putting them at their ease, finding and highlighting common ground between the two parties and, perhaps most importantly, using the same or similar communication signals. These inputs to achieving a state of rapport are shown in Figure 7.2 and the techniques which can be successfully employed are discussed throughout the remainder of this chapter.

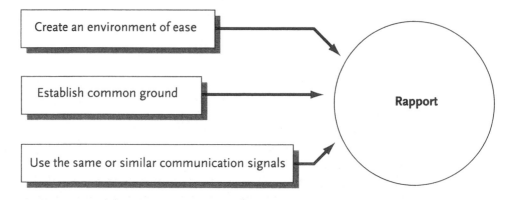

Fig. 7.2 *Inputs to achieving a state of rapport*

Ethical note

Achieving a state of rapport in personal communications is extremely powerful. Used wisely and professionally, it enables the sales person to be persuasive and influence the actions of the prospect/customer. However, when it is abused, the sales person can use the power to become manipulative. There is an ethical line which should not be crossed. To persuade and influence is on the right side of the line; to manipulate the thoughts and actions of others is on the wrong side.

Legislation and self-regulation by an industry will sometimes make it clear as to what is and what is not acceptable. However, on an individual level, each sales person must develop their own ethical code in this area. As a general rule, there should be a genuine need for the product/service being sold, and the solution provided by the sales person should provide real benefit for the buyer.

Long-term success needs to be based on good selling practice. This requires that the sales person provides their customers with genuine value for money based on their needs and desires.

7.3 Questioning and listening technique

In the preceding chapter, the importance of questioning and listening techniques were considered. In this section, we are more concerned with how one can develop these skills in selling situations.

Tutorial activity

In the preceding chapter, questioning and listening techniques were considered important to the need identification stage of the sales cycle. Given that these are the foundation of effective personal communication, for what other aspects of the sales cycle may these skills be important?

Discuss these thoughts with your tutor.

In personal communication, the good use of questions enables information to flow freely from the other person. Accurate and complete information is important to the sales person because it is based on this information that they are able to control and influence the sale.

Open questions encourage information to flow and closed questions can be used to control the conversation, highlight key points and demonstrate an understanding of the information which has been provided. In combination with these questions, soft and hard fact questions enable both emotional and logical information to be obtained.

Listening involves not only hearing words and sounds but analysing them so that they make sense. It is also important for the sales person to demonstrate their understanding through the use of appropriate linked questions, confirmatory closed questions and empathy statements. An empathy statement will often be used to summarise a batch of information by picking out key words and phrases used by the prospect/customer.

If a prospect/customer feels they are being fully understood, they will be at ease and become receptive to the suggestions of the sales person. This is achieved through active listening and appropriate response, the first stage of which is shown in Figure 7.3.

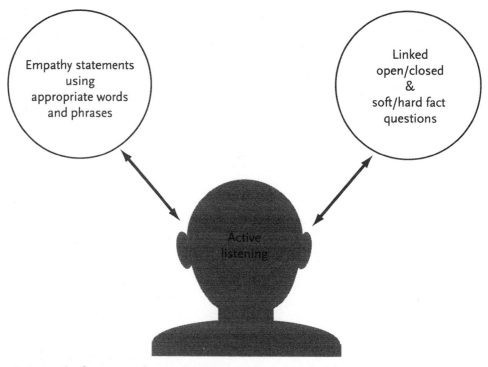

Fig. 7.3 *The first stage of active listening*

Practical activity 1

An awareness of questioning and listening techniques is a good starting point but the development of skills requires a practical approach. Of course, personal communication is not solely restricted to the selling arena and many social situations provide an ideal setting for these skills to be explored.

Over the next seven days, make a conscious effort to practise questioning and listening skills in a variety of social situations. Specifically, you should experiment with the following:

- *General open questions:* to encourage the other person to talk while you listen
- *Confirmatory closed questions:* to control the conversation and change direction
- *Soft and hard fact questions:* to gather a mixture of emotional and logical information
- *Empathy statements:* to demonstrate your understanding of the information which has been provided.

People tend to like to talk about their families, home, work and social activities. You should not necessarily restrict yourself to these areas but they will provide a good basis for starting conversations. Also, try to avoid gossip or the use of sarcasm in your discussions.

After each social exchange, try to note down your thoughts and observations. Particularly, you should consider:

- What worked really well?
- What would you change if presented with the same situation again?

Discuss this evaluation with your tutor at the end of the seven-day period.

7.4 Body language

The use of body and eye language has become commonly accepted as an effective tool in personal communication situations. For a wider appreciation of this area of personal communication, the student is recommended to follow a specific text. However, in this section, the key aspects of body language as they apply to the sales person are considered.

Open and closed gestures and clusters

Generally, body language gestures will be either open or closed, the latter involving crossed or partially folded arms covering the body, or another form of 'protection' such as a side-on stance. Closed gestures may also involve a crossing of the legs and the use of barriers. In the basic form, closed gestures are a negative signal which may indicate to the sales person that they are not being received favourably. Against this, open body language gestures may

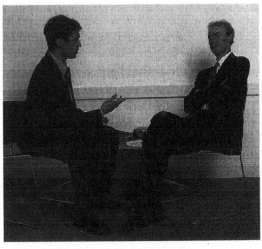

Fig. 7.4 *Open and closed gestures*

Fig. 7.5 *Thoughtful gestures tend to be hand to head gestures*

Fig. 7.6 *An untruth may often be followed by a hand to face gesture*

provide a positive signal. However, individual gestures should not be considered in isolation. A series or cluster of body language signals should be considered collectively to provide an overall picture. (*See* Figure 7.4.)

Thoughtful gestures

These tend to be hand to head gestures. Possibly, a rubbing of the head, a clutching of the forehead or a scratching of the chin as shown in Figure 7.5. Commonly, these gestures will be made after the sales person has asked a question and it is a sign that an answer is being considered. When a prospect/customer is in thought mode, they should be allowed to think, uninterrupted by the sales person.

Honesty gestures

The ability to know whether someone is telling the truth is important for the sales person. Much time and effort can be misplaced if one is pursuing a course of action based on inaccurate information. Children provide the basis for understanding honesty gestures. When a young child knowingly tells an untruth, it will frequently be followed by a covering of the mouth or face and may involve a degree of blushing and gulping. In adulthood, we learn to disguise our gestures. However, our natural instinct remains, and an untruth may often be followed by a hand to face gesture (*see* Figure 7.6), a speeding of the heart and breathing rate, and a delayed gulping action. Some aspects of eye language provide a useful support in this area, particularly given that it is far harder to disguise eye signals. (*See* Figure 7.7.)

Eye contact

Eye contact is important for both parties as it helps to build trust and respect. However, it should not be constant as this will result in an uncomfortable glare.

Fig. 7.7 *Possible dishonest eye language*

Fig. 7.8 *Handshakes should be neither too limp nor too firm*

Frequent eye contact combined with nods and encouraging noises will often enable the sales person to confirm they are listening. In reverse, they will be able to sense whether they are being received attentively.

Eye gestures

Eye gestures fall into two categories: eye movements and pupil dilation. It should be noted that the latter can be affected by factors of light but, putting this aside, large pupils tend to indicate a positive response and small the opposite. Eye movements tend to come in clusters and perhaps the most important to the sales person is the classic lie cluster, often accompanied by small pupils. It involves an upward glance as the untruth is created and structured, followed by a downward glance as it is delivered, after which eye contact may be restored.

Handshakes and power plays

Handshakes are very simple but nonetheless very important to the sales person. Given that a handshake will occur at the beginning and end of a meeting, it will form part of either the first or the closing impression. A handshake should not be limp nor too tight but, rather, it should be moderately firm as shown in Figure 7.8. It is also important to meet the other person head on and not turn or be turned to one side by the handshake. A handshake which aims to turn the position of the other person is one of a great number of power plays which can be used in personal communication. Others include leaning backwards, hands behind the head, feet on a desk or chair, or gaining a 'physical' advantage by standing up mid-conversation. If a state of rapport is to be achieved, the sales person must both be viewed as an equal and treat others equally. Therefore, an elimination or at least a minimisation of power plays is desirable.

Fig. 7.9 *Physical barriers should be removed at the earliest opportunity*

Fig. 7.10 *Look what happens when personal space is invaded!*

Barriers

The possibility of being sold to is often seen as a threat by many people. Frequently, they will seek to protect themselves from the threat by using a physical barrier. The most common in business situations is a desk. The larger the barrier, the greater the obstacle which the sales person has to overcome. Physical barriers should be removed by the sales person at the earliest opportunity. For example, a desk barrier can be removed by moving to the side in order to show a diagram or other visual sales aid. (*See* Figure 7.9.)

Personal space

Everyone has their own personal space, an area around them which they do not wish to be invaded. This will vary between social and business situations, with the latter usually requiring a greater space. The amount of personal space required may also be affected by one's upbringing. For example, an only child will often require more personal space than someone coming from a large family, and people raised in cities usually require less personal space that those raised in rural areas. The sales person should be responsive to an individual's requirement of personal space and take care not to invade it as shown in Figure 7.10.

Mirroring

Arguably, this is the most powerful aspect of body language as far as the sales person is concerned. It not only facilitates active listening but also enables persuasion to take place at a high level. Mirroring involves adopting similar

Fig. 7.11 *Adoption of similar body language gestures helps create a state of rapport*

body language stances and gestures to the other person. Subtlety is required and one should be careful not to rudely mimic others. When body language is mirrored, a state of rapport is almost inevitable. From this point, the sales person is able to lead the prospect/customer non-verbally by opening up their body language gestures and encouraging a positive frame of mind, receptive to their suggestions. (*See* Figure 7.11.)

The addition of body language provides us with the second stage of active listening. This is shown in Figure 7.12.

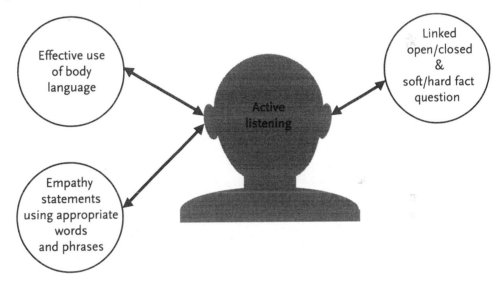

Fig. 7.12 *The second stage of active listening*

Practical activity 2

Using each of the sub-headings in this section, compose a list. For every personal communication exchange over the next seven days note down as many body language observations as possible. Try to note down the circumstances which gave rise to the non-verbal signal. For example, did it occur in response to a question? Was the subject threatened in any way, or particularly positive about something?

At the end of the seven-day period, discuss the contents of this list with your tutor.

7.5 VAK modes of communication

Relatively recent studies on personal communication have given rise to a number of mainly US authored texts on the subject of neurolinguistic programming or NLP as it is commonly known. For a more comprehensive understanding of this subject, further reading is recommended. In this section, the key aspects as they apply to the sales person are considered.

People have three modes of communication: visual, audio and kinesthetic (VAK). In other words, we all see, hear and feel things during communication exchanges. Although we all use all three communication modes, there tends to be an order of preference in which each of us use them. That is, we each have a primary, secondary and tertiary mode of communication and this may vary depending on the type of situation in which we are involved.

The sales person must first identify the mode(s) of communication being used by the prospect/customer, establish the primary mode and, in more lengthy exchanges, further distinguish between the secondary and tertiary modes. From this, the sales person can then adjust their communication transmissions accordingly.

Visual mode of communication

When someone is in this mode of communication, they are seeing or visualising images provoked by the exchange. Typically, breathing and heartbeat will be fast, talking will be rapid and hand movements will be exaggerated. The sales person needs to identify this mode and respond accordingly. This should include the use of visual aids and diagrams wherever possible, the phrasing of questions appropriately such as 'How do you see . . .?', and encouraging the prospect/customer to 'Imagine the effect of . . .' or 'Picture this . . .'. Additionally, the sales person should speak at a similar pace and exaggerate their own hand movements.

Audio mode of communication

This mode of communication involves a particular receptiveness to words and sounds and usually indicates a thoughtful and logical approach. The heartbeat will be slower, the breathing more controlled, there will be a steady pace to speech and measured hand movements. The response of the sales person to this mode of communication should be to select carefully the content of language, match the pace of speech and hand movements, use questions such as 'How does that sound to you?' and phrases such us 'I want to make this loud and clear . . .'.

Kinesthetic mode of communication

People in this mode of communication tend to be very relaxed, emotionally driven and are frequently prone physically to touch things, although this latter sign will often be restricted in business situations. Kinesthetic communication tends to be more commonly used in domestic situations, which is particularly useful for the retail sales person, as the nature of commercial situations will often dictate a different mode of communication. Pace of speech will often be much slower and the person may seem somewhat distant in mind, wrapped up in their own thoughts and feelings. The sales person should take a more laid back approach and will do well to retain control of the sale. Questions such as 'How do you feel about that?' and 'What are your feelings on . . .?' will be appropriate, along with responses which amplify the feelings of the prospect/customer.

Understanding and applying the VAK modes of communication in selling situations may be regarded as an advanced area of personal communication. It is somewhere to progress to rather than a starting point. The basic aspects of VAK will be achieved by mirroring body language and pace of speech together with empathy statements and linked questions which use similar language to that of the other person. Taken to a higher level, the use of VAK can provide us with our final model of active listening. This is shown in Figure 7.13.

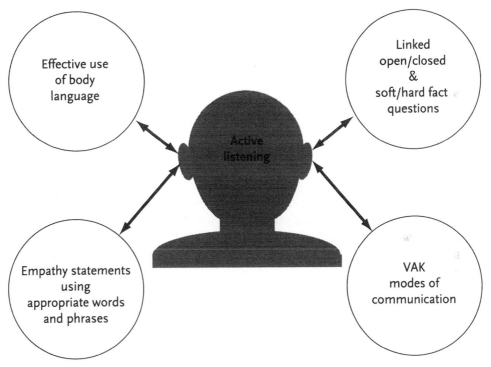

Fig. 7.13 *The active listening model*

Practical activity 3

In your lecture or seminar group, engage in an open-ended, round-the-table discussion based on a topic provided by your tutor. Try to act naturally in both asking and responding to questions. Ideally, this exercise should last for around thirty minutes but your tutor will guide you further on the time allowed.

During the discussion, try to identify different modes of communication around the table. At the end of the initial discussion, compare your conclusions with those of your peers and tutor.

A further important consideration of the active listening model is that it revolves around a two way communication process. It involves the use of a full range of transmission and feedback tools which can only be applied in their entirety in personal, face-to-face situations. The sales person may well find themselves in situations which do not allow the full range of tools to be used, the most notable of which will involve communicating by telephone or with groups. Both of these will now be considered in the remainder of this chapter.

7.6 Using the telephone effectively

The telephone has distinct advantages and disadvantages for the sales person. The greatest advantage is that it enables direct personal communication with a large number of people in the shortest amount of time. Against this, the major disadvantage is that it severely reduces the range of transmission and feedback tools at the sales person's disposal.

Initially, it may appear that only the questioning and listening tools are available. Indeed, it would be true to say that these will inevitably be the most prevalent. However, careful listening will enable the sales person to identify the likely mode(s) of communication based on the language used by the prospect/customer. Although incomplete, the sales person may be able to respond accordingly by, for example, trying to build a picture in the prospect/customer's mind using the telephone as the medium.

Further, body language has a partial role to play in effective use of the telephone as a selling medium. Although the sales person may not be able to see the body language of the prospect/customer, they are in control of their own body language. The sales person can enhance their performance on the telephone by using the same positive body language they would use for a face-to-face exchange. For example, smiling while talking on the telephone will be projected in the tone and pitch of the voice and this will be received accordingly by the prospect/customer.

Although the range of transmission and feedback tools is restricted over the telephone, the active listening model developed earlier in this chapter still applies. An additional skill which is required for effective telephone communication is the ability to focus on the call and exclude external activity. The sales person also has the task of maintaining the interest of the prospect/customer. The sales person has to build rapport quickly and ensure the conversation follows an expeditious path. Sales people working on the telephone tend to use a script to facilitate this.

Such scripts are not necessarily written down and should remain flexible within certain parameters. The script merely provides a framework for the sales person. This is not to be confused with the use of a standard inflexible script which tends to lead to a hollow and insincere sales call. Indeed many sales people using the telephone will frequently claim that they do not work to a script. However, if one were to listen carefully to these sales people, they will invariably use similar openings and introductions and certain phrases will be used repeatedly. The key is for each sales person to develop their own script or framework and remain sufficiently aware and flexible in order to respond to the needs of each individual call.

Practical activity 4

In your lecture or seminar groups, split into pairs and position your chairs so that you are back-to-back with each other. One of you take on the role of sales person and the other the prospect/customer. Use one of the telephone role-play scripts in Part V of this book or your own script relevant to a product/service with which you are familiar.

The position you are in has taken away the face-to-face transmission and feedback calls. The noise of your colleagues will provide a suitable distraction appropriate to most sales offices. Therefore, you have a simulated situation which enables you to practise your telephone technique. Continuously make your sales call(s) for fifteen minutes and then reverse roles.

7.7 Communicating with groups

Communicating with groups of people is not restricted to sales managers, lecturers, trainers or conference speakers. Many sales people will find themselves in various group selling situations, from presenting to a board of directors to seminar selling. The objective for the sales person when communicating with groups of people is to reach a state of rapport with all of them which, given that every person is different, may seem something of an impossible task.

Although the complete state of rapport which can be achieved in personal, face-to-face situations may not be possible, group dynamics enable an alternative state of rapport to be achieved. If sufficient numbers and influential members of the group are motivated, their enthusiasm can be encouraged and will have a knock-on effect.

The key tools for communicating with groups are now considered.

Planning and preparation

Presentations should be carefully planned, based on all available information, and should aim to achieve the sales person's objectives, such as generating enquiries or closing a sale. All presentation material and equipment should be prepared and checked in advance. Some people choose to rehearse their delivery, whereas others are more comfortable taking a flexible approach, using their plan as a framework.

Group objectives

The beginning of the group communication should seek to break the ice and achieve a set of objectives for the meeting which are acceptable to the group. The sales person needs to ensure that the group's objectives closely relate to their own.

Modes of communication

Accepting that within a group of people there is likely to be a mixture of preferred modes of communication, the sales person must attempt to deliver their presentation to the group using a combination of all three modes. The use of visual aids is important, but also the ability to vary the pace and tone of delivery is vital. The atmosphere created among the group provides a kinesthetic element and all three can be invoked by personal exchanges with individual group members.

Body language

Body language is very powerful in group situations. It enables the sales person to control and influence the group. Walking around, stances, hand gestures and eye contact all have a role to play. The sales person is also able to receive signals provided by the audience. Many of these are the same as in individual communication but the sales person should not be dismayed if a large number of people are sitting with their arms folded. In group situations, this is often a sign that people are listening closely to the points you are making and is often accompanied by a tilted head.

Play to the audience

In every group, there will be a mixture of characters and personalities. Everybody should feel that they are involved. Some will involve themselves naturally by asking or answering questions, whereas others will prefer to take a passive role. It is important not to communicate with the active members of the group at the exclusion of the passive ones. For example, a question posed by one member of the group can be expanded to involve the whole group. All questions and comments posed by the group members should be addressed, and those which are particularly important or positive should be highlighted.

Summary and action

At the end of a group communication, the sales person should summarise the key points discussed and confirm that the group's objectives for the meeting have been achieved. The sales person should then conclude the meeting by confirming the action which is to be taken. This action should relate directly to the sales person's own objectives.

Practical activity 5

Using either one of the group selling role plays in Part V of this book or a product/service with which you are familiar, prepare a presentation and deliver it to your lecture/seminar group who will act as your audience. The length of the presentation will be provided by your tutor.

Ideally, the presentation will be recorded on video for you to evaluate later; alternatively, one member of the group can be an observer, evaluating the performance of the sales person. The evaluation should include comments under the following headings:

- Did the sales person appear to be well prepared and have a plan for the presentation?
- Was a clear set of group objectives identified at the beginning of the meeting?
- Were all three modes of communication used effectively?
- Was body language used effectively?
- Was every group member made to feel involved?
- Was there a summary with confirmation that the group's objectives had been achieved?
- Did the sales person ask for appropriate action and did this match their own objectives?

Discuss this evaluation with your tutor.

7.8 Summary

This chapter started by looking at personal communication as a key skill area in implementing the sales cycle. The power of rapport was identified and its achievement through active listening. The final model of active listening incorporated the full range of transmission and feedback tools which can be used in personal communication. Finally, this range was adapted in consideration of telephone and group selling situations.

An awareness of the theory of communication is important but it can only provide a foundation. Skills need to be developed, and in this chapter there have been a number of practical activities which will help to do this by increasing one's appreciation in simulated or non-threatening situations. The sales person needs to develop further and improve these skills through practical application in the field and continuous self-evaluation. The context for applying these skills is provided by the framework of the sales cycle, as outlined in the preceding chapter.

Essay question

For a retail selling situation of your choice, discuss how the full range of transmission and feedback tools of personal communication can be successfully applied. The length of your essay should be between 1000 and 1500 words.

Further reading

Carnegie, D. (1965), *How to Win Friends and Influence People*, Angus & Robertson.

Covey, S.R. (1989), *The Seven Habits of Highly Effective People*, Simon & Schuster.

Drew-Morgan, S. (1993), *Sales on the Line*, Metamorphous Press.

Duncan, S. and Fiske, D.W. (1977), *Face-to-face Interaction*, Erlbaum.

Grinder, B.R. and J, and Stevens, J.O. (1979), *Frogs into Princes: neuro linguistic programming*, Real People Press.

Morris, D. (1967), *The Naked Ape*, Cape.

Morris, D. (1977), *Manwatching*, Cape.

Pease, A. (1993), *Body Language: how to read other's thoughts by their gestures*, Sheldon Press.

Robbins, A. (1988), *Unlimited Power*, Simon & Schuster.

Whitney, Hubin and Murphy (1978), *The New Psychology of Persuasion and Motivation in Selling*, Prentice-Hall.

Chapter 8

Qualities of a sales person

Learning objectives

By the end of this chapter, you should :

- Appreciate the essential qualities which every sales person should have

- Be able to consider the distinction between in built and acquired qualities

- Understand the variable qualities in relation to different types of selling

- Appreciate the importance of customer types in considering a sales person's qualities

- Have an appreciation of the different qualities required for both 'soft' and 'hard' selling.

8.1 Introduction

There is an ongoing debate within selling circles, indeed also within wider psychological fields, between 'nature' and 'nurture', that is, the personal qualities with which we are born and those which are acquired through personal development.

In considering this issue in wider psychological terms, one must consider life phases such as birth, infancy, early childhood, late childhood, teenage years, and so on. However, when viewing the qualities of a sales person, the debate is no longer strictly about nature and nurture. It becomes more a case of:

- What qualities does a person have when they enter the selling environment?
- What qualities can be acquired through training and personal development?

Within this chapter, the various qualities will be considered without specific reference to this distinction. Chapters 9 and 11 build on these qualities and go further towards considering whether good sales people are 'born' or 'made' through training and personal development.

Tutorial activity A

As you work through this chapter, consider which qualities you feel a sales person may acquire through training and personal development. Discuss these views with your tutor at the end of the chapter.

The author takes the view in this chapter that certain core qualities must exist in all successful sales people. A variable set of additional qualities can then be applied to different selling situations. These are considered in relation to:

- new business/account management
- telephone, field and retail environments
- product/service considerations
- customer considerations.

This builds on many of the issues and implications made in Chapters 5–7, further reinforcing a thorough appreciation of selling in practice.

8.2 The core qualities

Tutorial activity B

Before you read this section, jot down your own thoughts of the essential core qualities you feel every sales person should have. Compare these with those discussed by the author. If there are any differences, try to pinpoint them in the rest of the chapter.

1 **Interpersonal skills:** Every sales person must be able to communicate effectively. This relies on the ability to elicit, receive and understand information before applying it in outward communications which facilitate trust, empathy and persuasion. Some selling situations require more trust or persuasion than others, but in all cases, both factors, together with the overriding empathy considerations, form the basis of effective communication for all sales people.

2 **Adaptability and flexibility:** The behaviour of people is heterogeneous and, as a result, every selling situation is different. Given this, all sales people need to be flexible in their approach and be able to adapt to the variables which may arise in their environment. The degree of adaptability and flexibility required will vary from one type of selling to another but a core level is required in all cases.

3 **Honesty and trustworthiness:** Invariably, people will buy in an environment which makes them comfortable to do so. A key factor in creating this environment is the application of an open and honest approach by the sales person, building a relationship of mutual trust and respect between buyer and seller.

4 **Strength of character:** All types of selling carry a factor of rejection, some more so than others. Every sales person must have sufficient resilience and strength of character to absorb the level of rejection in their environment. Additionally, one must be able to receive constructive criticism in order to adjust and improve.

5 **Self-evaluation:** The most honest form of criticism is of oneself. The ability to reflect, analyse and evaluate one's own performance provides every sales person with a foundation for personal development and growth. In many respects this is an extension of the previous point. We all have the capability for self-evaluation but only those with sufficient strength of character will do so with honesty and purpose which results in an improved performance.

6 **Speed of thought:** We have already considered how every personal selling situation is different. Successful adaptation to varying situations often requires the sales person to 'think on their feet'. In many selling situations, the ability of the sales person to think quickly is a prerequisite.

7 **Self-motivation:** The need for this will vary from one type of selling to another, depending on factors such as isolation and managerial control. However, successful selling in any situation relies on the desire of the individual to perform well and achieve the desired results.

8.3 Account management, new business development and the combined role

The distinction between account management and new business selling was made in Chapter 5. The point was further made that many selling situations require a combination of both. In this section, the likely qualities of a sales person operating in each of these three categories are considered.

Account management

Successful account management or repeat selling relies on the ability to cultivate long-term relationships built on loyalty, trust and mutual respect. This requires an extension of the core interpersonal skills to incorporate friendliness, enthusiasm, perception and responsiveness. The development of long-term rapport requires an in-depth understanding of the customer, attention to detail and good personal organisation skills. The ability to follow routines and adopt a methodical approach to business activity is also likely to be a desirable quality.

New business development

The nature of acquiring new customers involves a greater degree of rejection for the sales person. As a result, they must be particularly resilient, highly self-motivated and determined to succeed. The ability to develop instant rapport requires something of a bold and gregarious personality involving strong belief in oneself and one's product/service. Interpersonal skills are likely to be tested to the maximum as are factors of confidence, speed of thought and flexibility. Persistency is often a prerequisite of the new business role along with a proactive, innovative and organised approach to business activity.

The combined role

Many sales people are employed in a capacity which involves a combination of both managing existing customers and actively seeking new ones. Few people will have all the qualities required for both types of selling. The key question to consider is how much of the role is devoted to each aspect. Common splits used in practice are 80/20 in favour of new business or vice versa, and 50/50 splits. These tend not to be scientific calculations but rather notional ratios used by organisations to place an emphasis on the split of responsibility.

Extending this practical approach, it provides us with a simplistic framework for considering the combined role, as shown below and in Figure 8.1.

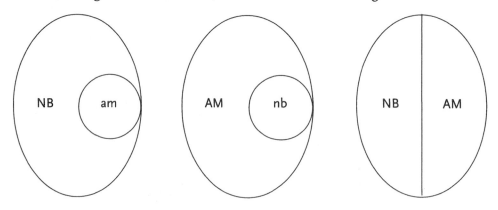

AM/am = Account management
NB/nb = New business

Fig. 8.1 *A practical framework for considering the combined roles of account management and new business development*

- Mostly new business, some account management: NB/am
- Mostly account management, some new business: AM/nb
- Equal split between account management and new business: NB/AM.

When considering the qualities of a sales person, this framework provides us with the ability to apply an appropriate combination of the qualities discussed previously under the respective headings of account management and new business development. Clearly, the NB/am and AM/nb situations require a majority of one set of qualities and a minority of the other, whereas the NB/AM role requires a good mixture of both sets. The precise combination of these qualities will vary according to the demands and requirements of each selling role, but the appropriate emphasis can be drawn from this framework.

Tutorial activity C

Scan job advertisements for selling positions and identify ones to represent each of the roles covered in this section, namely:

- NB only
- AM only
- NB/am
- AM/nb
- NB/AM.

From these advertisements, build a profile of the qualities required for each role. Present these profiles to your tutor in an appropriate format.

8.4 Teleselling, field selling and retail selling

This section enables us to look at the types of selling from a different angle. Here, we are concerned with the medium and environment in which the sale takes place. This can have an important impact on the qualities required of the sales person.

Teleselling

In Chapter 5, the definition of a true teleselling role was given as one where the sale is actually conducted and concluded using the telephone as the main or sole medium. For the purposes of this section, the term can be extended to include other telephone sales activity such as lead generation and after-sales customer support.

Using the telephone effectively as a selling medium introduces a whole new set of qualities. The ability to focus one's listening on an isolated verbal feedback tool is an essential factor. Additionally, the ability to project one's voice and express oneself using only verbal transmission is important. Working exclusively on the telephone also requires a high degree of self-discipline and can require a methodical or persistent approach.

Many of the mundane issues of working solely with the telephone conflict with the desire to have dynamic and enthusiastic sales people. Motivation in this area is vital. Many successful teleselling operations thrive on putting the sales people in close proximity to each other, with the collective activity producing a highly charged atmosphere. Although such an atmosphere can be highly motivational, it can also become very pressurised. The successful individual should be able to thrive on the high levels of pressure without the situation becoming stressful.

The pressurised environment of teleselling is perhaps one reason for the number of 'young' individuals employed in it, although there are other considerations. It provides an ideal training environment for sales people, as an on-site sales force is easier to manage and train than a remote one. Additionally, aesthetic qualities are restricted purely to the verbal, and the youthful looks which sometimes fail to gain respect from more mature buyers are eliminated from the equation. Although teleselling is not restricted to younger people (indeed there are many successful mature telesales people), it is certainly a common situation.

The use of the telephone also raises other issues. The lack of body language gestures and signals lead to faster verbal exchanges between buyer and seller. Therefore, speed of thought and issues of pace, tone and clarity become additional considerations. Additionally, use of the telephone as the selling medium usually leads to transactions being concluded more rapidly. The sales person must be able to work at this speed by being focused and concise.

Field selling

This takes us into a wider domain as there are many types of field selling. Most of the differences within field selling can be accounted for by considering the type of customer involved. Putting this aside until later in the chapter, there are some common qualities which can be applied universally to field selling.

Most notably, all the feedback and transmission tools of personal communication are available. The individual must be able to make maximum use of these tools. Additionally, the sales person is likely to work remotely and must be self-motivated, self-disciplined, well organised and a good time manager. Working, for the most part, in isolation requires that much personal development will come from self-evaluation. Successful development in field selling is often dependent on this factor.

Aesthetic issues must be considered. for example, how will the sales person be perceived by the customers? We have already seen how age may be a factor, but also personal appearance, such as appropriate dress, is an important issue. Additionally, the term 'field selling' indicates a degree of mobility. In most cases, this suggests the sales person must be able to drive and, therefore, the need for a current and relatively clean driving licence should not be overlooked.

Retail selling

Usually this presents a face-to-face selling situation. Therefore, many of the issues discussed in relation to field selling may also apply, particularly the full range of communication tools and aesthetic issues. Additionally, the training and development issues relating to an on-site sales force are worthy of note.

However, the main consideration in retail selling is that the sales person does not have to find the customer. Therefore, less rejection will be experienced and a less forceful character is required. Important qualities here relate to the ability to put the customer at their ease, be attentive to their needs and create an environment in which they are comfortable to buy.

Many of the qualities applicable to retail selling are similar to those required for customer care and after-sales service roles; that is 'soft' rather than 'hard' selling qualities.

8.5 Product/service considerations

This is an area which warrants special consideration. The type of product or service being sold can further differentiate the qualities required of the sales person. More specifically, the skills required of the sales person are likely to change in relation to tangibility. So, we can briefly consider the two categories.

Products

A key factor here is that the sales person can show or demonstrate the product. The customer can see and feel the product. On the surface this appears to be an advantage for the sales person and, indeed, in many cases it is. However, it can also require additional skills. Physical demonstrations and presentations will not be successful without skilful input from the sales person. They must be carefully planned and prepared. Even then, things can go wrong at a critical moment and the sales person must both anticipate and be able to act quickly in such situations. Customers will still need to be guided in order to appreciate the benefits but, also, the customer is provided with scope to highlight additional requirements and possibly specify product changes. The sales person must be able to identify these factors and act accordingly.

The efficiency of the sales person can also be enhanced if they are provided with a reliable product – one which does what it is meant to do and where quality control ensures a good level of reliability. Although this takes us more into the area of customer care and total quality management, the qualities of the sales person are relevant as they must be able to deliver this service element in conjunction with the product.

Services

The key difference between a product and service is its intangibility. If it cannot be seen or touched, the sales person will have to be able to communicate fully the benefits to the customer. Simple words and statements may be insufficient and the ability to facilitate VAK internalisation on behalf of the customer may be an important skill. This was discussed in depth in the preceding chapter.

Selling intangibles often involves concepts. Putting aside the VAK considerations, the ability to communicate fully concepts in a persuasive and convincing manner are prerequisites to success in this field.

8.6 Customer considerations

The final aspect affecting the qualities required in a sales person relates directly to the customer. It is important that a sales person is appropriate to the general customers they are likely to deal with. An admirable quality in a sales person is the ability to communicate at a variety of levels. For example, selling to garage proprietors requires different qualities than when selling to bank managers. In turn, different qualities are required in selling to academics, stockbrokers, office managers, architects, construction site managers, and so on.

Some of these qualities will come from a relevant background. For example, people with a university education are more likely to have an affinity with academics; an ex-mechanic may be appropriately matched to selling for a motor factory/parts supplier; and a trained draughtsman may be particularly successful at selling to architects.

Other qualities relate more to personality types than background. An ability to adjust to a variety of personality types is again an admirable quality which the sales person may possess. However, in many situations, it is possible to group customers into general personality types, although similarly this is usually achieved through occupations. Age, social background and status in the community can also be important factors when matching sales people to different customer types.

The overriding quality which a successful sales person will ideally possess is the ability to adapt to a wide range of customers in terms of communication and mutual respect.

A practitioner's tale

"A doctor made me give up smoking. This may come as no surprise to you but let me tell you this was no ordinary doctor/patient relationship.

I'd just started a new job as a pharmaceutical salesman and this doctor was one of the first calls on my territory. I'd done everything right: made an appointment at a quiet time of day, researched his file, ironed my shirt, polished my shoes. Imagine my surprise when I was dismissed from his office within the first minute. His words are so vivid, 'I don't buy from people who smoke, come back when you're no longer nicotine dependent.'

I don't know whether it was the implication that I was weak for being 'nicotine dependent' or my absolute desire to succeed in my new job, but that was the day I gave up smoking."

8.7 Summary

In this chapter, we have seen that there are a core set of qualities which must be possessed by sales people universally. The proviso to this statement is that each quality must be held to varying degrees in relation to different types of selling. Further, the type of selling opens up additional qualities which are likely to be necessary.

The core qualities can be summarised as:

- interpersonal skills
- adaptability and flexibility
- honesty and trustworthiness
- strength of character
- self-evaluation
- speed of thought
- self-motivation.

Further, looking at the different types of selling from a variety of angles provides us with an appreciation of the additional qualities. Specifically, these qualities relate to:

- new business and account management
- telephone, field and retail selling
- product/service considerations
- customer considerations.

Tip for success

Profile success and profile failure!

It is not uncommon for an organisation to build a profile of its ideal sales person. Doing so can assist with efficient recruitment and development of the sales force. A good method of building such a profile can be achieved with relative ease from within the existing sales force.

- Who are the most successful sales people and what common qualities do they possess?
- Who are the weaker or recently failed sales people and what are their common characteristics?

By profiling these extremes, it aids the recruitment process and provides a focus for training and development within the sales force.

Essay question

Based on organisations with which you are familiar or, alternatively, ones you have researched through job advertisements, identify one organisation which uses 'soft' selling and one which uses 'hard' selling. List and discuss the qualities which are likely to be required of the sales person in each situation.

Further reading

Gillam, A. (1982), *The Principles and Practice of Selling*, Butterworth-Heinemann, Chapter 1.

Lancaster, G. and Jobber, D. (1994), *Selling and Sales Management* (3rd edn), Pitman Publishing, Chapter 9.

Mercer, D. (1988), *The Sales Professional*, Kogan Page.

Stafford, J. and Grant, C. (1993), *Effective Sales Management* (2nd edn), Butterworth-Heinemann, Chapter 19.

Chapter 9

The 'psychology' of selling

Learning objectives

By the end of this chapter, you should :

- Appreciate the importance of psychological/sociological aspects in personal selling situations

- Have an increased awareness of the buying environment

- Understand the principle of mutuality in selling situations

- Appreciate the balance between logic and emotion in buying decisions

- Have an understanding of self-motivation.

9.1 Introduction

Essentially, 'psychology' in selling is about understanding how people think, both consciously and subconsciously. There are many skills which need to be acquired in order for the principles discussed in this chapter to be successfully applied in practice. Arguably, these skills are the most difficult for the sales person to master. It is virtually impossible to develop them in simulated situations and practical experience is the only path to follow. However, a critical appreciation of the issues involved will facilitate a faster acquisition of the skills.

The hallmark of a top quality sales professional will invariably show in this area. They will have many of the skills already covered in this text. Specifically, they will understand the key buying motivators of their customers and have excellent communication skills. The application of these skills in personal selling situations will result in a great deal of success. However, optimum success for the sales person will only be achieved when these skills are combined with the ability to understand how people think the ability to use this to their advantage.

There is a natural element to these skills. Some people are able to use them instinctively and have the ability to perceive the thoughts and feelings of others. Indeed, the use of one's natural instinct in personal selling situations should be encouraged and applauded. This leads us again into the great 'nature versus nurture' debate. Are we born with the ability to perceive the thoughts and feelings of others, or can we acquire and develop the skills required?

Although some people undoubtedly have a headstart in this area, the author takes the view that we all have the ability to improve on our natural qualities of perception. It is an ongoing learning process which underpins the aspects of personal communication, covered in Chapter 7. Evidence of this can be seen and heard in every sales office, team meeting, sales conference and convention up and down the country, as tales of success are enthusiastically exchanged. Frequently, these relate to psychological victories and powerful persuasion. Such tales are important, as they create excitement and a motivating environment. Additionally, and perhaps most importantly, they enable sales people to learn from the success of others.

Most of this chapter is devoted to the psychological and sociological exchanges between buyer and sales person. The final part considers the 'psychology' of self-motivation on the part of the sales person. The nature of the selling environment is one of extreme highs and lows for the sales person. The ability to maintain a balanced perspective and remain continuously motivated is arguably the most important skill a sales person needs to acquire in order to achieve sustained success over the long-term.

A practitioner's tale

"Sometimes you just have to let people discover for themselves what they want to buy. Last week a prospect came to my office wanting a quote for basic commercial buildings and contents insurance. I was the third broker they had visited and they had at least two more to see. Quite simply, they intended to buy from the person providing the cheapest quote. Now this is bad business for me because the only way I can provide the lowest quote is by slashing my commissions in order to win the business.

In the very early days of my career, I would have wasted a lot of time trying to persuade this type of buyer of all the good reasons why they should buy from me, such as the extra value which I could provide through offering high levels of service. Then I became wiser by reducing the amount of time spent on such prospects because of the low success rates. I would give them their quote, outline the advantages of dealing with me and send them on their way. My conversion ratios remained exactly the same and I wasted less of my time. Now I have found a new way of handling these situations which involves even less of my time and produces an improved success rate.

I sat this prospect down in a quiet office and explained that I could not provide them with a quote until I knew exactly what they wanted. So, I handed over a pen and a piece of paper and asked them to write a list under three headings:

- What would happen to my business if the building was destroyed?
- What would happen to my business if all the capital equipment were stolen?
- What would happen to my business if I were successfully sued for £1 million?

I left the room saying I had to make an urgent call. Ten minutes later, I returned knowing the answers to all three questions would amount to substantially reduced profits and possible business failure. I then asked what the prospect would want to happen if any of these disasters were to occur. Again, I knew the answer would be to eliminate the risk.

Once I explained that the cheapest policy I could provide would not actually eliminate the risk, they became more interested. 'How much will it cost me to eliminate the risk?' was music to my ears. Making the sale from that point was a formality.

Now that is efficient selling. The prospect effectively sold to themselves while, for the most part, I was somewhere else doing something else."

Tutorial activity A

The practitioner in the above tale states that making the sale was a formality after the prospect asked 'How much will it cost me to eliminate the risk?' Consider why this was the case and how the sale could be achieved in terms of a simple dialogue. Discuss these conclusions with your tutor.

9.2 What do people buy?

It could be argued that people *want* to buy things which they feel they *need* and can *afford*. Although this may be true, it is too simplistic in considering personal selling situations. People must also be comfortable with the environment and manner in which they are buying. Notwithstanding the physical environment provided by the organisation, the sales person is responsible for the intangible environment.

It follows that before someone will buy anything, they must first 'buy' the sales person. This requires that the sales person must gain the trust and respect of the buyer and retain them throughout the sale. Factors which may affect these aspects are:

- a balance of enthusiasm and sincerity
- professional competence
- comprehensive product knowledge
- honesty
- reliability.

If this can be achieved on an ongoing basis, the customer will become loyal to the sales person. They will buy from them because they are comfortable doing so, trusting them and respecting their views.

Tip for success

People buy people first and products second!

Given this, the sales person must build and maintain a genuine rapport with the prospect and be sufficiently perceptive to the signals provided by them. This requires enormous skill and flexibility on behalf of the sales person. The perfection of such skills will never be achieved, as one will never be able to please all of the people, all of the time. However, in terms of personal development, it provides a valid goal to work towards.

9.3 Creating and controlling the buying environment

There have been several references in this book to the sales person creating an environment in which the customer can buy. This is particularly relevant to the UK market, as there is something of a cultural resistance to being sold to. However, such an approach also travels rather well and can be applied as good selling practice to many markets around the world.

Establishing this principle is fine, but how can a suitable buying environment be created? There are two levels of input and several considerations:

The organisation

The sales person cannot create a suitable environment on their own; the organisation has a role to play. Specifically, there is the responsibility for an appropriate physical environment, name awareness, corporate image and identity, quality of products and after-sales service. If these factors do not exist or are lacking in any way, the sales person is presented with an additional hurdle.

In sales-orientated organisations, some of these factors may be overlooked or remain inconsistent with the requirements of customers. The increasing influence of marketing on the selling function has seen enormous advances in these areas in recent years, and the widening philosophy of marketing looks set to see continued improvements.

Even with the positive influence of marketing, sales people have to accept that perfection will not always exist. There will be times when an organisation will receive some bad publicity, a product will be faulty, a member of the support staff will have a bad day, or any number of other problems. It is important for the sales person to appreciate the efforts of their organisation and to adjust their tactics in the field accordingly.

The sales person

The sales person is responsible for creating the intangible environment based on the needs of each individual customer. This will involve the creation of rapport and putting the customer at their ease. Beyond this, it is important for the sales person to be honest and build a relationship of mutual trust and respect. Potentially good relationships can be destroyed by making false claims about the product, making rash or offensive statements and comments, pushing too hard or trying to close a sale too soon.

In order to be totally effective, the sales person must act as a facilitator to the buying process. The customer should be guided along the path of the sale, one step at a time. Ideally, the customer should feel that they are in control of the buying decision throughout, whereas the reality is completely the opposite, with the sales person retaining control.

Tutorial activity B

How can the sales person retain complete control of a sale while at the same time enabling the customer to feel that they are in control of the buying decision?

Make notes on how you think this can be accomplished and present them to your tutor for an open discussion.

Good sales and long-term relationships are based on the customer having a full appreciation for the product they have purchased, including its capability, limitations and value. Ultimately, having considered these factors, the customer should feel totally comfortable with the decision they have made. Post-purchase dissonance is a well recognised problem experienced by customers. In order to limit the impact of this, the customer should be reassured by the sales person and the organisation at every opportunity.

9.4 Mutual respect and benefit

A selling myth

The customer is always right!

Nothing could be further from the truth, as the customer is rarely right. Sales people must be careful in their efforts to satisfy the customer, as it can result in the customer buying the wrong product and weakening the position of the sales person. However, the customer's views and feelings are extremely important. Argumentative confrontation and belittling the customer should be avoided. Instead, customers need to have their feelings and views redirected by the sales person.

Good sales are rarely made when one party is placed in a weaker position than the other. A business transaction should take place between equals in an environment of mutual respect. It is not vital for the customer to like the sales person, although it helps. However, it is imperative for the customer to respect the sales person in their professional capacity. Similarly, the sales person needs to respect the views and opinions of the customer, even if they do not totally agree with them.

Building on this principle, a good transaction must result in mutual benefit for both buyer and seller. In the long run, it benefits neither party for the wrong product to be purchased or for the right product to be purchased at the wrong price. The customer should be expected to pay the right price for the right product based on their needs and the value which will be derived from the purchase. Further, this should be consistent with the needs of the sales person and their organisation.

A practitioner's tale

"I never let people buy from me until I'm ready to sell to them. Now, this is harder than it sounds. Picture yourself in this situation.

You have been with a prospect for thirty minutes. You have introduced yourself and your company, begun to build a rapport, identified their outline needs and tried to develop these needs further by producing some samples or product literature. The prospect says, 'I want this one, how much is it?' With all the rejection we take as sales people, nobody could blame you for quoting a price and attempting to close the deal. But the deal isn't ready to be closed as you have not presented the prospect with any value."

Tutorial activity C

In the scenario presented by the practitioner above, how would you proceed in order to build real value into the sale? Discuss these thoughts with your tutor.

9.5 Balancing logic and emotion

In Chapter 4, reference was made to how buyers base decisions on logic and emotion. Specifically, the point was made that domestic consumers tend to make buying decisions based mainly on emotion, whereas commercial and trade buyers are more likely to make decisions based on logic. It could be further argued that trade buyers need to use an even higher degree of logic compared to many commercial buyers.

However, it can be dangerous for the sales person to generalise buyers in this way, as all buyers, whether consciously or not, will use a combination of logic and emotion in a buying situation. The sales person must anticipate the motivation of each individual customer, and achieve an appropriate balance of logical and emotional reasons for the buyer to make an affirmative purchasing decision.

Building on some of the communication principles established in Chapter 7, one can say that logical reasons are based on *hard facts* and emotional reasons on *soft facts*. Use of appropriate soft and hard fact questions will enable the sales person to establish the depth of logical and emotional needs in each individual situation.

As we saw in Chapter 6, once the real needs of the prospect have been established, a successful sale can be concluded by matching these needs in the form of *benefits*.

Tutorial activity D

In this section, it was inferred that trade buyers apply a greater degree of logic to their buying decisions than do commercial buyers. In approximately 500 words, present an argument to your tutor which either agrees or disagrees with this viewpoint.

9.6 Disturbing the customer

The thought of disturbing a customer may appear somewhat contradictory to the objectives and principles of selling. However, in many selling situations, it can be one of the most powerful methods of making a sale.

It is particularly relevant to concept selling and selling services. Although appropriate to all three types of buyer, disturbing a customer has the tendency to create an emotional impact and, therefore, it is particularly common in domestic buying situations.

Ethical note

The power of creating an emotional disturbance in a prospect should be used wisely. If misused, it can lead to very hard, unethical selling. Used appropriately, it can enable the buyer to appreciate fully the value of their purchase.

Therefore, care should be taken not to make false or exaggerated claims and for the sales person not to apply undue amounts of pressure.

Essentially, a customer is disturbed when they become aware of the consequences of not buying. For example, what would be the consequences for someone not to make a will?

The answer to this question will vary according to each individual situation. In the case of many simple estates the consequences may be relatively minor, but in the case of more complex ones, there may be major implications.

Regardless of the product/service being sold, the sales person should ensure that the consequences of not purchasing are fully understood by the person making the buying decision. In this way, they can become fully aware of the benefit which will be derived from the product/service.

A practitioner's tale

"One of the hardest products to sell is life assurance. It is a concept which many people are uncomfortable with and this is understandable, as it involves thinking about death. But when you see the financial destruction of a family unit caused by an untimely death, compounding the grief which is experienced, you learn to appreciate just how important life assurance is. I cannot remove the emotional difficulties which death causes, but I can reduce the impact by eliminating the financial burden.

If that means disturbing my customers a little now, I'd rather that than face up to a widow who faces losing her and her children's lifestyle in addition to their burden of grief. If I can see a clear, logical need but the prospects can't appreciate my point of view, I ask them if they would mind humouring me with a little role play.

Assuming they are agreeable, I produce a little box from my pocket and explain to the breadwinner of the family that they are to imagine they are in it. I then ask their partner what they would do next. Based on their response, I proceed to have a full discussion with them to establish the circumstances which would prevail. If at any point the 'deceased partner' tries to enter the conversation, I stop and explain that they must be quiet because they are supposed to be in 'the box'. If they don't buy, that's fine, so long as they understand the consequences of not doing so.

This method rarely offends, although frequently it disturbs my customers. I am comfortable with their being disturbed. I can provide a solution to their problem and if they don't want my solution, at least my conscience will be clear. It also enables me to demonstrate that the problem I am solving is not only achieved with a product but a service as well. If they have bought me, then not only will I sell to them now but they will become my client for life."

9.7 Reverse psychology

Sometimes a very soft yet powerful approach is required. This can be achieved by using reverse psychology.

Reverse psychology is achieved by providing reluctant or hesitant buyers with the option not to buy. By ensuring that they feel there is always a way of not purchasing, they can be guided along a path of appreciating the benefits of the product/service being sold.

Using this method requires a lot of skill, as the customer must be given reasons and options for not buying while at the same time creating an environment in which the sales person can demonstrate the need for and the value of their product/ service. However, when such techniques are skilfully applied the impact can be very powerful.

Prospects can be encouraged to buy without feeling under pressure to do so. They are able to appreciate fully the benefits and the value of the product/service, because they are at their ease and receptive to the sales person's advice and guidance.

A development of this is where the sales person tries to 'take the sale away' from the buyer once a strong need has been established. Making the customer 'reach out and buy' in this way can provide a powerful method of closing the sale.

9.8 Self-motivation

Selling for a living tends to produce a working environment of emotional highs and lows. There can be excitement at closing deals, exhilaration at overcoming challenges and a feeling of success when things are going well. However, the feeling of failure when opportunities are missed or when being repeatedly rejected can be overwhelming. To compound the effect of this, many sales people spend large periods of their working lives in isolation from the support of their colleagues.

In the preceding chapter we saw how the sales person must have a sufficiently strong character for the demands of their selling role. Invariably, strength of character involves the ability to motivate oneself and minimise the impact of negative emotional influences. Motivational speakers and managers will frequently refer to the need for a *positive mental attitude (PMA)* which has given rise to sayings such as 'there are no problems, only solutions' and 'for every negative there is also a positive'. Whether or not one chooses to accept the complete philosophy of PMA, there are some universal factors which positively influence self-motivation for the sales person:

1 **Belief in oneself:** Self-confidence is vital. It is important to believe in one's ability which includes an acute awareness of one's own strengths and weaknesses. Wherever possible, the strengths should be used to the maximum and exposure to the weaknesses should be minimised. If this is achieved, self-belief is a natural progression.

2 **Belief in one's product/service:** Over a sustained period of time, it is virtually impossible to motivate oneself to sell a product or service in which one has no belief or confidence. It becomes difficult to remain enthusiastic, and therefore difficult to persuade and motivate buyers.

3 **Self-evaluation:** Continuous and honest self-evaluation can be a powerful tool of self-motivation. Evaluation facilitates change and improvement, which in turn increases achievement, which inevitably will provide motivation.

4 **Driving force:** Arguably, the most important requirement of a sales person is to have a strong driving force. This involves setting personal goals which, when achieved, will deliver real personal benefit. Both long-term and short-term goals should be used; the former will provide the underlying driving force, and the short-term goals will confirm that progress is being made and help to identify when changes need to be made.

Personal goals should be based on the specific *key motivators* of each individual. For example, some sales people are motivated by ego and status, some by lifestyle, others by competition, and so on. The goal must be sufficiently important to the individual in order for its achievement to be valuable and meaningful.

A practitioner's tale

"The long-term goal is the most important. It is that shining light at the end of the tunnel; the purpose of the journey is to reach it. The short-term goals provide the route which needs to be followed, at first step-by-step, then section-by-section. Every step or section takes you closer to the light. It starts as a direct route. Every so often, there is a twist or turn or an obstacle which you hadn't anticipated. You overcome the obstacle, adjust and refocus on the light. The nearer you get to the light, the more determined you become to reach it. My advice to you is – don't ever let that light go out and when you reach it, find another tunnel and aim for another light."

9.9 Summary

This chapter has provided a practical view of some of the key psychological and sociological factors for the sales person to consider. Psychological and motivational theories provide a huge area for academic consideration. However, in the context of selling in practice, the aspects covered here provide a sound basis for the sales person.

An awareness of the issues, applied in a variety of practical situations, combined with the tales and inspirations of others, will lead to success in the field of selling. The ability to perceive the thoughts and feelings of others and respond accordingly is one of the hardest and, therefore, one of the most valuable set of skills which a sales person will acquire.

Essay question

The concluding paragraph of the Practitioner's Tale in section 9.6 reinforces many of the key psychological and sociological issues involved in selling situations. In the form of an essay, discuss how this practitioner appears to have a comprehensive appreciation for the 'psychology' of selling.

Further reading

Allen, P. (1993), *Selling: Management and Practice* (4th edn), Pitman Publishing, Chapters 5 & 10.

Gillam, A. (1982), *The Principles and Practice of Selling*, Butterworth-Heinemann, Chapter 5.

Pease, A.V. (1976), *The Hot Button Selling System*, Elvic & Co.

Robbins, A. (1988), *Unlimited Power*, Simon & Schuster.

Robbins, A. (1992), *Awaken the Giant Within*, Simon & Schuster.

Stafford, J. and Grant, C. (1993), *Effective Sales Management* (2nd edn), Butterworth-Heinemann, Chapters 30, 32 & 33.

Case study: Kewill-Xetal Systems Ltd.

Background and instructions

Kewill-Xetal Systems Ltd. is a wholly owned subsidiary of Kewill Systems PLC. It provides Electronic Data Interchange (EDI) software solutions which enable electronic business transactions, such as orders, invoices, credit and debit notes. This case study relates to a specific selling situation which occurred.

Initially, you are required to familiarise yourself with the first and second phases of the selling strategy provided. You are then to complete Task 1 which asks you to consider an appropriate third stage, given the problems which have arisen. After you have completed this task, your tutor will be able to tell you how the problem was actually solved by the sales people of Kewill-Xetal.

The second stage of the case study goes on to look at the structure of the sales force and the resources it has available. You are given the selling processes used in the first and second phases of the strategy and are required to propose a selling process which can be used for the actual third phase. After you have completed this task, your tutor will be able to show you the actual selling process used by the sales people of Kewill-Xetal. For those students using this book on a self-study programme, the actual selling process used is summarised in the solution document.

Your final task is to evaluate your own solutions in comparison to those selected by Kewill-Xetal and its sales people.

Phase 1

Following an analysis of the market, Kewill-Xetal (KX) developed a software solution which could be used by major consumer retailers. The concept is that EDI replaces common paper-based messages, such as orders, invoices and statements, with electronic ones on a secure network. The resultant benefit is that the efficiency of the retailer is significantly enhanced. However, the full benefit to the retailer relies on each and every supplier using compatible software. KX offers a standard EDI solution to the retailer's suppliers based on the bespoke needs of the retailer, but there are other competitive EDI solutions which can be customised to achieve compatibility.

The first phase of the selling strategy was to target selective major retailers which were carefully researched. A lengthy selling process was necessary in order first to sell the concept and then facilitate purchase by building relationships. The decision on behalf of the retailer would be a strategic one and would be taken at a very senior level. In effect, the decision to proceed would lead to a strategic alliance or trading partnership between the two organisations.

Phase 2

One major organisation to be convinced of the benefits which could be gained by using KX's software solution was Asda Stores PLC. A strategic alliance was formed. Asda agreed to use the EDI software supplied by KX. Further, the two organisations embarked on a joint operation to ensure Asda's suppliers were all using compatible systems within eighteen months.

Asda divided its suppliers into two categories: major and minor. The first stage of the operation was to ensure all major suppliers were using compatible systems within nine months, and the second stage was to ensure the same for all minor suppliers within the following nine months. In effect, these two stages of the joint operation are the second and third phases of KX's selling strategy.

Asda's major suppliers were generally very keen to purchase a system supplied by KX or allow KX to customise their existing EDI software to suit Asda's requirements. KX's full software solution could be provided for a price of between £2000 and £5000 with a further £1000–£2000 for training and support services. Asda made it clear that suppliers *must* have a compatible system if trading links were to continue. The costs incurred by the major suppliers were minimal in relation to the value of their continuing relationship with Asda, and selling was relatively straightforward and profitable for KX.

Phase 3

Problem

Six months on, sales to major suppliers were going well and nearing a conclusion. KX and Asda were looking ahead to the second stage of their joint operation, the minor suppliers. Minor suppliers included two sub-groups: small businesses with limited capacity, restricting trade to relatively low volumes, and larger companies trading with Asda on a limited or occasional basis. Both sub-groups presented a selling problem. The value of continuing trading links with Asda would not necessarily exceed the cost of purchasing KX's system.

Again, Asda made clear that use of the system was essential if trading links were to continue but it was also keen not to alienate its minor suppliers. As the situation currently stands, the small business minor suppliers cannot generally afford the systems, and the larger-sized minor suppliers are not likely to be sufficiently motivated to purchase. The effort and time spent by KX's sales force to convert these two prospect groups into customers would be disproportionate to the profits which would be obtained.

Currently, the price of the standard software which is totally adequate for the minor supplier is approximately £2000 and the costs to KX are:

Direct costs of sale £600
Packaging and distribution £10
Sales support costs £290

Additionally, each piece of software needs to be supported, the costs of which are as follows:

Installation and training £100 (for one day)
Maintenance contract £ 50

At present, these latter costs are covered through the additional sale of training and a support contract, priced at around £1000.

The total price of £3000 is too high in relation to the willingness and ability of the prospects to buy. Additionally, the sales effort required to convince these prospects to buy produces a less than acceptable return on time spent in terms of profitability. This is reinforced by the fact that only 50 of Asda's 300 minor suppliers are likely to purchase, even with this level of selling effort.

Asda wants to increase the number of minor suppliers using the system to at least 100 and KX wants to ensure more profitable sales in relation to its selling and service effort. Asda has a cashflow reserve of £40 000 which can be used temporarily in an effort to find a solution, and the company is also prepared to second three members of staff into sales support roles for a nine-month period.

Task 1

Your task is to think of a solution to this third phase of the selling strategy.

Tip: Consider the following selling processes before reaching a conclusion.

Organisational structure of KX

Wherever possible, KX tries to relate all its sales and service costs directly to results. It retains the services of three highly experienced and skilful field sales people who work on a commission-only basis against sales generated. Similarly, consultants are used to install the software and provide the basic one-day training programme. They are paid a daily rate of around £100 by KX. Four internal sales and customer support staff are employed by the company.

Selling process/tactics: Phase 1

The sales support staff conduct desk research in order to target customers and, in consultation with the field sales people, write personal letters of introduction. The field sales people make direct contact with the major retail organisations and arrange meetings. The concept sale is then conducted over several meetings with the lead time for the whole sale running from three to six months. During this time a strong relationship is formed and a successful sale will invariably lead to some form of strategic alliance between the two organisations. As a result, the sales people will be in close contact with these customers long after the initial sale is concluded. This process is shown in Figure A.

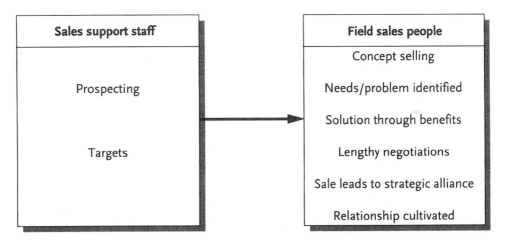

Fig. A *Selling process for Phase 1*

Selling process/tactics: Phase 2

Asda sends out letters of introduction to major suppliers, outlining the importance of meeting with the KX sales person. KX sales support staff call and

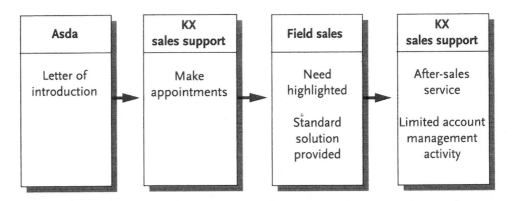

Fig. B *Selling process for Phase 2*

make appointments. Field sales staff visit and offer a standard solution, usually conducted over one appointment. Customers are supported by KX's internal sales support staff. This process is shown in Figure B.

Task 2

At this stage you should be aware of the Phase 3 strategy adopted by KX in conjunction with Asda. Your task is to suggest a suitable selling process/tactics which could be used. Present this in the form of a brief narrative and diagram for your tutor.

Task 3

At this stage you should be aware of the Phase 3 strategy and the actual selling process/tactics used by KX. Your task is to evaluate critically your own work by direct comparison to the solutions and methods which were used in reality. This evaluation should be concluded with a discussion of whether you believe KX were right in their strategy and tactics or rationale supporting a better alternative.

Task 4

The three freelance field sales people involved with KX are highly experienced and skilled. Their range of selling is conducted at three different levels. Imagine you were asked to recruit a fourth field sales person. What key qualities would you look for?

Managing the selling function

Chapter 10

Sales force organisation and structure

Learning objectives

By the end of this chapter, you should :

- Appreciate the strategic requirements of structuring a sales force

- Appreciate the operational nature of organising a sales force

- Understand the various levels of selling and sales management in the organisational context

- Understand the principle of territory planning and the most common inputs

- Begin to consider the growing importance of team-based selling efforts.

10.1 Introduction

The decision as to whether personal selling is appropriate to the needs of the organisation and its customers is a strategic one. Further, the organisation must develop its strategic thinking to incorporate the most appropriate structure for its sales force. This will involve consistency with the other components of the marketing mix, including the specific role of the sales force, together with consistency with the distribution strategy of the organisation.

The operation of the sales force should be efficient and profitable. This starts with developing a structure consistent with the sales and distribution strategy; and continues with good organisation, planning and management control. The successful implementation of this strategy and the integrated operational plan revolves around good management practice in terms of recruitment, training, motivation and communication.

Given these considerations, this chapter provides the context in which the remaining chapters of this third part should be placed. The role of sales people and sales managers alike is dependent on the strategic objectives of the organisation and, operationally, how these objectives are best achieved.

10.2 Efficiency and performance

In line with current marketing philosophy and good business practice, the sales force should be both efficient and profitable. Sales people and sales managers need to provide an optimum return of sales revenue in relation to the expenditure of the organisation. This needs to be targeted in the form of:

- *Income:* What sales revenue do we require? and
- *Expenditure:* How much will it cost to achieve this revenue?

By achieving the targeted income within the expenditure budget, a sales force will be profitable. Logically, this can be broken down, ultimately, into a targeted return and outlay for each member of the sales force and support personnel. If each active member of the sales force produces their targeted level of **profitable sales**, the net result is a successful one for the organisation.

In order for this principle to work, the expectations of each individual, and therefore the sales force as a whole, must be realistic. This realism should include their level of remuneration and the support costs/benefits of the operation. For example, sales people working with the support of national television advertising or a telemarketing team can be reasonably expected to return a higher level of sales revenue. Further, the organisation should consider the most efficient use of their resources. For example, a sales person earning £40 000 per annum may well be effective in prospecting and making their own appointments but is it efficient for them to be doing so? Perhaps, the delegation of this task to a telemarketer, releasing the sales person to spend more time with customers, may be more efficient and produce an increased performance in terms of overall profitability.

These are the sort of considerations which need to be given to the structure, expectation and organisation of the sales force. The management role throughout the sales force is to plan and manage results which are consistent with the needs and expectations of the organisation, making optimum use of all available resources. This needs to be broken down into every level of sales management and selling within the sales force in order to deliver the strategic and operational objectives of the organisation.

10.3 Levels of sales management

The management structure of the sales force needs to be relevant to its size and demands. A very small sales force may require only one sales manager/director but as size increases, so further layers or levels need to be introduced. In the case of a small sales force, there will be a responsibility for performing both strategically and operationally, whereas as the number of levels increases there is a diminishing responsibility for strategy and an increasing requirement for operational performance, at the lower levels.

An additional consideration relates to the demands of a sales force. A sales manager responsible for a team of only very experienced sales people is likely to be able to manage more of them than if the team comprised less experienced sales people, requiring more individual attention and guidance. Also, particularly at lower levels, sales managers may be required actively to sell in addition to their management duties. This, too, will limit the number of sales people they can manage effectively.

The variables involved in structuring a sales force make it difficult to specify universally correct ratios for developing layers within the management structure itself. Perhaps the most comprehensive analysis which has occurred in this area can be drawn from the financial services industry. As a result of the industry being regulated, organisations had to scrutinise their sales forces and amend their operations and practices to satisfy the industry regulator. A well-trained and closely managed sales force became a key focus of their efforts.

Flexibility allowed for the scope of experience within each team and limits were placed on team sizes, in the interests of complying with minimum customer quality levels. The outcome was a range of between eight and twelve team members for every sales manager, at every level. Higher level sales managers would manage teams purely of sales managers; middle level managers would have teams made up of a mixture of sales managers and sales people; and junior sales managers would manage teams purely of sales people. In each case, the team size would be variable within the specified range, dependent on the team's experience level and that of the sales manager.

Tutorial activities: scenario

For the purposes of the following tutorial activities, an assumption will be made that the optimum size of a sales team is eight team members plus the sales manager. Further, it will be assumed that each team carries two team members at each of four notional levels of personal development:

Level 1: New to the role (first year)
Level 2: Between one and three years' experience in the role
Level 3: Between three and five years' experience in the role
Level 4: Over five years' experience.

Senior and middle managers are assumed to have additional responsibility for their functions, such as strategy development/delivery and liaison with other management/marketing functions. Therefore, their direct span of control will range between five and seven more junior managers.

The focus of the sales force is growth – through winning new customers and developing/maximising existing ones. In pursuit of this, sales people are responsible for both new business development and account management, that is, they have a dual role to play. Sales managers are responsible for running and developing their teams, and have no direct, personal selling responsibility.

Unless directed otherwise by your tutor, assume that the company is a capital equipment manufacturer, supplying the commercial sector directly.

Tutorial activity A

Purely in terms of field management activity, apportion the time a sales manager should spend with each of eight team members, working to the notional levels of personal development provided in the scenario. Present these conclusions to your tutor in the form of a pie chart.

Tutorial activity B

The sales force has a total size of 139 active members (sales people and sales managers), including the Sales Director. Applying job titles as appropriate, plot an organisation chart for the sales force.

Extended tutorial activity C

Based on either your own organisation chart or one supplied by your tutor (from the tutor's guide), plot a possible career path from newly appointed trainee through to:

(a) Sales Director   (b) National Accounts Manager.

10.4 Territory planning

Apart from being broken down into manageable team sizes, sales forces need to be divided into appropriate territories. There are three main inputs to this exercise: namely geographical considerations, customer types and product types. In most cases, a combination of all three will be used in dividing the responsibility of each team member in relation to their so-called territory. Further, these inputs will impact upon the structure of the sales force itself, specifically the levels of selling within it. Each of these key inputs is now considered.

1 **Geographical area:** The distribution strategy of the organisation will have a major influence on this aspect of sales force organisation. The geographical area for each sales person and sales manager needs to be logistically manageable in terms of customers and potential customers. If a sales person is responsible for a handful of large customer accounts, they are likely to be able to cover a larger geographical area than the sales person responsible for multiple smaller customer accounts. Similarly, sales managers need to be allocated geographical areas which enable them to perform their field management responsibilities in relation to the personal development needs of their team.

2 **Customer types:** It has been common practice for many years that sales territories are allocated in relation to customer types. For example, there have been key or major account sales people, a general sales division, retail sales division, trade sales division, and so on. The influence of marketing on the selling function has further developed this practice, by providing a more comprehensive analysis of customer types in relation to efficiency and profitability. Seen by the author as an evolutionary influence on selling practice, more detailed consideration is given to this area in Part 4 of this book.

3 **Product types:** It is unusual in a large sales force for all sales people to sell the whole product range of the organisation. This may be influenced to some extent by customer types and logistical considerations, but it is also relevant in its own right. Sales people acquiring specialist knowledge of a product or closely related range of products are often able to achieve a competitive advantage. When dealing with more technical products, it is often essential for sales people to carry a specialist knowledge; and an organisation with a large product portfolio may well have more than one sales person covering the same geographical area, possibly even calling on the same or a crossover of customers.

10.5 Levels of selling

Within most sales forces it is likely there will be a range of selling levels. The basis for this is likely to relate closely to the stage of personal development of each sales person but is also likely to be reflected in the type or number of customers involved. Whatever the basis for structuring the sales force, there is a universal factor which applies. That is, the higher the level of the sales person, the higher the expectation in terms of profitable return to the organisation. Necessarily, an increased expectation and profitable return must also take into account a higher remuneration package to provide suitable differentiation among the levels of selling.

The very best sales people often do not become good sales managers. This problem is generally peculiar to the selling profession, and the structure of the sales force should take account of this by making provision to appoint the most suitable sales managers whilst retaining motivation and profitable return from the best sales people. Many organisations have found value in acknowledging this principle and developing levels of selling which, in terms of both rank and remuneration, go beyond the lower levels of sales management. In some organisations, the highest paid employee is the best sales person. Although this latter scenario may not be reflected in rank, it demonstrates the value which can be placed on top quality sales people.

A good practice within a large sales force is to focus personal development along two distinct career paths: a sales management route for appropriate individuals who achieve relative success in selling performance, and a selling route for successful sales people whose performance can be developed still further. As an extension to this, it is important for a sales manager to have personal experience and proven performance for the level of people they are responsible for managing. That is, they must be able to earn respect from their team and respond to their personal development needs.

A practitioner's tale

"In soccer, it takes a top coach to get the best out of top players. You don't have to have been the best player to become the top coach but you do need to have played. Take Terry Venables, previously head coach for the England team. He was a good player but never the very best. As a coach, he went through a range of experiences, achieving success at home and abroad. All the best players respected Terry Venables because he could help them to develop their game still further.

The same applies to selling. You need selling experience in order to manage sales people but you don't have to have been the best. Similarly, a junior sales manager will not have the respect of the best sales people as they will be limited in their ability to assist the development of their staff. The best sales managers need to be at the top of the tree, managing the best sales people.

If this philosophy is adopted for structuring a sales force and due attention is given to the personal development of each person within it, a self-evolving structure will be achieved."

Advanced tutorial activity D

Conduct an analysis of a large fast-moving consumer goods (FMCG) organisation. If you work within this sector, the scenario can be a real one or, alternatively, you can construct an organisation based on your own awareness of the market place. Consider:

(a) how the sales force may be divided in terms of product type
(b) how the sales force may be divided in terms of customer type
(c) how the sales force may be divided in terms of geographical area.

Based on these considerations, draw an organisation chart of the sales force, applying appropriate job titles.

10.6 Team selling

Increasingly, team selling is becoming a feature of the UK selling environment. In part, this has been brought about by the influence of the marketing philosophy; that is, the efficient application of resources in pursuit of the most profitable return. It has led to the devolution of selling roles, with specialist skills being developed at all levels of selling.

For example, one customer may be approached by a telemarketer, may first buy from a new business executive who is supported by a technical expert, and then be managed by an account executive who utilises the services of the technical support department, as appropriate. In this example, there are three active members of the sales force and at least two support personnel involved in the application of the selling process. In order for the customer to receive the best service and the organisation to achieve the best results, they must all fulfil their obligations to the team effort. This involves being proficient in their individual roles and collectively as a team.

Management systems, control and active channels of communication are prerequisites of effective team selling. It is only through effective team selling that the benefits of efficiency and increased customer satisfaction will be realised by the organisation.

Putting aside the evolving influence of the marketing philosophy, team selling has been a feature of many selling environments for some time; for example, where technical products are involved or in the negotiation of large contracts. Regardless of the rationale behind team selling, the principles of effective application remain the same. That is, each person must perform individually and link with other team members coherently to produce an effective collective effort.

Remuneration for sales people is covered in Chapter 12, but when considering team selling situations, special consideration needs to be given to both the motivation of sales people and the needs of the organisation.

Within team selling situations, it may be appropriate to reward the team collectively or by each individual effort. Both systems are fraught with difficulty. From the sales person's perspective, a team payment is dependent on the performance of other team members, regardless of their own performance individually. From the organisation's point of view, they will not want to reward individual efforts if, collectively, the performance is below par. That is, they require a direct relationship between some of their costs and overall performance.

A compromise approach of rewarding individuals partially for their own performance and partially for the overall team effort is likely to provide motivation on two levels, individual and group, whilst also being acceptable to the organisation, as there is a direct outlay against results.

10.7 Summary

In this chapter, we have seen how there is a strategic nature to structuring a sales force and an operational nature to organising it. Higher level sales managers will be primarily concerned strategically with an overview of operations; and lower down the scale, sales managers in the field will have an operational outlook with perhaps a remote input and appreciation for the strategy.

Both sales people and sales managers will tend to work within territories which will be based geographically, and take into account customer types, product types and the personal development requirements of individuals.

The personal development needs within a sales force require, in many cases, differentiation between levels of sales person. A view has been expressed in this chapter promoting the benefits of a sales force structure which focuses on two distinct career paths: sales management and selling. Further, one may choose to add a third career path of sales training. Although many organisations already recognise sales trainers as part of their management structure, the continuing emphasis on personal development and the specialist skills required of sales trainers give rise to the possibility of a discrete career path.

Team selling is an ever increasing area for consideration. Used wisely, it can provide the increased efficiency demanded by a marketing philosophy, differentiation between selling levels and opportunities for personal development.

Each organisation must develop a structure and operational practices which are effective, efficient and meet the needs of its customers and potential customers. The result of achieving this is a **profitable sales performance**.

Essay question

The practitioner telling a tale in section 10.5 of this chapter, put forward a philosophy for structuring a sales force. It was claimed, if combined with due attention to personal development, 'a self-evolving structure will be achieved'.

In the form of an essay write a critical evaluation of what is implied by the statement and conclude your piece with either a justified agreement or disagreement of the practitioner's philosophy.

Further reading

Allen, P. (1993), *Selling: Management and Practice* (4th edn), Pitman Publishing, Chapter 17.

Lancaster, G. and Jobber, D. (1994), *Selling and Sales Management* (3rd edn), Pitman Publishing, Chapter 11.

Strafford, J. and Grant, C. (1993), *Effective Sales Management* (2nd edn), Butterworth-Heinemann, Chapters 10, 12 & 13

Chapter 11

Recruitment and training

Learning objectives

By the end of this chapter, you should :

- Understand the recruitment and training process as a framework for good practice

- Be aware of the cyclical nature of this process in terms of personal development

- Have an appreciation of the key tools at the sales manager's disposal

- Have an appreciation of the skills required of the sales manager as a recruiter

- Have an appreciation of the skills required of the sales manager as a trainer.

11.1 Introduction

It has been said that some sales people succeed *because of* their sales manager and others *in spite* of them.

Unlike other occupations, the nature of a sales person leads to an element of truth in this statement. Throughout Part II of this book, we saw how sales people will tend to have a high degree of self-motivation and will learn many of their skills through practical experience. This includes learning from mistakes as well as from successes. The net result is that a poor sales manager can still develop a sales team which produces acceptable results and, in some cases, this can go undetected for lengthy periods.

This chapter and the following two chapters consider good sales management practice in operational terms; that is, methods which encourage sales people to succeed *because of* their sales manager and, from this, sales teams which produce quality results over the long-term.

A practitioner's tale

"Any of you who have teenage children will know exactly what I mean. You can tell a teenager why they should or shouldn't do something based on your own life's experiences and acquired wisdom. However, they will often ignore your advice and insist on learning inevitable lessons the hard way. Good parents learn that there is a way of communicating with teenagers which enables persuasion and influence to be exercised much of the time.

Sales people are similar to teenagers. If they are to avoid many of the pitfalls, they should learn from the mistakes and experiences of others. Creating and managing an environment in which this occurs is a key skill which sales managers must acquire. It involves earning their respect and being able to communicate with them in a persuasive and influential manner. If you can achieve that, you will have a loyal and motivated team."

Historically, selling has been considered something of a 'numbers game'. Earlier in this book, we have seen how good practice and the integration of selling within the wider marketing function can improve the efficiency of the sales person. Similarly, the role of the sales manager in recruiting and developing successful sales people can be something of a chance operation. As with selling, this chance element can never be entirely removed, but good practice and acquired skills on behalf of the sales manager will enhance efficiency and performance in this area.

The framework for this practice is provided by the recruitment and training process which is shown in Figure 11.1. This chapter then proceeds to consider each element of the process and its practical application.

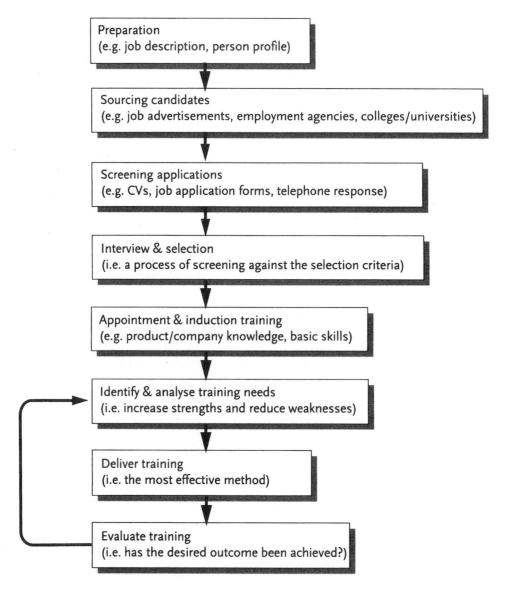

Fig. 11.1 *The recruitment and training process*

11.2 Job descriptions and person profiles

This is a traditional and widely accepted area of recruitment practice. However, it is often seen as an administrative burden by recruiting sales managers and may be ignored in reality. This is unfortunate because, used wisely, these documents are the foundation of good recruitment practice.

Recruit objectively!

Too many sales managers are misguided as recruiters. There is a natural tendency to recruit in one's own image and to base decisions on subjective personal feelings rather than objective reasoning. A good recruiting sales manager will be able to view candidates objectively in relation to the demands of the post and the person best equipped to meet the responsibilities and challenges.

Job descriptions

Each position should be individually analysed and described. Ideally, one will not wait until a vacancy arises before producing a job description, with the exception of new positions. In this way, the incumbent job holder can input to the document. This said, it is the responsibility of the sales manager to ensure the accuracy of the job description and the role of the personnel function to oversee the process, providing support and guidance where necessary. Preferably, a job description should be reviewed annually and whenever a vacancy arises. The following should be included in the document:

- job title
- grade (if applicable)
- package (usually broken down as basic salary, on target earnings and additional benefits)
- hours of work (usually expressed as a minimum number and stipulating the need for flexibility)
- department/division (including the general function)
- place in the organisation structure:
  (a) to whom responsible
  (b) number and job titles of subordinates
- objectives of the job
- main responsibilities and tasks
- occasional tasks and any special responsibilities
- any additional or general comments.

Source: This list is drawn from guidelines produced by the Institute of Personnel & Development.

Tutorial activity A

For a selling position with which you are familiar or, alternatively, one of the sales management role plays in Part V of this book, produce a comprehensive job description. Submit this document to your tutor at their direction.

Person profiles

Completion of this document should follow immediately from the production of a job description and be reviewed at similar intervals. That is, once the job has been analysed and described, one must decide on the ideal person to fulfil the role. The sales manager may choose to include the incumbent job holder in this process, although care should be exercised, as their objectivity may be limited and, further, training needs for existing personnel may be highlighted during the process. The following should be considered when producing a person profile:

- physique (including health, appearance and age, as relevant)
- attainments (education, training and qualifications)
- background (work experience and acquired skills)
- general intelligence (including ability to benefit from training)
- special aptitudes (for example, numeracy)
- disposition and personality (for example, acceptability, reaction to stress, motivation, diligence)
- circumstances (such as mobility, ability to work irregular hours).

Source: This list has been drawn from guidelines produced by the Institute of Industrial Psychologists.

As the perfect candidate rarely exists, a person profile should include both *essential* and *preferred* characteristics from the above list. For example, previous sales experience may be essential but experience within the same industry may only be preferred.

Group tutorial activity B

A number of recommended inclusions in a person profile may evoke an emotive response (for example, age) or may raise questions as to their relevance. At the direction of your tutor, engage in a group discussion to debate the relevance and objectivity of each component of the above list.

Tutorial activity C

In relation to the job description produced in the Tutorial Activity A, draft a profile of the person you feel ideally suits the position, including a breakdown of essential and preferred characteristics. Submit this document to your tutor at their direction.

11.3 Methods of sourcing candidates

When a vacancy has arisen, the job description and person profile have been prepared or updated, the next stage is to encourage suitable candidates to apply for the post. There are a number of sources which can be used to reach prospective candidates:

National newspaper advertisements

A relatively expensive form of recruitment advertising which will encourage a large number of responses. They are applicable where several vacancies exist over a range of geographical areas and for senior or specialist vacancies where suitable candidates may be relatively few in number.

Trade publication advertisements

These reach specialist audiences and are appropriate where a specialist background is required. This could include experience of working in a particular industry or a specific type of training and related skills.

Local and regional newspaper advertisements

A relatively inexpensive form of recruitment advertising, relevant to recruitment in a specific geographical area, where a general rather than specialist background is required.

Employment agencies

Arguably, one of the most misused methods of sourcing candidates. In 'above the line' terms, an employment agency will seem very expensive by comparison to direct advertising. However, fees tend to be paid on results and, moreover, used wisely an agency will substantially reduce the time spent on recruiting by the sales manager. The value of this time must be taken into account when deciding upon the use of an agency. Specialist agencies are likely to be more beneficial than the so-called 'high street generalists', due to their understanding of the client's specific requirements and the base of candidates registered with them. Using a sole agent may be appropriate, particularly if they are retained for a specific assignment. This scenario aside, it is rarely wise to use agencies in addition to one's own advertisement, as this encourages confusion and a breakdown of the service which will be provided. However, a tactic used by some recruiters is to utilise agencies as a contingency, in the event of recruitment advertisements failing to provide suitable candidates.

Head-hunters

These are extremely specialist recruitment professionals. At the lower end of the spectrum, the specialist employment agency operates in a dual role as an extension to the core service which is offered. However, this area is more appropriate to high level and specialist positions in either selling or sales management and involves the use of exclusive head-hunting consultants. The fees charged are extremely high but this method may prove the most appropriate to sourcing and approaching high calibre individuals. Invariably, the relationship between the head-hunting consultant and client company will be extremely close and the service provided should be relevant to the level of fee involved.

Sales manager direct efforts

In many situations, the sales manager can be effective through personal sourcing efforts. On the one hand, they can act in a head-hunting capacity which will involve making a direct approach to successful individuals, usually working for competitors but sometimes for suppliers or clients. In these latter scenarios, care should be taken not to disrupt the trading relationship and it is often more appropriate to use a head-hunting consultant to make the initial approach. Additionally, sales managers can engage in a form of 'prospecting' activity for recruiting more general sales people, perhaps from other industries or, in the case of trainee sales people, from other environments. The degree to which it is appropriate for the sales manager to engage in such activity revolves around how efficient and profitable they will be by devoting their time to this direction.

Group tutorial activity D

In the context of the sales manager's direct efforts, discuss how is it that they may be effective in recruiting sales people but that equally it may not be efficient or profitable for them to do so.

What personal efforts could a sales manager make to recruit sales people for general or trainee roles? Discuss this question in your groups and prepare a comprehensive list for presentation to your tutor.

Referrals from existing employees

Often, this will relate to the existing sales people or those who work in the sales office. If motivated to do so, they can be very effective and efficient in this area. An appropriate incentive should be offered, perhaps in the form of a 'finders fee', a commission override or gestures of thanks such as weekend breaks, meal and clothes vouchers.

Colleges and universities

Traditionally, these have been relatively under used as sources for recruiting sales people. Graduate trainees can be extremely appropriate, as selling becomes more and more of a profession. Marketing trainees have been drawn from these sources for several years and the continued integration of the two areas makes this an important consideration. Additionally, there are progressively more selling courses being run by both colleges and universities for part- and full-time students. This is a largely untapped source of suitable candidates for trainee or general sales positions.

Personnel database

Many organisations receive speculative approaches from job seekers. Often a vacancy does not exist or a candidate is inappropriate for one position but may be suited to an alternative one. A suitable system of recording and storing candidates' details can prove extremely valuable. The use of a computerised database is likely to increase the efficiency and effectiveness of such a system.

Job centres

Rightly or wrongly, many sales managers tend to avoid recruiting from this source. The justification is that they rarely find suitable candidates and save little time on the selection process. An extreme view is that the nature of a sales person, such as their drive and determination, means they are unlikely to remain unemployed other than for short periods. However, there are some notable exceptions to be considered. Trainee sales people may be suitable from this source and also more mature sales people with enormous experience who have passed the 'magic age' and find it more difficult to become re-employed. In both cases, the sales manager should be concerned with how much effort has been made to find a suitable post. For example, has the individual taken advantage of the retraining facilities which are available to unemployed people?

Career counsellors

Effectively, these are employment agencies in reverse. An individual pays a career counsellor to guide their career and possibly introduce them to prospective employers. One should remember that they work on behalf of the individual and not the employing organisation. Therefore, the sales manager will have little control over the screening process and the efficient use of their time is an important factor.

Outplacement consultants

These are similar to career counsellors, indeed, they are often the same organisation. The difference is that they are contracted by responsible organisations when shedding employees. Consultants are brought in to provide career guidance to the outgoing member(s) of staff.

Professional institutes and trade associations

It is common for such bodies to offer a career service to their members. This is likely to be free to the individual but there may be a small administration charge to the employing organisation. It is unlikely that any form of agency agreement will exist either with the member or employing organisation, and the professional body is more likely to act as a medium for the exchange of contacts. As with the use of career counsellors and direct advertising, little screening will take place. Again, the sales manager should consider both the efficient and effective use of their time.

Armed forces

This is a large single source for recruiting trainee sales people. Relatively mature individuals leave the armed forces in search of second careers. They are likely to have acquired a variety of professional and trade skills. Also, many have developed personality characteristics which are appropriate to selling, such as the ability to take rejection or work under pressure. The resettlement packages offered to departing services personnel often include a provision for retraining which can be enormously beneficial to the sales manager. Again, effectiveness and efficiency must both be considered but, certainly, many sales managers have made good use of this method of sourcing suitable candidates.

11.4 The selection process and technique

In the preceding section, frequent reference was made to the sales manager being both effective and efficient in their recruitment activity. The process which they use to select suitable candidates will be driven by the method they use for sourcing them.

From the recruitment process we can see that:

- applications need to be screened
- appropriate candidates need to be interviewed and tested
- appointments need to be made which lead to induction training.

In this section we shall consider the first two stages of the selection process, with the final stage being covered separately in the following section.

Screening applications

Depending on the method of sourcing suitable candidates, the sales manager may find themselves considering a large number of applications. It is only likely to be appropriate for a small number of candidates to be considered for interview. Assuming a two interview process, the sales manager will want, say, eight to twelve candidates interviewed on the first round, reducing to a shortlist of between two and six for the second round.

Here, we are concerned with how applications are screened prior to interview, with the interview process itself providing two further levels of screening as part of the selection process. Applications may come from a variety of sources but essentially they will be screened by either a third party or the employing organisation.

Third-party screening

Most commonly, this will be an employment agency or head-hunter. To a lesser degree it may also include some other methods of sourcing candidates such as the use of a job centre, university or college. The level of screening should be appropriate to both the fee being paid and the expertise of the screener. In the case of specialist screeners, as a minimum they should be expected to deliver only suitable candidates for first interview, which can extend to actually conducting the first interview and advising throughout the selection process. More general third-party sources may only be expected to filter applications for more detailed consideration by the sales manager.

First-party screening

The sales manager will either decide to conduct this personally or use an administrative employee either from the sales office or personnel function.

Whichever path is followed, the screener should work in relation to the person profile which, in turn, is based on the job description. Applications may be made by curriculum vitae and personal letters of application, the use of standardised application forms or by telephone. Regardless of the mode of application, the screener should first ensure that the candidate meets all the essential characteristics of the person profile. Depending on the number of candidates remaining, it may then be appropriate to screen further on the basis of matching candidates against the preferred characteristics.

When the number of candidates is reduced to a suitable number, they should be invited to attend an initial interview.

Interview and testing

The sales manager may conduct the initial interview or, alternatively, delegate this task to another employee or fee-based third party. In many respects, this stage of the selection process becomes a two-way selling situation. First, the candidate should be encouraged to sell themselves by demonstrating their appropriateness to the needs of the employer but, also, the employer needs to ensure suitable candidates remain positive about the organisation and the position. Therefore, an interview for a sales person closely relates to the need identification and satisfaction stage of the sales cycle on both sides, which can be achieved by using the range of personal communication skills discussed in Chapter 7.

During the first interview, it may be appropriate for the interviewee to be formally tested. This may take the form of a basic intelligence test, an awareness test or psychometric personality test. The results of these tests are likely to be analysed in conjunction with the interviewer's observations and conclusions to decide on the most appropriate candidates to shortlist.

If the second interview is a personal one or on a small panel basis, it may be appropriate to interview only a small number on the final round, say two or three. In recent years, many organisations have found benefit in incorporating the second interview within a group assessment programme. Although this exercise is more costly, the value can be enormous. In terms of making a recruitment mistake, the training expenditure and loss of sales revenue can make errors very costly affairs. Group assessments enable candidates to be observed over a longer period in a more natural environment. They are likely to include group exercises, social interaction, an individual interview and further individual tests and exercises. Generally, a larger number of candidates will be invited to a group assessment session. Around six is the optimum number for a single post.

Whichever method is available to or selected by the sales manager, the objective is to discover as much as possible about each shortlisted candidate in order to choose the most appropriate one for the post. Inevitably, the sales manager will want to be sure there is a good rapport with their prospective employee but, moreover, they should try to be sufficiently objective in their decision making by recruiting against the criteria from the person profile in direct relation to the demands and requirements of the position.

Practical activity 1

Split into groups of three within your lecture or seminar groups. Based on one of the sales management role plays in Part V of this book, you are required to simulate an employment interview. One person will take on the role of sales manager, one will play the candidate applying for the position, and the third person will observe the interview.

At the conclusion of the interview, the observer should provide both parties with feedback on their performance. This should include both the good points and areas which require improvement. Specifically, one should be concerned with the quality of information which is exchanged and how it is applied. Roles should then be rotated twice to ensure everyone plays all three roles.

Tip: It may be helpful for the sales manager to produce a job description and person profile prior to this exercise, and for the sales person to produce a curriculum vitae for their role.

Advanced tutorial activity E

At the direction of your tutor break into small groups. Based on one of the sales management role plays in Part V of this book, design and plan a group assessment programme for shortlisted candidates.

Extension: At the direction of your tutor, you may be able to test the programme, using one of the other groups as your candidates. If you conduct this extended activity, be sure to evaluate the successes and failures of your programme, preferably in written form to your tutor.

11.5 Appointing, induction training and probationary periods

The recruitment process does not end with the decision to appoint the most suitable candidate. They must be formally offered the position, accept it and ultimately join the organisation. There are still many things which can go wrong at this stage.

Formal offers should be made subject to references. Many organisations will only provide or accept formal written references. However, there is a limit to how much information will be provided in such a reference and, on a personal level, the sales manager may be well advised, where possible, to take up informal verbal references. Indeed, such conversations can be quite revealing and serve to reinforce the selection process.

Further, candidates may change their mind. Most commonly, they are persuaded to remain with their current employer, although they may also receive offers for other positions they have applied for or be adversely persuaded by friends and family. The skill of the sales manager is tested at this point. Ideally, they would have sold the position and the organisation well enough during the selection process to avoid the situation arising. However, there may still be a need to persuade or counter negotiate after an original offer has been made. Success in this area will often revolve around the quality of rapport which has been developed between the two parties and its power should not be underestimated.

A practitioner's tale

"Selling requires an enormous personal commitment if one is to be successful. The long hours and emotional pressure require a supportive family environment. Without this, it will not be long before the sales person experiences personal stress and this will negatively impact on their performance.

When I am employing a sales person, I insist on meeting their spouse or partner. I need to be as sure as I can that they are fully aware of both the pressures and benefits which come with the job. With a supportive spouse or partner at home, my role as a motivator becomes so much easier."

Good recruitment practice extends to the first day of employment and the induction of an individual into the organisation. Whether the sales person is highly experienced or a trainee, they will need information and support in order to settle quickly into their role. This may take the form of a formal training programme laid on by the organisation or, more informally, the responsibility may lie with the sales manager on a local level. Key aspects which should be included when inducting sales people are:

Company history and background

Although much of this may well have been covered during the selection process, it is important for a sales person to be fully aware of the company history and general background information. This will include how long the company has been established, its growth and development in recent years, its mission statement, philosophy and organisational structures.

Staff handbook

Good employment practice dictates that a staff handbook is an ideal tool for providing uniformity within the workforce. It may include a proforma of the employment contract for the post and the job description. It should certainly include health and safety regulations, disciplinary procedures, grievance procedures, and general information about the organisation such as its objectives and the standards which are expected from its employees.

Administrative procedures

Every organisation will have its own management processes and administrative procedures. It is important for all employees, including sales people, to be made aware of them in general terms and, more specifically, how they apply to their own roles.

Product training

It is vital for sales people to be totally familiar with the products of the organisation. In the first instance, this will relate to the specific products they are expected to sell, but further, they should be aware of the wider range of products offered by the organisation.

Quality standards and procedures

In these days of Total Quality Management (TQM) and customer care programmes, most organisations have a set of quality standards and procedures. Incoming sales people should be fully aware of their responsibilities and expectations in this area.

Skills training

This will depend on the level of sales person which has been recruited. In some cases, the sales person will have been recruited on the basis of the specialist skills which they possess, making the need for skills training redundant in terms of the induction programme. However, in many cases, the new sales person will not yet have developed the full range of skills required. In this scenario, attention needs to be given to some key skills training as part of the induction programme. The range of tools available for providing skills based training is covered later in this chapter.

Introductions to other employees

Starting a new job can be quite daunting for many people. Although by nature sales people are likely to be more extrovert than many other employees, they should still be made to feel welcome, and being introduced to other employees with which they are likely to have contact in their early days is important. A formal introduction and welcome at the next sales meeting is also important.

Agreeing expectations

Like all employees, sales people are entitled to know what their manager expects of them in terms of performance, attitude and day-to-day working practices. Although sometimes overlooked, it is important for the sales manager to know what each sales person expects of themselves. From this, initial targets and performance criteria can be agreed and the sales manager can identify the personal goals of the sales person as a basis for motivating them.

Many organisations engage in the practice of probationary periods for new employees. Such periods generally run for anything up to one year and should be regarded as a two-way trial. The probationary period often carries shorter notice periods for either party wishing to terminate employment, and successful completion is frequently accompanied by an enhancement of the remuneration package.

The probationary period provides a formal framework for the sales manager to assess the sales person, and, in turn, for them to assess the organisation and their role. However, within this framework, there should be frequent communication between the two parties based on agreed expectations and performance.

This practice extends to formal appraisal of all sales people. When a formal appraisal scheme is in place, assessment should not rely on formal interview every six or twelve months, but rather the appraisal should be ongoing, based on continuously agreed expectations and performance, adjusted as necessary. Further, success in this area is dependent on expectations and performance being a two-way process between sales person and sales manager. That is, what do they expect of each other and how does performance relate to these expectations? For such an honest exchange to take place in a motivational environment, it is important for the two parties to have a high level of rapport and mutual respect.

11.6 Identifying and analysing training needs

Ongoing communication between sales person and sales manager based on mutual expectations and performance is likely to give rise to a general training need being identified. There follows a more detailed consideration of how this may occur.

Performance ratios

Regular reporting of performance is covered in more detail in Chapter 13 of this book. In essence, the sales manager needs to be aware of the sales person's performance based on a range of criteria. This could be converted sales against sales calls made, prospects converted into appointments, and so on. Further, such ratios may be broken down into different client types, such as new and existing. If both parties agree that an expectation or target is reasonable and it is not being achieved, corrective action needs to be taken. In the first instance, it is likely that a general training need has been identified and this should be explored further.

Self-evaluation

Sales people should be encouraged to evaluate their own performance. This should not solely be in terms of formal reporting to their sales manager but also on a regular basis following sales appointments. They should be encouraged to focus on both the positive and negative aspects in order that they can develop the positives and eliminate the negatives from their selling practice. Honest evaluation will often result in a sales person identifying their own training needs. This will then need to be explored further by the sales manager.

"I arranged for all of my sales people to be issued with a 'dictaphone' machine. After each appointment, I asked them to answer two questions for me:

- What was really good about that appointment?
- What went wrong or could have been better?

Every week, I ask them to summarise their recordings into a list of good points and bad points about their week's activity. In conjunction with their statistical reports, I use this as a basis for our weekly meetings. In the six months I have been using this system, there has been an average month-on-month increase in sales turnover of 10 per cent.

Many of the negative practices become self-eliminating. Other negatives identify a training requirement and I can help with that. But it goes further; they actually focus on all the positive things they are doing, do them more often and ask me to help them get better at doing them . . . I can help with that too!"

Customer feedback

This will often identify a general training need. Historically, this may have revolved around the purely negative feedback of customer complaints. Recent advances towards a marketing-orientation by many organisations has led to the development of systems for gathering objective customer feedback, that is the positive experiences as well as the negative ones. Although the sales force may provide a medium for obtaining some customer feedback, it is also important to gain feedback about the service delivered by the sales people. This may take the form of a mailed questionnaire, a call from the quality or customer service department and possibly random quality visits by the sales manager. Sales people should not feel threatened by such actions, and the risk of this can be minimised by giving them a chance to review customer feedback which has been received and ultimately using the feedback positively as a means of identifying and developing training needs.

Observation

Observing a sales person in action can provide an enormous insight for the sales manager. The danger is that it is perceived as a threat by the sales person and their usual performance alters negatively for the observed sales call. Against this, the sales person may be particularly pleased to be receiving individual attention and their performance alters positively. The key is for the sales manager to encourage the sales person to perform as though they were not there. This requires a good rapport to exist and involves explaining the purpose and objectives of the observation, gaining the customer's agreement, being unobtrusive during the observation, which includes avoiding active participation, providing early feedback to the sales person in the form of a debrief and agreeing action which needs to be taken by both parties. Observations can be used in the first instance to identify that a training need exists, but further, they provide a useful method of analysing the specific training needs of a sales person.

Simulations

Again simulations or role plays can be used to identify general training needs and also they can take the process a stage further by providing the sales manager with a method of analysing a sales person's specific training needs. To work effectively, they should be made as realistic as possible in terms of structure, content and selling environment.

Organisational and product changes

Any change in this area gives rise to a need for management communication. However, major changes by their nature lead to a specific training need for the sales force. Further, the sales manager should be vigilant in identifying any individuals who may require additional training and information beyond that given to the whole sales force.

Once a general training need has been identified, it must be analysed into a specific form. For example:

- Ratio of closed sales against sales calls made is lower than agreed = *General training need identified*.
- This is because they need to improve their personal communication skills = *Specific training need identified*.

Tutorial activity F

In this section, we have seen how observations and simulations can be used, not only to identify a general training need, but also to analyse it into a specific form. What other methods are there of analysing an individual's general need for training so that it becomes a specific requirement? Discuss these thoughts with your tutor.

11.7 Product training

A practitioner's tale

"People ask me why I am so successful, so I tell them how I learned how to sell. It may seem a little bizarre to some of you, but bear with me.

I stood in front of the mirror for an hour a day over a two-week period, searching for a part of my body which I could consider perfect. It took me so long because every time I found a part which I started to like, I would be critical of it and it would no longer be perfect. Eventually, I had a short list of six aspects of my body which I really liked, albeit I could criticise each of them in a minor way.

Over the next six weeks, I continued to stand in front of that mirror for an hour every day. Each week I took one body part from the shortlist and tried to sell it to myself. I would raise objections or criticisms and try to overcome them, and I would keep doing so until I could no longer criticise. I was successful for one of the first three weeks and on each of the second three weeks. At the end of the six weeks, I knew I could sell four parts of my body to anyone because I had already made the hardest sale to the harshest critic.

All I had to do now was find a product I totally believed in . . ."

The need for a sales person to have belief in a product is a major reason why product training is so important. A thorough understanding of and belief in the product enables its benefits to be enthusiastically communicated throughout the sales cycle. Additionally, good product knowledge enables requests for information from customers to be successfully handled and the sales person is able to ensure that the customer receives the right product in relation to their needs.

Product training should include not only the organisation's own product range but that of its competitors and, more specifically, the positive benefits or USPs in comparison.

Tip for success

Never knock a competitor!

It is unprofessional for a sales person to talk badly of a competitor or its products. It can be off-putting to customers and endangers the development of mutual trust and respect which the sales person wishes to accomplish. It is far better to acknowledge the merits of the competitor but also highlight the weaknesses through the promotion of one's own product benefits and USPs. For example:

'XYZ are an excellent company with a very good product but I believe ours is even better. Let me show you why . . .'

There are many ways in which product training can be achieved. It could involve workshops, seminars and briefings, supplier presentations, product samples for personal use, product brochures, newsletters and updates. The method selected will vary according to the nature of the product and the needs of the sales people but, regardless of the method, it remains vital for sales people to have a thorough understanding and total belief in the product they are selling.

Incidentally, the product offered should be regarded as including any customer care programme provided by the organisation and, therefore, product training should incorporate any quality issues which are important for the service to be delivered.

11.8 Skills training

Throughout Part II of this book we saw that the skills requirement of sales people is very high. Many skills are required to master the art of selling and these are often developed through personal experience in the field. Earlier in this chapter we considered how some sales people may succeed because of their sales managers and others in spite of them. Perhaps one of the greatest ways a sales manager can help a sales person to succeed is to assist and guide the development of their skills. In itself, this assistance can also be highly motivational for the sales person and enhance the relationship of mutual trust and respect.

Sales people need to buy into the concept of training and appreciate the need for it in relation to how it will benefit them. In this way, they will be motivated to learn and, moreover, implement and practise the skills they have learnt. Successful implementation also requires that sales people are able to place the skills in the context of their roles. The sales manager or trainer may need to provide guidance in this area or, alternatively, the sales person should be sufficiently aware to do so for themselves.

Skills training can be provided in many ways. Good training requires a structured approach aimed at producing specific learning outcomes and objectives relating to improved performance in the field. Further, successful training delivery depends on excellent communication skills with both individuals and groups. Regardless of whether or not the sales manager is delivering the training, they must be supportive of the objectives in order to encourage implementation. Methods of skill-based delivery include:

- lectures, seminars and workshops
- sales meetings and peer-group discussions
- observations and demonstrations
- individual coaching
- role plays and simulated exercises
- third-party delivery such as video and audio recordings.

Of course, the method selected will vary according to the training needs. For example, if there is an individual need, the sales manager may address it by coaching or through the use of a peer group, whereas a wider skill need may be better addressed through a training course internally or with a firm of specialist external training consultants.

Training and personal development takes many forms and one must be careful not to regard it solely as the formal session or course. It is an ongoing process which both the sales person and sales manager must accept positively in pursuit of their goals and targets.

11.9 Evaluation

The final stage of the training process highlights the cyclical nature of it, as was shown in Figure 11.1. Training must have measurable learning outcomes and objectives for improving performance in the field. Immediate learning outcomes can be measured shortly after the training has been delivered, either through group questioning or an individual debriefing interview. However, improved performance needs to be measured over a longer period as skills are developed through practical application.

It is the responsibility of the sales manager to facilitate the implementation of the training outcomes and actively encourage practical application. This application should then be monitored. Initially, this will involve the use of observations, simulations and feedback based on self-evaluated performance. Over a longer period, the performance ratios should show an improvement in terms of conversions, sales turnover, customer retention, account profitability, or whatever is the appropriate measure for the training which has been delivered.

The methods for evaluating the success of training are extremely similar to those which were used to identify the training needs in the first place. This supports its ongoing and cyclical characteristics.

Tutorial activity G

Make a note of the answers to each of the following:

- Stage 1: Think of something you are really good at.
- Stage 2: How did you become good at it?
- Stage 3: How do you know you are good at it?

Discuss these conclusions with your tutor.

11.10 The value of psychometric testing as a recruitment and management tool

Psychometric or personality testing systems have become commonplace as a recruitment tool. They are proven to be highly accurate and can help the sales manager with the recruitment decision. One is able to take a snapshot of the key personality characteristics which an individual possesses, their ability to withstand pressures, any current stress they are experiencing and their core motivators. There are self-mark systems available which often incorporate consultancy and support services, and in recent years many systems have been offered in a computerised format.

Somewhere during the rapid growth of these products, their full value to industrial users has been lost. It is true that, used wisely, they are a very valuable recruitment tool but equally, and perhaps more importantly, they can serve as an extremely powerful management tool. Both applications for psychometric testing systems are considered in this text.

As a recruitment tool

It is unwise to recruit on the basis of a psychometric test alone. Indeed, no recruitment technique is foolproof and there will always be a risk element to recruitment decisions. However, organisations and sales managers can develop systems and techniques which increase the opportunity for good decisions to be made. Interviews, group assessment programmes and cognitive tests all have a role to play, as well as psychometric or personality based tests.

Candidates should be put at ease about completing the test and instructed precisely. Every effort should be made to encourage accurate responses, as many tests available will effectively seek out inconsistencies. The accuracy of the tests should not be taken for granted. Rather, their accuracy should be confirmed through interview and/or group interaction.

In a two-interview situation it is perhaps most appropriate to test at the end of the initial interview. The test can then be marked and analysed prior to the second interview. In group assessment programmes it allows not only the personal interaction of an interview, but the observation of effective characteristics such as dominance, receptability, creativity and the ability to influence and persuade others. Throughout the interview or group situation, the recruiter should look to test key characteristics highlighted in the analysis, including both negative and positive points.

A practitioner's tale

"I use a psychometric testing system to help me recruit the right people but I can't bring myself to rely on it. For example, if the test tells me someone has a high drive, a quality which is essential for selling in my industry, I have to confirm it for myself. When I interview them the second time, I put lots of barriers and hurdles in their way – nothing major but things that make them work harder to persuade me of their suitability. If they keep overcoming the hurdles it tells me that they do, indeed, have a high drive, but if they fall down at the first hurdle, then I know that either the test was lying or they were."

As a management tool

Although many organisations and sales managers use psychometric tests as a recruitment tool, few use them wisely as a management tool. It is in this area that increased benefit can be derived. If sales people are tested during their selection and then at regular intervals of between three and twelve months, changes in their profile can be monitored by comparison with previous tests.

Many tests will be able to indicate whether the individual is motivated, experiencing personal stress, fulfilling their potential, and so on. Some changes may be desirable, as they indicate positive personal development, often in relation to planned training objectives. However, negative changes effectively flag a warning to the sales manager of a potential problem and guide them in the direction of the solution.

In order for this practice to be successful, the tests must be used in a positive and non-threatening environment. For example, a decision to retain or release a member of staff based purely on the result of a psychometric test would be misguided. Like other employees, sales people should be debriefed on the outcome and analysis of their tests. Positive changes should be praised and encouraged. Negative changes should be highlighted and discussed with a view to finding an appropriate solution. The solution may lie in the sales manager's control or they may be able to direct the sales person towards a solution. Alternatively, the solution may indicate a wider training need.

In its role as a management tool, psychometric testing can be validly placed in the training process as a method of identifying training needs and also assisting with the evaluation of personal development or training programmes. Beyond this, it can also assist sales managers in motivating their sales people by verifying the success or otherwise of existing motivational practices.

11.11 Summary

For all levels of sales manager, recruiting the right people is extremely important. Making the wrong recruitment decision will result in wasted 'above the line' expenditure, in addition to wasting the time of the manager and any relevant specialist training or development staff, and a likely loss of sales revenue. One could further argue that employing the wrong person may potentially damage the relationship between the organisation and some of its customers.

Beyond this, good recruitment decisions alone will not produce a successful sales force. Every individual in the sales force must be developed in line with the needs of the organisation and its customers. With change being a constant factor, this development or training must be an ongoing process.

The recruitment and training process put forward in this chapter provides a framework for good sales management practice. Its successful implementation depends to a large extent on the skill of each individual sales manager. Some of the skills are similar to those required of the sales person, most notably, excellent communication skills. However, there are additional skills which the sales manager must acquire and develop in order to apply good recruitment and training practice in the field. In turn, higher level sales managers have the responsibility of appointing the right people to sales management roles and developing their skills and awareness accordingly.

Many of the skills required of a sales manager are contained in this chapter, either explicitly or implied within the text. Similarly, other skills which are required are covered in the remaining chapters of Part III.

Essay question

In relation specifically to the sales manager as a recruiter and field trainer, list the typical skills which they will need to possess in order to be successful. Justify the components of this list.

Further reading

Allen, P. (1993), *Selling: Management and Practice* (4th edn), Pitman Publishing, Chapters 16 & 19.

Lancaster, G and Jobber, D. (1994), *Selling and Sales Management* (3rd edn), Pitman Publishing, Chapters 9 & 10.

Stafford, J and Grant, C. (1993), *Effective Sales Management* (2nd edn), Heinemann , Parts 3 & 4.

Weymes, P. (1990), *Handbook of Sales Training and Development*, Kogan Page.

Chapter 12 # Reward and motivation

Learning objectives

By the end of this chapter, you should :

- Appreciate the variety of remuneration packages in relation to the needs of the organisation and the sales person

- Have considered the key motivators for all sales people

- Understand that each person has individual motivational needs and the implications of this in terms of good sales management practice

- Appreciate the value of personal goals as a primary motivational influence

- Begin to consider the complexity and dynamics of motivating teams.

12.1 Introduction

All employees need to be motivated in order to perform their employment duties and fulfil the responsibilities of their role. However, when managing sales people, there are special considerations.

Some sales people work in isolation in the field, which significantly changes the traditional perception of a working environment. Certainly, many more work from a branch or regional office base which, again, provides a different working environment. The continued advancement of teleworking in the UK is resulting in an increasing number of workers experiencing what sales people have known for many years. That is, working in isolation or remotely from the main office potentially damages morale, as peer-group interaction, management and administrative support are substantially reduced.

Moreover, the nature of selling, whether on a remote or more integrated basis, gives rise to extreme emotional pressures. We all have good days and bad days in our working lives, but for sales people, these highs and lows are exaggerated. They must remain positive and enthusiastic when dealing with customers. Necessarily, this requires something of a passionate approach to their work. The so-called 'buzz' of making a good sale provides a sense of satisfaction and achievement which most workers are unable to relate to. Against this, a sales person on a 'bad run' will experience a sense of dismay, despair and personal frustration, peculiar to the role of selling.

Some selling roles involve a lot of rejection and, although sales people will be encouraged to view such rejection as being aimed at the product or the organisation, human instinct makes it difficult for one not to take it personally. Additionally, sales people will experience frustration with administration, order processing, product delivery, and so on. Whether these problems are real or perceived in the mind of the sales person, they do, nonetheless, provide further negative influences.

The value of a positive mental attitude and the need for sales people to discover methods of self-motivation are considered in Chapter 9. This chapter focuses on the role of the sales manager and the organisation in continuously motivating the sales force and individuals within it.

12.2 The package

A practitioner's tale

"Good management practice dictates that an organisation should provide the lowest possible value of package in order to attract and retain motivated personnel. That is, the natural forces of the employment market should dictate the remuneration for each role.

Generally, I do not disagree with this approach. However, when employing sales people, the word 'motivated' is critical. In order to produce the required level of performance, sales people need to be highly motivated. Money is not the only motivating factor, but it is an extremely good starting point.

The very best sales people should earn a lot of money and, more importantly, they need to be seen to earn a lot of money by those aspiring to become better sales people"

Performance-related pay (PRP) has become increasingly common in the work place. It has met with much resistance, with the most convincing counter arguments relating to the method by which performance is measured rather than the principle of PRP.

Measuring the performance of a sales person is relatively straightforward. They should have a known expectation in the form of a target and they can be paid in direct relation to performance against this target. To what extent they are solely responsible for their own performance should also be taken into account. For example, does the marketing function support the selling process in terms of lead generation, customer care, product development, and so on? In Chapter 10, we saw how the responsibilities of team selling questioned sole responsibility for performance.

There are a number of components which should be considered when formulating a package for sales people. It is unusual for any single component to be used in isolation, and for most sales forces a combination of remuneration components is required to achieve optimum performance levels. The application of each component is now considered.

Basic salary

Sales performance rarely remains stable throughout the year. There will be seasonal fluctuations, motivational fluctuations, and so on. Further, the performance of the sales person may not solely relate to bringing in sales revenue. Many sales people are also expected to provide a service to existing customers and maintain existing sales revenue. Although this may be considered an intrinsic part of their role, service activity may well detract from new business selling activity.

Most sales people will have personal financial commitments. Indeed, it is desirable for the organisation that they do have commitments such as a mortgage, a family, and so on. A basic salary provides an assurance to sales people that these commitments will be met; that is, it provides them with stability throughout the year. Although some may argue that it is motivational for sales people to need to perform in order to pay their mortgage or feed their family, the personal stress which can arise as a result of this pressure is likely to have a negative impact. The pressure to sell may result in the sales person applying undue pressure or appearing over-anxious in selling situations. Neither scenario is likely to be in the interests of customer satisfaction nor, therefore, in the interests of the organisation.

A basic salary provides the sales person with a financial cushion in the form of a stable income. Pitching the basic salary at the right level is a motivational art. It must be sufficiently high as to encourage the right calibre of people to join and remain with the organisation. However, if it is too high, there is a danger that sales people will fall into a comfort zone and optimum performance will not be achieved.

One formula is to provide a basic salary which is aimed at covering the typical basic financial commitments of that calibre of sales person. The improved lifestyle which they strive for can then be achieved through performance-related payment methods. However, uniformity of financial commitments throughout the sales force is unlikely, and some will find themselves under immediate pressure while others experience a degree of comfort.

Another method is to provide a basic salary which is consistent with the service needs of the organisation. This may be based on the number of customers in a territory, the volume of business, and so on. Commission can then be paid for additional business which the sales person brings in, directly related to targeted performance.

A further practice is to have a fluctuating basic salary year-on-year. That is, the performance of a sales person in one year will dictate their salary for the following year. In terms of both motivation and sales force retention, this method has visible benefits in pursuit of continuous performance.

Whichever method is selected for calculating an appropriate level of basic salary, it is rare for it to be used in isolation without a performance-related element. One could argue that a sales person's position is only secure if they perform, but such a view tends to disregard the pursuit of optimum performance, and the role of payment directly related to results is an extremely motivational influence.

Tutorial activity A

In this section, it was stated that it is desirable for the organisation for sales people to have personal financial commitments. Consider why it is desirable and then discuss these conclusions with your tutor.

Commission

A common method of rewarding sales people is through commission. Historically, this has been based on sales revenue, particularly relevant to the procurement of new customers. More recently, the focus has become the production of profitable sales revenue.

If it is paid on every sale, the notion of rewarding in relation to targeted performance is called into question. More commonly, and when a basic salary is also being paid, there is a threshold imposed, say at 75 per cent of targeted performance. Below this threshold, no commission will be paid, which ensures a basic performance level before additional reward. It is also common to reward exceptional performance; that is, performance which exceeds the expectations/ targets of the organisation. This can be achieved through an enhanced commission payment or the use of bonuses.

Few sales managers would doubt that the use of commission provides an extremely effective base for motivating sales people towards optimum performance. Unlike many other employees, it provides the organisation with an employment cost directly related to the value of return which is received. Perhaps the key to using commission effectively as a motivational tool lies in the way sales people are set targets. Although the practical aspects of this are covered in the following chapter, it requires some consideration at this stage.

A good target is one which extends the sales person but is achievable, based on their skills and level of personal development. An unachievable target can be demotivational, as can a target which is relatively easy to achieve. The application of targets which meet the needs of the organisation, and its customers and takes into account the personal development of individuals is desirable. Indeed, when such targets are directly related to the remuneration package, it is also good employment practice for these targets to be mutually fair and reasonable.

However, some well recognised supporters of motivation theory may question the validity of targeting in this way. It could be argued that by setting a target for performance, the potential for excelling is given a psychological limit. The use of enhanced payment for performance which exceeds the target goes some way towards addressing this issue. However, sales managers also have a role to play in this area. Additional motivational influences need to be applied which not only encourage targeted performance to be achieved but also facilitate performance which exceeds these boundaries. These non-monetary aspects of motivation are the focus of sections 12.3 to 12.5 of this chapter.

Bonuses

Bonuses are distinct from commission in that they represent specific performance criteria. The application of commission thresholds leads to some crossover in this area but, generally, bonuses are the reward for consistent performance over an agreed period. There are several ways in which bonuses may be appropriate.

One use of bonuses is to reward above-target performance over a period of between, say, one and three months. Additionally, they may be used for maintaining or increasing sales revenue from existing customers over, say, a full year. They may be used in conjunction with promotional campaigns such as launching a new product or targeting a specific customer group. That is, additional bonuses may be paid for selling a particular product or procuring customers from a specific group, throughout the length of the promotional campaign, in addition to usual commissions.

Bonuses have become more appropriate as the focus of selling activity has moved towards producing *profitable* sales revenue. Many sales people find themselves being considered as an individual profit centre. They are paid bonuses in relation to their profitable performance against target, with factors such as sales revenue, personal remuneration, vehicle costs, contribution to wider promotional efforts, and hospitality expenditure all contributing to the profitability of the sales person.

One problem with annual bonuses is that they provide limited motivational impact on a day-to-day basis. That is, many sales people require more instant reward for their efforts in order to remain continually motivated. Systems of remuneration which provide a revenue- or profit-based sales commission on a monthly basis and bonuses related to profitable performance over a sustained period of between three and twelve months, are likely to provide the right motivational balance in relation to the needs of the sales force and the performance requirements of the organisation.

Company car

Field sales people require mobility in order to reach customers. In some densely-populated urban areas public transport may be more appropriate but, on the whole, the use of a car is imperative. Traditionally, this has been provided by the company and perceived as a necessary benefit by sales people.

Motivationally, cars can be used as a status symbol within the sales force to differentiate between the levels of selling. However, they are expensive for the organisation, and the personal taxation treatment of them in recent years has eroded some of the value derived by sales people. Increasingly, the company car is being replaced by an allowance which compensates the sales person for using their own vehicle in addition to covering the fuel costs incurred.

A practitioner's tale

"In our company, we have a bright red, top of the range Porsche. Every month, the top sales person is given it to drive around in for the following month. It is more motivational than you would imagine. The top sales person doesn't want to give it up and the rest want to get it. Success is rewarded by status and it is there for all to see."

Additional benefits

The most common additional fiscal benefits which should be considered are pension and healthcare schemes. The true value of these is not necessarily appreciated by young single people, but maturity and family commitments lead to these being seen as extremely valuable additional benefits. For the sales person they demonstrate a commitment on behalf of the organisation which provides an air of security and leads to increased loyalty. The benefits to the organisation may relate to increased staff retention and long-term motivation which, in turn, facilitate continuous customer relationships and loyalty, reduced recruitment and reduced training costs. Additionally, long-term absence will be minimised by the healthcare provision. The value derived from providing these benefits must be considered against the financial costs to the organisation.

Traditionally, sales people will also receive so-called 'perks of the job'. These may take the form of product discounts, free samples, or the outcome of winning a sales competition, such as a weekend break. Many of these are valid in motivational terms but, again, their value should be considered in relation to the financial costs to the organisation.

A further area for consideration is that of entertainment expenditure. In many selling environments, this is an important part of relationship cultivation. Expenditure in this area should be carefully applied and monitored by the organisation. The value which will be derived is difficult to measure, although the application of focused selling and servicing efforts based on customer groups provides a useful framework. This is considered in Chapter 16.

Sales managers

In order to achieve motivation throughout the sales force, it is vital that sales managers are highly motivated. Just as with sales people, the starting point for motivation is with the remuneration package which is provided. A basic salary serves a similar purpose. Commission can be paid on personal sales performance and in the form of an override on the team's performance. Sales managers should be expected to take a longer-term business view than sales people and the application of bonuses in relation to sustained, profitable performance is extremely appropriate.

Developing the best remuneration package for a sales force is a difficult task. A package must be provided which enables the organisation to attract the right people, retain and motivate them. Achieving this balance is in itself a very difficult task but, additionally, the costs of providing a sales force remuneration package must be carefully considered against the benefit which will be derived.

For some organisations, this will call them to question the extent to which a sales force should be used, but for most, it will encourage them to ensure the sales force operates efficiently and profitably. This is likely to involve effective management systems, an integrated marketing effort and the application of an effective personal development programme, all combining to achieve sales force retention, continuous performance and the development of long-term customer loyalty.

Tutorial activity B

For an organisation of your choice, analyse the remuneration package which is applied to the sales force. Consider how this is motivational to the sales people and sales managers, and how it serves the needs of the organisation in relation to its operational practices.

Present this analysis and your findings in the form of a brief report to your tutor.

12.3 Key motivators

In 1991, the author had access to a private commercial survey in which over 400 sales people at a variety of levels and from a range of industries participated in individual interviews. A confidentiality agreement prevents the detailed results by industry and type of sales person to be shown, but an overall picture of the combined results can be considered. The top ten motivators in descending order of importance, as defined by the sales people themselves, were:

1. **Job satisfaction:** This included reference to 'the buzz of selling', 'the thrill of the kill', 'being on the road' and 'meeting people'. Collectively, responses provided the view that the primary motivation for salespeople was enjoying their work.
2. **Performance against peers:** Internal competition was cited as the second most popular motivator.
3. **Achieving goals/targets:** Most sales people felt good when they achieved personal goals and sales targets. In turn, this was cited as the third most popular motivational influence.
4. **Good support:** This related to administration, management effort, training support and sales support, such as lead generation and point-of-sale material. Collectively, under the broad heading of 'support', these factors were rated fourth most popular motivator. However, individually, no single support factor was in the top ten.
5. **Money:** Often regarded as being the single most important motivational influence, this was not the case for many of the sales people surveyed. Although more important in some forms of selling and, similarly, at various levels of selling, there were several groupings who regarded it to be only important up to a certain point, after which other motivational factors became more important.
6. **Status:** Varying degrees of importance were placed on this as a motivational factor. For those citing it as important, the recognition of their performance and visibility of their success were both popular responses.
7. **Fear of dismissal:** Generally, sales people are aware that under-par performance places their job at risk. This relative insecurity was regarded as motivational by some.
8. **Merit-based promotion:** Good promotional prospects were generally regarded as important but sales people specifically cited the need for merit-based rather than time-served or favoured promotion.
9. **Participation in setting targets:** The ability to have a say in their own destiny was regarded as important by some sales people. An input into their own sales targets was desirable as a motivational factor on the basis that it would lead to fair and reasonable expectations.
10. **Customer satisfaction:** Only the tenth most popular motivational factor. Even within this grouping, many sales people felt that customer

satisfaction was only important because it enabled them to secure more business. There were other motivational factors which did not make the top ten but, nonetheless, this placing of customer satisfaction may raise an eyebrow or two.

There are other studies which have been conducted in this field which provide a more comprehensive analysis than this summative view. Lancaster and Jobber[1] refer to several studies, one completed by sales managers, and a comparison between a survey of industrial sales people and a survey of consumer sales people. The findings bear an interesting comparison with the overall results presented in this text.

12.4 Motivating individuals

Appropriate application of the key motivational factors provides an environment of motivation within the sales force. On a day-by-day basis, the sales manager needs to use these factors selectively to maintain the motivation levels of each sales person.

It is a key principle that every person has individual motivational needs. With sales people, many of these needs will be met through self-motivation; more specifically through the development and achievement of both long- and short-term goals. It is these goals which provide an individual's driving force and they will normally indicate to the sales manager the specific motivational forces which need to be applied.

For example, a sales person with a goal of buying a new prestigious car by the end of the year may well be motivated by the status factor. A sales person aiming to qualify for a sales convention may be motivated either by the status which this will give them within the organisation or by the competitive nature of performing better than their peers.

The sales manager is effective by recognising the goals of each individual and encouraging the sales person to achieve them. Further, the sales manager should understand the methods which will derive a positive response from each team member. Indeed, the ability of the sales manager to achieve this variety of motivational methods, based on individual needs, is an important skill which needs to be acquired and developed.

Practical activity

This exercise may take you some time to complete, as it requires a high degree of thought and consideration. You are to consider the following questions:

- Where do you really want to be and what do you really want to be doing three years from now?
- Why?

- How are you going to get there?
- Working backwards from your three-year goal, plan what you need to achieve over each of the next three years.
- What are you going to do to achieve each of your annual goals?
- How could your manager help you to achieve these goals?
- What changes in your behaviour and practices are you going to make as a first step towards achieving this year's goal?

Extension: If you are employed in a sales management capacity, ask each of your team members to complete this exercise, encouraging them to think carefully about what is important to them. Analyse these goals with them, taking care to understand what their key motivators appear to be. Use their planned achievement and key motivators to motivate them, and continuously evaluate your effectiveness.

12.5 Motivating teams

Given that each individual within a team will have their own personal goals and a variety of motivational influences, the idea of motivating a team collectively becomes more complex. Obvious factors such as team competitions and recognition of performance among the peer group are likely to play a role. Care should be taken to recognise not only the best performers but also improved performance and personal achievement.

However, teams should also have collective goals. The vision for these goals is likely to come from the sales manager, but team members are likely to have an input. Team incentives may be offered but this will depend on the nature of the selling environment. More importantly, the sales manager will need to create an environment which balances friendly and motivational competition with production of team spirit and collective loyalty.

Perhaps the way in which a sales manager can be most effective in motivating their team is to present and deliver their vision and team goals in the form of collective benefits to team members. An ideal platform in which to launch and manage team efforts is through the medium of a sales meeting, although the individual management interview may also be used as a supporting medium. Both of these are discussed in more detail in the following chapter.

12.6 Summary

In this chapter, we have considered the components of a remuneration package and their application in rewarding a sales force in a motivational environment. We saw that money was perhaps not the most important motivating influence for sales people, as many observers perceive it to be. However, it would be fair to say that an inappropriate package is likely to be demotivational and detract from a basic objective of achieving optimum performance within the sales force. Therefore, achieving the right remuneration package for the sales force is of crucial importance.

Beyond this, one can consider there is a set of key motivational factors which can be applied in the selling environment. This text provides a suggested set and further identifies other studies which provide similar considerations.

The final sections of this chapter focused on the application of motivational techniques to sales people as individuals and collectively within teams. The media through which motivational communication can be both transmitted and received are discussed in the following chapter.

Essay question

The practitioner in section 12.2 of this chapter stated 'an organisation should provide the lowest possible value of package in order to attract and retain motivated personnel'.

In the form of a short essay, critically evaluate this statement and suggest ways in which it can be improved in considering the remuneration of a sales force.

Reference

1. Lancaster, G and Jobber, D. (1994), *Selling and Sales Management* (3rd edn), Pitman Publishing, Chapter 10.

Further reading

Herzberg, F., Mausner, B. and Bloch Snyderman, B. (1959), *The Motivation to Work* (2nd edn), Wiley & Sons.

Robbins, A. (1986), *Unlimited Power,* Simon & Schuster, Section III.

Stafford, J. and Grant, C. (1993), *Effective Sales Management* (2nd edn), Butterworth-Heinemann, Part 6.

Vroom, V.H. (1964), *Work and Motivation,* Wiley & Sons.

Chapter 13 Management communication and control

By the end of this chapter, you should :

- Appreciate the benefits of effective management communication

- Understand the communication dynamics of the management channel

- Have a practical appreciation of the key media for management communication

- Understand the importance of and method for controlling performance

- Understand the importance of and method for controlling quality standards.

13.1 Introduction

In Part II of this book, we saw how communication and psychology provided the key to successful application of the selling process. They are key skills which the sales person must acquire and develop in pursuit of optimum performance. Similarly, these skills provide the basis for success in terms of management performance.

Sales managers have an advantage over other managers, as they have already acquired many of the key skills through their selling experience. The main development for sales managers is learning how to re-apply these skills in a different context. They must learn when to be supportive, when to be didactic, how to encourage others to achieve their maximum potential, when to take a democratic approach, when to take an autocratic approach, and so on.

Against this, sales managers have a disadvantage over other managers. The role becomes more structured in terms of systems and procedures, administration, reporting and taking responsibility for the actions of others. The nature of sales people makes the transition into this environment more difficult, as it involves an adaptation and development of one's attitude and skills.

Many of these issues are discussed in this chapter in addition to the overriding consideration of management communication, including the re-application of skills which the sales manager will have previously acquired.

13.2 The management channel

In all but the very smallest sales forces, there will be more than one level of management. The addition of levels gives rise to a structure and it is through this that a management channel is formed. For example, a sales person may report to an area manager, who reports to a regional manager, who in turn reports to the sales director. It is imperative for communications within the channel to be transmitted and received at each appropriate level, according to the line management responsibility.

In the interests of expediency, there may sometimes be a temptation to bypass a level but, in most cases, this has a negative impact, as response and control mechanisms become devolved. The exception to this principle is when a group communication is transmitted. For example, a sales director may address the whole sales force at a conference, or a regional manager may communicate with all sales people and sales managers in their region at a quarterly meeting.

The principle of good communication remains the same as previously considered in Chapter 7. That is, a message must be transmitted, received and, ultimately, feedback must be obtained. A direct line management communication is likely to be aimed at either selling performance or the provision of quality standards to customers. The communication itself will be transmitted and received with a certain degree of instant feedback. However, total feedback or, rather, confirmation that the communication was successful, will only be received when a resulting change or continued excellence in performance or standards is achieved.

Most managers will want to retain a degree of communication with a level below their direct line management responsibility. Direct personal communication in this form is likely to be less formal with wider objectives, such as rapport building or morale boosting. Opening a channel of informal communication in this way also serves to provide an indication of the interim manager's performance in terms of team spirit, motivation, and so on.

Appreciation for the management channel and its dynamics provides a framework for the practical application of management communication and control techniques. Although formal written communications have a role to play, the majority of management communication in the selling environment will involve personal interaction between the two parties. The remainder of this chapter focuses on personal line management communications and control or feedback mechanisms.

13.3 The sales meeting

A sales meeting has the same framework as any other meeting, in that it requires an agenda, summative minutes and, most importantly, an action plan or series of performance outcomes. It is there that the similarities end, as the content and environment of a sales meeting are unique.

The sales meeting will be chaired by the direct line manager of the core attendance. For example, an area manager will chair a meeting for all their sales people, or a regional manager for all their area managers and sales people. In the former situation, the regional manager may well attend the meeting as a guest speaker or observer, which reflects the less formal nature of their communication objectives.

Above all, sales meetings need to be motivational. Any change in practices or procedures should be sold to the delegates in the form of the benefit which will be derived by them. New products or product developments need to be presented in the form of customer benefits, highlighting unique selling points and emphasising the exciting opportunities which have now been created. Achievement should be recognised and rewarded. Tales of success may provide inspiration for others. One can also consider competitions, customer feedback, hospitality and collective objectives as possible additional features of a good sales meeting.

The physical environment in which a sales meeting is conducted is important. The sales office may be appropriate, but it is often beneficial to remove the team from its working environment by holding the meeting at, say, a country club or hotel. Seating should be comfortable, the meeting should be of an appropriate length to the attention span of the audience, and the use of good visual aids, acoustics and positive body language remains the same as for any other group communication. The establishment of common rapport is less of a problem, as all active members of the sales force should want to be successful and the meeting will be aimed at assisting them. Quantified team objectives may also serve to enhance the rapport among a peer group.

Sales meetings become ineffective when run poorly and sales people will come to see them as a chore which impinges on their valuable selling time. However, a good motivational sales meeting will be viewed differently, accredited value by sales people in pursuit of improving their performance and enhancing their success. The ability to plan and deliver a good sales meeting should be regarded as a key skill which sales managers at all levels must acquire and develop.

Practical activity 1

This activity may be based on the team role play scenario in Part V of this book or any variation which you care to apply. Working in your lecture or seminar groups, plan a monthly sales meeting. Attention should be paid to detail, including timings, as the meeting should last for one hour. Plan to use as many motivational forces as you can during the meeting, turning any potentially negative factors into positive ones.

Extension: Allocate a role to each person in your group. Present the entire meeting as it has been planned and try to create a motivational environment. This exercise should be followed by a collective evaluation of the meeting, primarily in relation to its motivational impact and possible improvements.

13.4 The management interview

Personal communication between a sales manager and their team members will be ongoing. Much of this communication will be informal, providing encouragement, support and inspiration. However, it is also important to have a formal communication on a regular basis. This may be to consider performance over a targeted period, evaluate a training course or debrief an observation visit.

The nature of the circumstances giving rise to the meeting will dictate the focus and objectives of the communication. For example:

Weekly performance meeting

The focus will be on achievement this week against targets or goals which were set the previous week. The overall objective of the sales manager is to ensure performance regularly meets expectations. Any over-performance should be applauded and under-performance discussed. In both cases, an analysis of reasons behind the performance should be made. From this, further goals and targets should be set for the following week, and the sales person should leave the meeting feeling motivated and capable of achieving them.

Training evaluation

Any team member returning from a training programme should be formally interviewed by the sales manager. The reasons for their attending the course would have been identified previously in terms of what they were hoping to achieve from the programme. Their expectations should be discussed in relation to what they have actually gained. As we saw in Chapter 11, training is wasted unless it brings about a positive change in performance. Therefore, the conclusion of this meeting should aim to quantify ways in which performance will improve, in order that the effectiveness of the training may be measured.

Observation debrief

Field management often involves observing a sales person in either a real or simulated situation. The purpose and objectives of the observation should be identified in advance and the sales person should be encouraged to behave normally during it. In every case, such an observation should be followed by a formal debrief. This will involve a discussion of what the sales manager observed in relation to what they were trying to discover. This may relate in the early days to the general conduct of a sales person, but with more experienced sales people, it is likely to relate to specific performance areas. The outcome of the observation needs to be addressed in terms of personal development. This may be handled with instant coaching or, alternatively, a wider training requirement may be identified.

Tip for success

Telling is not selling!

As we have seen, this is a fundamental principle of any selling environment. Sales management is no different. If people are told what to do, they are unlikely to be committed to the cause. They must identify problems for themselves and be encouraged to find and apply the solutions in terms of corrective action. The sales manager facilitates this.

If successful selling is about creating an environment in which people want to and do buy, then sales management is about creating an environment in which people want to and do perform.

We can consider that there are some common features of all formal sales management interviews, including a good level of rapport centred on the individual's needs, with the sales manager guiding the individual along a path which encourages a solution to be found and motivating action which improves performance. Classic personal communication techniques, as discussed in Chapter 7, should be applied. A record should be kept of the outcome of the meeting, identifying any agreed action and revised performance goals. From this, a clear focus or set of objectives should be provided, against which effectiveness can be measured.

Identifying mutually agreed performance objectives is the basis of personal management communication. Measuring actual performance against these expectations provides a control mechanism by which results can be managed and the sales manager can optimise their own effectiveness.

Practical activity 2

This activity is to be based on one of the sales management role plays in Part V of this book or, alternatively, a role play based on the specific nature of your own organisation's environment.

Working in groups of three, one person should act as the sales manager, another the sales person and the third as a critical observer. Conduct a management interview with the purpose of identifying ways in which selling performance can be improved, agreeing appropriate action and setting clear, measurable goals. Roles should then be rotated until all three roles have been played by each person.

At the end of each role play, the observer should critically evaluate the performance of the sales manager.

Extension: When the observer is evaluating the performance of the sales manager, this could form the basis of a second role play. The observer can play the role of a regional manager observing the performance of their sales manager. The evaluation can take the form of a debriefing interview and the original sales person can observe and evaluate this additional management communication.

A practitioner's tale

"Whenever I have a formal meeting with one of my sales people, I always finish with a stock question, 'Is there anything else I can do for you?' It sounds simple and obvious but it is amazing how powerful it can be.

At the very least it confirms we are both satisfied that everything has been covered. It also reaffirms to them that I am on their side. But the real value is in the throw-away comments which are made at this stage. They ask for leads, ask me to make a call for them, comment about administration or any number of other support requests. Sometimes it is a valid request for me to do something and other times it uncovers areas on which I need to focus.

For those of you who have ever used the so-called 'Columbo' close to uncover a hidden objection, this serves exactly the same purpose in a management interview."

13.5 Setting targets and monitoring performance

As will become clear in the following chapter, there are two forms of performance objective with which we are concerned. The first may be referred to as an operational target and is an annualised figure contributing to the target of the whole sales force. This will usually be broken down into a monthly target for each individual, often taking account of factors such as seasonal fluctuations, planned promotional campaigns and planned growth through personal development throughout the year.

The formal operational targets need to be broken down into smaller tactical goals, agreed on a less formal basis between sales manager and team member. These shorter-term tactical goals are the second form of performance objective. They still contribute to and work towards achieving the operational target, but they have different characteristics. They provide day-to-day motivation, are an early indicator of longer-term performance, identify personal development needs and confirm appropriate progress is being made.

Targets which are imposed can often be demotivational or ineffective. If a sales person is told what is expected of them, they are less likely to be committed to achieving results than if they develop the expectation for themselves. Ultimately, operational targets are set at a senior management level as they will apply to the whole sales force. Sales managers throughout the management channel will then be expected to allocate their portion of the overall target to individual team members. Although inputs from the sales force would have been part of the original decision-making process, other factors such as organisational objectives and wider marketing mix considerations would have also contributed.

In most sales forces, there is an air of anticipation leading up to delivery of the annual sales targets. The task of setting the right targets throughout the sales force is a massive one and, inevitably, there will be disappointments and anomalies. Often there is a period of consultation whereby some targets will be adjusted for various individuals, although the overall sales force target is unlikely to be adjustable.

The skill of the sales manager at this point is to convince each team member of their ability to achieve the target. Annual sales targets usually take the form of an overall sales figure based on either turnover or, more recently, profitability. For most sales people, their new target will represent an increase on existing performance and the overall target will often seem comparatively high. The sales manager must convince them that it is achievable. Methods for this vary but, generally, encouragement and faith are transmitted together with the development of a personal plan of action.

A plan of action involves breaking the target down into smaller, quantified portions. This will often result in demonstrating the target in the form of what must be achieved every day or week. In this way, the large annual figure becomes much smaller in the mind of the sales person. They can begin to visualise how the target will be achieved. This, of course, is merely a process of outlining the shorter-term goals which need to be achieved throughout the year.

Ideally, the sales manager will be aware of the personal qualitative goals of the sales person and will be able to relate the overall target and quantitative breakdown against the long- and short-term personal goals, respectively. After this annualised process, the performance needs to be managed throughout the year. This is achieved with regular performance meetings, usually on a weekly basis.

Weekly performance meetings will not merely focus on the sales which have been produced but, rather, on how they have been achieved. This involves breaking down the sales person's role into, for example:

- *Prospects:* How many people have been available for you to contact this week?
- *Contacts:* How many people have you contacted?
- *First appointments:* How many people agreed to meet with you?
- *Second appointments:* How many people agreed to see you again?
- *Closed sales:* How many people have you sold to this week?
- *Sales value:* What are these sales worth in terms of order value or profitability?

This will usually take the form of a sales reporting form, which provides the basis for the formal management interview. The precise components of the form will depend on the specific nature of the selling environment and the sales person's role within it. A similar format may also be used for sales management reporting purposes but, again, the components will vary according to the role and responsibilities of the manager.

The outcome of a meeting in one week forms the basis for expectations in the following week. That is, there will be two columns on the form: targeted and actual performance. The sales manager should be concerned not solely with the quantitative aspects of *how many?* but also with the qualitative aspects of effectiveness of each stage of the selling process. For example, what is the ratio of appointments gained to people contacted? In this way, *motivation* can be measured in terms of effort or activity, with *effectiveness* being measured by the performance ratios. This will provide a good indication of where management effort needs to be directed and will serve to highlight the personal development needs of each individual.

An alternative method of delivering a weekly performance interview is to reverse the process to focus on the needs of the sales person rather than the needs of the sales manager/organisation. Most reporting forms present the information in such a way that it measures and controls performance in direct relation to the overall operational sales target. In itself, this is fine, but from a motivational point of view it is often better to start with the needs of the sales person in the actual face-to-face meeting. For example:

- *How much commission do you need to earn?*
- *How much revenue/profit does that represent?*

- *How many sales is that on current order values/ margins?*
- *How many presentations do you need to make that many sales?*
- *How many contacts do you need to make to achieve this many presentations?*
- *How many prospects do you need to gather in order to contact this number of people?*

Quite simply, the information the sales manager requires is gathered in reverse order, addressing the needs of the sales person as an internal customer. The process may be preceded by a discussion of the sales person's ongoing goals (Why do you need to earn that much commission?) and concluded by gaining a commitment from them (What positive action are you going to take towards achieving your goals this week?).

Tutorial activity

For an organisation with which you are familiar, design a sales force reporting form. Present this form to your tutor, justifying its relevance and commenting on its application.

Extension: If you are a practising sales manager, design a form for your own role or, alternatively, critically evaluate the form which is currently being used. In either case, focus on its relevance, application and likely effectiveness.

13.6 Setting and maintaining quality standards

Achieving quality standards is not peculiar to the sales force. In customer-orientated organisations, there is a need for quality standards to be laid down and achieved. This should be *total* throughout the organisation, usually taking the form of a *TQM* programme, as discussed in Chapter 2.

In relation to the sales force, quality standards will relate to two main areas.

Sales people and support staff

These people will be expected to provide a level of service to customers in support of the selling process. This will include follow-up calls, after-sales service, technical support, efficient order processing and service calls, which enhance relationship cultivation. Sales managers will agree the standards which need to be achieved in relation to the range of responsibilities of each active sales force member; for example, call frequencies, delivery times, response times, and so on.

Measuring these standards is somewhat more difficult. Frequently, one must trust the honesty of sales people and support staff. However, sales managers may be well advised to confirm the accuracy of reporting with random checks and field accompaniments. The nature of these accuracy controls should not detract from an environment of mutual trust and respect, which is a prerequisite for a successful working relationship.

The development of customer service levels in direct relation to customers' needs and those of the organisation is discussed in Chapter 16. This extends current practice to consider the most profitable and efficient service levels based on a long-term perspective, and students are encouraged to expand their understanding in this area to reflect the direction of modern thinking and practice.

Sales managers

In addition to ensuring customer quality standards are achieved and maintained, sales managers have to deliver their own services to team members. That is, sales people and support staff need to be viewed as internal customers. They require support from their sales managers in order to be both effective and efficient in their roles. This may take the form of personal development, administrative support, support in applying components of the selling process, motivation, advice and guidance. Quite simply, this relates to good sales management practice. In turn, the quality of internal service delivery should be monitored throughout the management channel.

13.7 Summary

In this chapter, we have considered the dynamics of the management channel. This channel is formed on the basis of the sales force structure, and provides the framework for management communication and control. Sales management communication will usually take place on a personal basis, although the effectiveness of this communication is measured with performance controls, necessarily in documented form.

The key communication media are group or team sales meetings and the formal management interview. The focus and methodology of both have been considered but, students have been encouraged to develop their skills in this area through simulated exercises.

Of equal relevance to students studying this subject as part of a wider course of marketing or management is the second part of this chapter which looked at measurement and control systems used within a sales force. How they are used as performance indicators and provide managers with feedback that their communications and actions have been effective were key issues. Also, the potentially positive and negative impacts of performance expectations and measurement systems were highlighted. Specifically, it was concluded that a sales person must regard targets and goals as being fair and achievable, if they are to be fully committed and motivated to perform.

The role of the sales manager in transmitting these messages positively is crucial. Delivering the required performance levels revolves around good management practice, which has been the focus of this and the preceding three chapters. In line with modern thinking, sales people can be viewed as internal customers, accorded appropriate levels of service and support by the sales manager on a local level and by the organisation on a wider scale.

Essay question

Reference has been made in this chapter to the sales person being regarded as an 'internal customer'. In the form of an essay, consider this perspective and how it relates to 'good sales management practice'. The length of your piece should be between 1000 and 1500 words.

Further reading

Allen, P. (1993), *Selling: Management and Practice* (4th edn), Pitman Publishing, Chapters 18 & 19.

Lancaster, G. and Jobber, D. (1994), *Selling and Sales Management* (3rd edn), Pitman Publishing, Chapters 12 & 13.

Stafford , J. and Grant, C. (1993), *Effective Sales Management* (2nd edn), Heinemann, Chapter 40.

Wilson, M. (1983), *Managing a Sales Force*, Gower.

Chapter 14 Planning

Planning

Learning objectives

By the end of this chapter, you should :

- Understand the principle of the planning model and appreciate its practical application

- Appreciate the nature of the strategic plan and its delivery

- Appreciate the role of the operational plan within the strategy

- Appreciate the use of tactics within the operational plan

- Be aware of the various inputs and outcomes of planning from a sales management perspective

- Understand the need for expenditure budgets and their application to the sales force strategy.

14.1 Introduction

Planning is a key function of any management role, from senior executive through to field level. The principle of planning remains the same for all managers, the only difference being the scale of the plan. Indeed, planning extends to sales people, not only the targets agreed with their managers but also personal goals, as discussed in Chapter 9.

A practitioner's tale

"Planning occurs not only in business but in many things we do. Think of a recent journey you went on, perhaps somewhere you had never been before. You decided on where you were going and then worked out a route for the journey, including an estimate of how long it was likely to take you. Along the way you may have experienced some unforeseen events, such as roadworks, flight delays, and so on. You deal with these obstacles, remaining focused on reaching your destination, perhaps adjusting your travel plans along the way.

The world of business is no different. You need to start with an *objective* – where are you going or what are you going to achieve? Then you develop a *plan* of action which will enable you to achieve this objective – how are you going to get there? The plan is then *implemented* – starting the journey. Along the way, you will encounter difficulties and obstacles, the reaction to which requires an *adjustment* to the plan. If you had anticipated a potential problem, you may have built in an adjustment mechanism in advance, known as a *contingency*. Whether through a reactive adjustment or a preplanned contingency, you must remain focused on achieving the original objective.

OPIAC provides us with a planning framework and I regard it as fundamental to the performance of my sales force. As I say to my sales people, if you don't know where you are going, how do you know when you've arrived?"

In this chapter, we will consider the planning model as it specifically applies to the sales force. The sales manager has a role to play in both the planning process and its delivery; that is, inputs to the plan and producing a successful outcome. The level of sales manager will dictate the scale of their involvement but the principle of planning remains the same throughout all levels.

14.2 The planning model

In the business environment, plans can be broken down into three forms:

1 The **strategy** aims to achieve strategic objectives over the long-term.
2 The **operational plan** aims to achieve a stage or segment of the strategy via operational objectives. These have a mid-term timescale.
3 A series of **tactics** work towards the operational objectives by achieving short-term goals.

For example, a three-year marketing strategy may be broken down into operational plans over three years. Each year, there will be, say, a sales

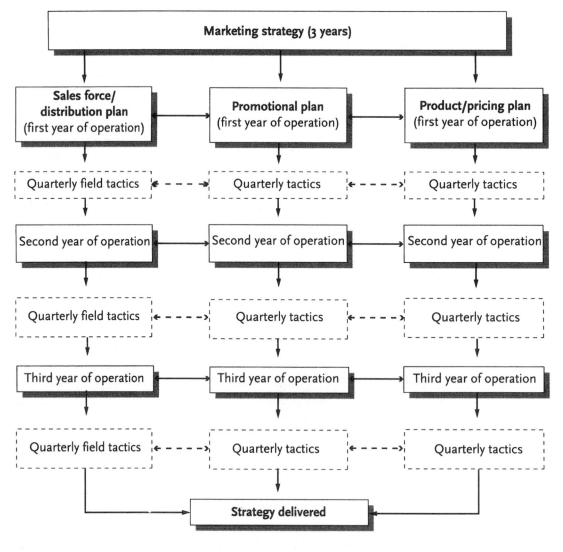

Fig. 14.1 *A simplified marketing strategy*

force/distribution plan, a promotional plan and a product/pricing plan. Therefore, the overall strategy will be achieved through the successful implementation of nine operational plans. There will be, say, quarterly tactics within each operational plan, all interdependent in ultimately delivering the overall strategy. This simplified marketing strategy is shown in Figure 14.1.

In this example, we can see that there is a set of components which all work towards the delivery of the marketing strategy – essentially, three separate strategies: sales force/distribution, promotional and product/pricing. Besides these being broken down into three operational years and a series of quarterly tactics, there is an interrelationship between them at each stage of delivering the strategy. The strength of this internal communication and interdependency is greatest at the strategic level, reducing operationally to only limited interdependency at a tactical level. That is, on a day-to-day basis, the three functions will each be working relatively independently of each other, but operationally and strategically, respectively, there is an increased interdependence and reduced independence. This principle is shown in Figure 14.2.

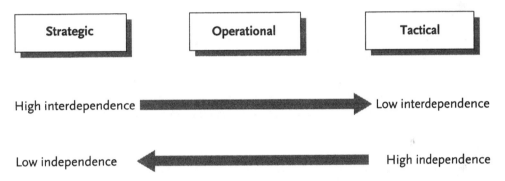

Fig. 14.2 *The dependence relationship between discrete functions within the marketing strategy*

The example used in this text serves to illustrate the principle of the planning model. In reality, a marketing strategy will be more complex with a wider range of discrete functions and a longer timescale – say, five years. Each function will fulfil its own strategy with an operational plan year-on-year but, within this, tactics are likely to be more frequent than quarterly.

Tutorial activity A

Maximising profits is often regarded as the key objective or strategic aim of a commercial organisation. However, in itself, this is inadequate. What other strategic aims/objectives may an organisation have?

Build a list of these possibilities for presentation/discussion with your tutor.

14.3 Strategy

Strategies are developed and delivered at a senior management level. The organisational strategy will occur at board level and, say, the marketing director will have an input to and responsibility to deliver their segment of that strategy. From this, the marketing strategy will be developed and the heads of the various marketing functions, including, say, the national sales manager, will have an input to and a responsibility to deliver their portions of the marketing strategy. This will give rise to the sales force strategy, which will require input from the regional sales managers, who will be responsible for delivering the strategy operationally.

Within a typical organisational structure this represents the depth of strategic development and delivery; that is, three layers of strategy before operational plans are developed. In very large or multinational organisations there may be more strategic layers, and in smaller organisations there may be two layers or possibly only a single one.

As we have seen, a strategy is a long-term plan. Traditionally in the UK, organisations have worked to a five-year strategic plan, although this has been criticised as being too short-term for larger organisations. Despite these criticisms, many UK firms are opting for an alternative approach to meet the demands of the dynamic business environment of the 1990s. Increasingly, we are seeing the use of a three-year rolling strategy, updated annually. The longer-term direction is provided by the mission statement or corporate philosophy but, within this, the strategic objectives are reviewed and amended year-on-year, this having a knock-on effect for the existing two years of operational plans and the development of the rolling third year of the plan.

14.4 Operations

The preceding four chapters have been dominated by operational considerations of the sales force. Although reference has been made to strategic issues and consideration has been given to field tactics, the operational focus is indicative of the nature of the majority of sales management roles. In terms of the sales force strategy, it is the sales managers within the sales force who are responsible for inputting to the operational planning process and delivering performance which satisfies the requirements of the plan; that is, they are responsible for achieving the budgets and targets on an annual basis.

So, whereas senior managers or executives may be regarded as having a strategic role, middle levels of sales management have an operational role. Invariably, operational plans are made annually and the performance of a sales manager will be measured on this basis. Within an operational plan, tactical indicators will be included which provide an early warning signal if things are not going according to plan.

Sales managers will be interested in these tactical indicators to ensure that the operational plan is delivered. Strategic managers though will have less interest in tactical indicators and will use operational performance as the main tool for developing and delivering strategy.

Practical activity 1

If you are pursuing a career in sales management or indeed any management career, there is an important consideration at this stage. Progression through management levels involves taking a wider and longer-term view of business activity.

In relation to your own role, consider how your line manager has to consider wider issues and take a longer-term view than you do. What skills and experience do they require in order to accomplish their responsibilities? Evaluating yourself, what additional skills and experience do you need to acquire in order to progress your career?

Discuss this analysis with your line manager and/or tutor.

14.5 Tactics

Field sales tactics are planned and delivered by the lower levels of sales management and all sales people within the sales force structure. Occasionally they will be quarterly but usually they will be more frequent. Typically, tactics will be measurable on a weekly or monthly basis. The practical application of breaking down performance targets into tactical segments and monitoring these at field level was considered in depth in the preceding chapter.

It is the practical application and monitoring of these tactics which enable the sales manager to make the required level of contribution to the operational plan. In turn, this is achieved by ensuring that each member of the sales team makes the level of contribution which is required of them individually. Although some tactical issues have been considered in this section of the book, many more were considered in Part II, both explicitly and implied within the text.

14.6 Inputs and outcomes

In order for successful strategies, operations and tactics to be developed and delivered, some preconditions exist. First, they must be accurate and realistically attainable, based on all relevant factors which are either known or likely to exist. Second, they must be consistently integrated so that tactics achieve operational objectives, which in turn deliver strategic objectives. Further, there must be consistent integration with the wider strategies of the organisation. Finally, employees at all levels must be motivated to make their required level of contribution to the total organisational performance.

Tutorial activity B

In the introduction to this section, the author has suggested four preconditions which exist in order for successful strategies, operations and tactics to be developed and delivered. Before continuing with this section, consider how these preconditions can be accomplished in the specific context of a sales force strategy. Compare your conclusions with the comments made by the author in the following narrative.

Accuracy

Basing decisions on accurate information is the key to developing plans which are realistically attainable. Relevant information will need to come from a variety of sources. Feedback from the sales force itself is important: both quantitative in the form of statistical reporting and qualitative by encouraging an upward flow of (albeit subjective) feedback. Other sources will include market analysis (customers and competitors); product development and innovation; promotional initiatives; economic climate; and personal development issues within the sales force, including matters of recruitment, retention and training. It is only by putting accurate and relevant information into the planning process that realistically attainable plans will result.

Micro-consistent strategy

It is no use having tactics which fall short of achieving the planned operational performance, and, similarly, senior managers should not accept an operational plan which does not meet the requirements of the strategic plan. The numerous tactical and operational plans within any strategy must be mutually consistent. Ultimately, this requires skilful management at the senior level, but prior to this, there should be appropriate inputs from sales managers and sales people within the sales force. This requires accurate communication to be transmitted and received at all levels within the management channel, as discussed in the preceding chapter.

Macro-consistent strategy

Apart from being consistent within itself, the sales force strategy should be consistent with the strategies of all other relevant functions. In an organisation which has a marketing-based structure, this process is likely to be driven by the marketing director. The role of the marketing director is to ensure each function head communicates effectively in developing individual strategies which are mutually consistent. As we have seen, the level of interdependence at this point is relatively high. Each function head will then need to ensure that mid-level managers are aware of the strategic interdependence and encourage operational communication, as appropriate.

Motivation

From a field management perspective, we have already seen how an imposed target can lead to a demotivated or under-committed sales person. The same principle applies throughout the sales force. Ultimately, targets will be decided by the most senior sales manager as they develop the sales force strategy. However, members of the sales force are likely to be more committed to achieving their targets if they feel their views have been considered as an input to the planning process and the outcome they are presented with represents what they consider to be a realistically attainable target.

14.7 Expenditure budgets

People with a selling perspective often see expenditure budgets as the constraints within which they have to work. That is, they will tend to focus on the turnover which can be produced based on how much they have available to spend. Historically, it is the sales revenue which sales managers have tended to manage rather than the profitability.

More recently, sales managers have taken responsibility for managing profit to a certain extent, although this often entails an expenditure budget, imposed by the finance function. The integration of selling into the wider marketing effort has transformed thought and approach in this area. By taking an overview of wider business activity, the marketing director is more likely to be saying to senior decision makers, 'This is the sales revenue we can generate and this is what we need to spend in order to accomplish it. Therefore our proposed profit is . . . and our risks are . . .'.

By integrating the marketing efforts, focusing on efficiency and encouraging a high degree of both internal and external communication, the overall profitability objectives can be delivered and improved. In organisations where personal selling is the main promotion and distribution tool, Sales Director or Sales and Marketing Director may be the title applied to the most senior manager responsible for the sales force. The principle of looking at expenditure positively in this way as a tool for increasing profitability remains equally valid. The following chapter considers this evolving relationship between selling and marketing, specifically the inputs which are required for increased profitable sales to result.

14.8 Summary

In this chapter, the model and process for sales force planning have been considered. The chapter represents a culmination of a variety of issues which have been covered throughout the first three parts of this book. Terms such as 'strategic issues' and 'field tactics' have been commonly used. Although a general understanding of these words and terms is assumed to have existed, the detailed consideration of planning provides a context for many issues which have been covered previously.

Strategies, operations and tactics are all relevant to the role and responsibilities of the sales manager. The degree of involvement with each planning component will be driven by the management level at which they are operating. Regardless of the level, the principle of planning remains the same. The practitioner quoted in this chapter relates the planning principle to the mnemonic **OPIAC**. A simplified strategic model has been presented to demonstrate the levels at which this principle can and should be applied.

The author suggested four preconditions which must exist in order for successful strategies, operations and tactics to be developed and delivered, specifically in the context of a sales force strategy. This was followed by an analysis of the key issues which enable these preconditions to be achieved. In summary of this analysis we can say that a variety of inputs to the planning process is required before a successful outcome or plan can be achieved. This requires skilful management and excellent communication.

Finally, expenditure budgets were considered, specifically how they can be used positively to increase profitability. The following chapter develops this issue and Chapter 16 further considers the relationship between costs and profitability in the modern selling environment.

Essay question

Some senior managers expect a year-on-year increase in sales revenue. This has been referred to as a practice of 'blind targeting'.

In the form of an essay, present an argument which counters this viewpoint, presenting an alternative view which has more validity as a planning philosophy

Further reading

Allen, P. (1993), *Selling: Management and Practice* (4th edn), Pitman Publishing, Chapter 18.

Chisnall, P. (1987), *Strategic Industrial Marketing*, Prentice Hall.

Greenley, G.E. (1986), *The Strategic and Operational Planning of Marketing*, McGraw-Hill.

Heibing, R. and Cooper, S. (1991), *How to Write a Successful Marketing Plan*, NTC Business Books.

Lancaster, G. and Jobber, D. (1994), *Selling and Sales Management* (3rd edn), Pitman Publishing, Chapters 12 & 13.

Case study: Dudley Stationery Ltd.

Martin Guntrip, Sales Director of Dudley Stationery, takes something of a modern approach to managing his sales force. That is, sales people are empowered to make appropriate decisions relating to customers, and sales managers are empowered to make appropriate decisions relating to sales people. This involves *delegation of authority* but not *delegation of responsibility*. It requires that members of the sales force are well trained and trusted to do the job they have been trained for.

Information technology plays an important role and provides sales people with a range of customer information, which enables them to be micro-business managers. This system also enables sales managers to focus on the performance of their sales teams, addressing areas of concern/weakness, identifying general training needs, and highlighting areas which merit praise.

The sales force system can be broadly considered as follows:

Sales people manage customers: Objective = optimise profitable sales revenue.

Sales managers manage sales people: Objective = optimise opportunity to perform.

Empowerment, in the context in which it is used by Dudley Stationery, does not mean total or, rather, blind faith. The performance of all individuals within the sales force must be measured to ensure the objectives and, therefore, targets are being achieved. Specifically, the performance of sales people is measured by four key business areas:

- sales
- profitability
- account base
- platform activity.

Under-performance in any of these business areas is likely to result in the sales person's targets and, therefore, organisational objectives not being achieved. At a formal, monthly reporting meeting between sales manager and sales person, under-performance needs to be highlighted and corrective action needs to be taken. Similarly, both on-target and over-target performance need to be discussed, lessons drawn and praise given. Overall, this provides an environment of motivation and continuous improvement. Ultimately, both the organisation and its customers benefit.

Task 1

In considering empowerment, what is the difference between delegating authority and delegating responsibility?

Task 2

Sales managers at Dudley Stationery manage the sales force performance in four key business areas. Using these as main headings, what sub-headings or, rather, detailed performance criteria would you measure?

Task 3

The reporting system and skilfully managed monthly meetings provide an environment of motivation and continuous performance. What other main ingredient is required to motivate a sales force and how would you address it in the case of Dudley Stationery?

Part IV

The future of selling

Chapter 15 # The evolving relationship between selling and marketing

Learning objectives

By the end of this chapter, you should :

- Have been introduced to an alternative strategic model

- Appreciate the role and scope of selling within the strategy

- Be encouraged to evaluate critically the model in relation to wider marketing considerations.

15.1 Introduction

Throughout this book, the relationship between selling and marketing has been explored. This has been based on a foundation of academic theory and principles, combined with a realistic overview of practical considerations. An integrated effort has been encouraged. Aspiring marketers have been provided with an insight into the role and application of selling in their environment. Similarly, sales people and sales managers have been provided with an education and training programme which places their modern role in the context of a wider marketing effort.

In the first chapter, emphasis was placed on the needs of the customer providing the key to successful business activity. These changing needs have led to the strategic influence of marketing in the organisational structure. In some cases, this calls into question the need for an organisation to use a sales force in marketing its products. Indeed, this was confirmed by the case study at the end of Part I. If personal selling is deemed necessary, it is considered as a part of the promotional mix and a channel of distribution by the marketer.

However, in some industries and organisations, selling plays a key role in the organisation's success. Much of the time there is unease between the sales force and the wider marketing effort. This leads to potential inefficiency in achieving an integrated approach, with duplication of effort and less appropriate application of resources. Mutual appreciation between sales people, sales managers and marketers is essential if progress is to be made.

It is increasingly common to see the job title 'Sales and Marketing Manager/Director'. This title implies an organisation which relies heavily on a personal selling effort but which also has a wider appreciation of other marketing influences. Other organisational structures tend to opt for a more traditional view of marketing as the main strategic management role. This gives rise to the title of 'Marketing Director' who has overall control of the sales force and other marketing functions such as research, advertising, distribution, pricing, and so on.

With the increasing influence of the marketing philosophy, aspiring sales managers have had to acquire a wider appreciation of marketing in order to enable career progression. Indeed, many such people are likely to be studying texts such as this one, to facilitate career development. A strategic role of 'Marketing Director' or 'Sales and Marketing Director' is the ultimate career goal. This will involve a responsibility for the full range of marketing functions, including the sales force. Mutual dependency and full integration is an ideal which has been achieved by some organisations in the past decade, but many others have found this harder to achieve.

In the US, the terms 'sales' and 'marketing' are seen as mutually dependent. Sales people appreciate wider marketing issues and fulfil a wider role in pursuit of the organisation's objectives. Many marketers have reached their senior career positions through a selling route but, regardless of background, there is a greater appreciation of the role of the sales force. It is not seen merely as a tool for promoting and distributing the organisation's products, but as fulfilling an important research and service function. Sales people and marketers alike are perceived as professionals, not only in their own organisations, but also in the wider society. Where personal selling is of strategic significance, full integration has to be a key objective for many UK companies.

In this chapter, two strategic models are presented which can be applied by organisations with a dependence on personal selling. The first is summarised in Figure 15.1 where personal selling is the primary promotion and distribution tool. It contrasts with the second model which is summarised in Figure 15.2, a more traditional approach adopted by UK organisations seeking to adopt a marketing philosophy. The suggestion is that this latter model is only appropriate for organisations with a secondary or minor dependence on personal selling.

For those organisations with a primary dependence on personal selling, adopting the first model will facilitate a smoother and successful transition to marketing/customer-orientation. Chapter 16 builds on this strategic model to consider its successful application in achieving enhanced profitability through full integration.

15.2 A strategic customer based model

In this section, the two strategic customer-based models are put forward. The first is where personal selling provides the main impetus in providing profitable sales revenue. The second considers situations where personal selling is a secondary tool in favour of alternative promotional and distribution approaches to business activity, but where the provision of customer service is paramount to the organisation's success.

In both cases, marketing research is assumed to underpin each component of the strategy, and the role of sales and service personnel is considered crucial if the strategy is to be successfully delivered. The first model, with personal selling as a primary factor, is shown in Figure 15.1.

The model provides a focus or strategic objective based on customer satisfaction and profit maximisation. There are four key inputs to the strategy: market, sales, service and product management. In terms of human resources, the actual management structure may or may not fit into these four discrete areas and it is for each organisation to develop its own management structure. The crucial factor is that each of the four inputs must be identified independently as separate strategies before being integrated and managed as one complete strategy. The typical content and coverage of these inputs can now be considered.

Market management

This requires an overview of all relevant areas of the market place. Specifically, it concerns customers and competitors. Through a process of continuous analysis, market management seeks to provide a focus for selling efforts; that is,

Fig. 15.1 *A customer-based strategic model (primary selling dependency)*

accurately targeting those customers which are the most profitable for the organisation, positioning the company's products in relation to these target groups, enhancing the efficiency of sales, service and product efforts.

Sales management

This involves managing all activity which is directly related to producing profitable sales revenue based on a personal selling effort. Clearly, the sales force is an important consideration, but beyond this, one should be concerned with wider distribution and promotional efforts and aspects of sales support, such as point-of-sale material and lead generation. It is through a collective effort in these areas that a sales force will be effective. Increased efficiency requires integration with the three other strategic inputs.

Service management

This encompasses all the key issues of customer service provision which are seen as being increasingly important to an organisation's success.

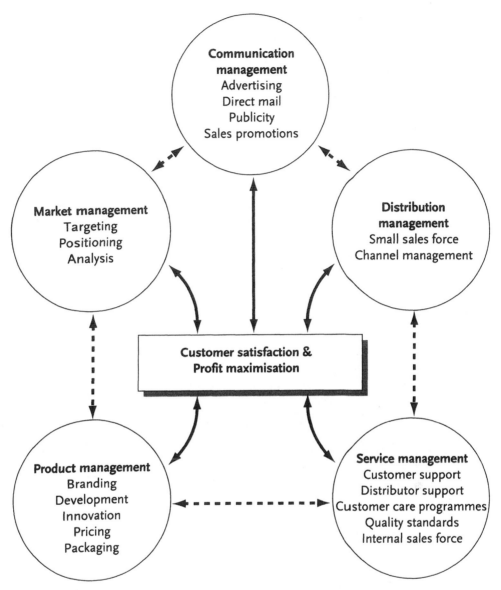

Fig. 15.2 *A customer-based strategic model (selling as a secondary tool)*

Specifically, we are concerned with efforts to support the customer, providing wider customer care programmes and maintaining quality standards. Additionally, service efforts are primarily responsible for ensuring repeat business from existing customers. Certain 'high value' customers may require personal attention from the external sales force, but many can be successfully serviced from a distance. Service provision must remain consistent with the product, market and sales strategies in order to be both effective and efficient.

Product management

This involves traditional marketing considerations which facilitate the application of the other three strategic inputs. Developing the right products to meet the needs of the right customers is a key principle. Following this, branding, pricing and packaging the product(s) appropriately contribute to efficiency of the sales and service efforts.

The second model, with selling as a secondary tool in favour of other promotional and distribution approaches, is shown in Figure 15.2.

There are more similarities than differences between the two models. Product and market management issues remain the same. Service management remains similar, but its scope widens to support the distribution network as well as direct customer-based service. A smaller sales force is required, perhaps being solely responsible for managing the distribution channel, and customer demand is generated through wider communication activity. In this scenario, sales force efforts are driven by other marketing communications rather than the reverse. The use of an internal, service-based sales force is appropriate if the organisation wishes to market its products directly, in addition to the use of channel intermediaries. This will be particularly relevant to repeat business with existing customers and shares a close relationship with communication efforts.

Advanced tutorial activity A

Based on your general awareness, think of an organisation to which the first strategic model could be applied and, similarly, one to which the second model could be applied. Discuss these thoughts with your tutor.

15.3 The role of selling within the strategy

Within this strategy, the role of all personnel in each strategic area is important. In considering selling personnel, we are primarily concerned with the areas of sales and service management. This is particularly true of the first model, but in the case of the second, service management provides the main focus with the additional consideration of managing the channel structure.

When personal selling is the primary function through which an organisation transacts its business activity, it drives and influences the other functions. The sales force provides a focus for most of the organisation's marketing efforts, as it is they who enjoy a close relationship with the customers. The market, product(s) and service levels should all be managed to meet the needs of customers but this should be in direct support of the sales force efforts.

When demand is generated through wider marketing communications and a more complex distribution structure, the role of the sales force becomes secondary. It remains important to establish and manage intermediaries within the structure but this is very much in support of the primary customer communication efforts. Other selling efforts are closely linked to repeat business with existing customers and can be regarded as service based.

Advanced tutorial activity B

For each of the two strategic models, build a general profile of the person who is most likely to be suited to the role of Marketing Director. Present these two profiles to your tutor together with a rationalisation of the key differences.

15.4 Successful implementation

In the following chapter, practical application of these customer-based selling strategies will be considered in relation to selling and service efforts, targeted specifically in relation to the profit contribution of customers. That is, resources need to be applied in a manner which is consistent with the costs being incurred.

The first stage of delivering such a strategy is to have management systems and processes which facilitate its implementation. This may involve a revision of current systems or a degree of re-engineering. Many of these processes will be standardised but provision should be made for flexibility in the field to accommodate local or regional variations. This will require high quality communication at both a strategic and operational level.

The second stage is to ensure selling and service personnel are fully aware of their duties and responsibilities, suitably equipped with the relevant skills and motivated to perform. This involves excellent management communication, a first class training and personal development programme at all levels, and reward mechanisms which recognise profitable performance.

Successful implementation of this strategy involves a total commitment from the top of the organisation and throughout all levels. However, that is where the

Advanced tutorial activity C

For an organisation with which you are familiar, and in direct relation to the organisational structure which is currently in place, consider:

(a) ways in which the key inputs discussed in this chapter could be independently identified in the design of an overall marketing strategy
(b) the management systems which would be required to facilitate implementation
(c) which of the two strategic models is most appropriate and, accordingly, any possible changes in the management structure.

Be prepared to justify these thoughts when debriefed by your tutor.

similarity with other strategies, such as total quality management (TQM), ends. TQM focuses on providing high levels of product and service performance to all customers. This alternative strategic approach actively discourages some aspects of this philosophy. Rather, it focuses on providing even higher levels of service to the most valuable customers and reduced levels of service to the least valuable. In this way, resources are applied in a manner which maximises profitability.

15.5 Summary

The future of selling is currently under the microscope. The influence of marketing has instigated a great deal of change in terms of the role which selling has to play in delivering an organisation's overall strategy. Although change has been necessary, many organisations still do not make optimum use of their sales force. Costs are being minimised and controls tightened with an ever increasing demand for more productivity and increased service levels. Although such ideals are valid to a degree, there is room for further improvement.

Clearly, sales and marketing need to integrate, and practitioners need to acquire a wider appreciation of the principles and practices of both. More importantly, there needs to be a new strategic approach. In this chapter, we have seen an alternative strategic model. Profits are maximised through customer satisfaction which requires mutually dependent inputs. In the first model, the organisation has a primary dependency on personal selling and the inputs may be considered as: market, product, sales and service management. In the second scenario, the organisation has only a secondary dependency on personal selling and the key inputs are: product, market, service, communication and distribution management.

Regardless of the model which is being used, the emphasis is on identifying the best customers, providing them with product(s) they require and relating sales and service efforts directly to the value which is provided to the organisation. This contradicts the principle of TQM which seeks to provide a high quality service to all customers and the marketing principle which sees selling as part of the promotional mix. Certainly, when the organisation has a primary dependency on personal selling, the sales force is much more than a promotional tool. Rather, it has a vital link with customers which should be fully utilised for the purposes of feedback and service provision.

A development of this strategy in terms of applying sales and service efforts in the most profitable way is considered in the next chapter.

Essay question

In this chapter, the author has challenged some established UK business practices. Specifically, the principle of TQM has been questioned and the view of selling solely as a promotional mix component has been regarded as too narrow.

In the form of an essay, write an evaluation of the first strategic model put forward in this chapter, concluding your piece with a justified opinion as to whether this represents an improvement on current principles and practice.

Further reading

Doyle, P. (1994), *Marketing Management and Strategy*, Prentice-Hall.

Fraser-Robinson, J. (1994), *Total Quality Marketing*, Kogan Page.

Skinner, R. (1993), *Integrated Marketing*, McGraw-Hill.

Wilson, G. (1993), *Making Change Happen*, Pitman Publishing.

Chapter 16

Maximising profits by providing optimum customer value

Learning objectives

By the end of this chapter, you should :

- Appreciate the principle of targeting customers in direct relation to their current and future profit contribution to the organisation

- Understand the strategic application of selling resources

- Understand the strategic application of servicing resources

- Understand the need for operational flexibility

- Have an appreciation for the typical tools which can be used to differentiate selling and service efforts in relation to customer value

- Appreciate the importance of human resources in delivering the strategy and consider an alternative model for developing these human resources

- Appreciate the potential benefits of strategic alliances/partnerships with other organisations.

16.1 Introduction

In the preceding chapter, an alternative strategic model was put forward. From the range of inputs discussed, we are specifically concerned in this chapter with the areas of market, sales and service management.

In terms of market management, the organisation should not only consider who their customers are but, further, analyse them in terms of their current and future profit contribution. Accordingly, selling efforts need to be focused on customers with the most potential for profitable growth and reduced for those customers with the least potential. Similarly, servicing efforts should be aimed at customers currently producing the most profit for the organisation and reduced for the ones which produce the least.

In order to be effective in maximising profits, this philosophy needs to be strategically driven but also must allow scope for operational flexibility based on field conditions. An inflexible approach which does not allow for regional or local circumstances will limit the impact of the strategy and potentially lead to missed opportunities, under-resourcing and over-resourcing. Specifically, this can be achieved by taking a quantitative position strategically and a qualitative position locally. Operationally, this will be visible by the range of tools which are used and how they are employed to differentiate between selling and service levels for the various target groups.

This chapter explores the key issues and considerations for gaining the maximum profit over both the short- and long-term by providing optimum customer value.

16.2 Customer profiling

Many organisations target specific customer groups through a variety of market segmentation systems. Marketers will seek to offer appropriate value to customers based on factors such as their perceptions, product benefits, price, and so on. There has also been a concerted effort in the past decade or so to increase customer value by providing higher levels of service through the use of TQM and customer care programmes. Although these business approaches have been largely successful, there remains scope for further improvement.

Change is not only inevitable but essential if organisations are to compete in the modern business environment. Ever increasing consumer awareness and national and global competition require an organisation to perform better and better in order to survive and thrive.

A practitioner's tale

"Are you being asked to produce more and more sales revenue with static or reducing budgets? Ask yourself, why? You have probably all reached the same conclusion – your company needs to make more profit on sales performance in order to cover increased costs of people, product development, advertising, the competition squeezing profit margins ... and the list goes on.

How can you possibly keep pace with these increasing demands? Well, you've just got to keep getting better and better at what you do. The things that work best and produce the best results have got to be done more often. The things that don't work very well and produce minimal results have got to be done less often or maybe you should even stop doing them."

A model for profiling customers is shown in Figure 16.1. It is based on a notional three-level dimension, although in practice the number of levels may increase or decrease depending on the range and scope of the organisation. This notional dimension is used to provide a context for specific selling and service considerations.

Category A customers are those with the highest profitable growth potential. This could be as a result of developing a need which is known or anticipated by the selling organisation or by winning business currently held by competitors.

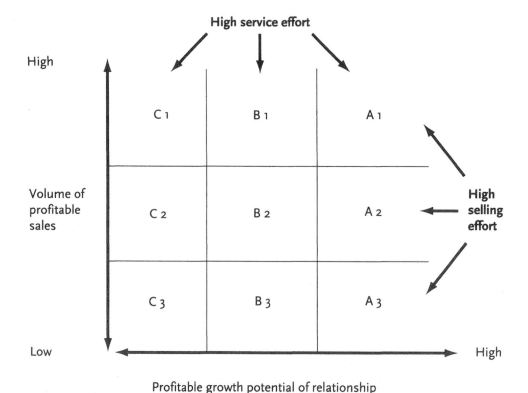

Fig. 16.1 *The customer profile matrix (notionally three-level dimension)*

On a sliding scale, *category C* customers have the least profitable growth potential. Selling efforts should focus primarily on *category A* customers, secondarily on *category B* customers, with minimal effort for *category C* customers.

Category 1 customers are those producing the highest volume of profitable sales, and on a sliding scale, *category 3* customers provide the lowest. Service efforts should focus primarily on the *category 1* customers, secondarily on *category 2* customers, and the need to service category 3 customers will either be minimal or subsumed by the selling efforts which are being made.

Treatment of customers in this way provides a level of selling and service effort which is consistent with satisfying the needs of customers but which is provided in direct relation to their value to the organisation.

16.3 Application of selling resources

Targeted customer groups need to be accessed and a level of selling effort, relevant to the profitable growth potential of the customer, needs to be exerted. This will involve developing a need, providing a solution and encouraging a positive buying decision. The separate consideration of servicing requirements enables a modified selling process to be considered. This can be summarised by the mnemonic **TANSE**:

> **T**arget customer groups
> **A**ccess customers
> **N**eed identification and development
> **S**olution provided
> **E**ncourage a positive buying decision.

Tutorial activity A

For an organisation with which you are familiar, consider how the profitable growth potential of customers could be quantified and, therefore, how appropriate groups could be profiled and targeted.

Discuss these conclusions with your tutor.

The key to profitable success in this area is to ensure the level of selling effort is relevant to the profitable growth potential of the trading relationship. Achieving this balance in practical terms will involve a variety of efforts from the sales force and support functions. An example of how this may be achieved is shown for each customer sales category:

A customers: *Targeted* by corporate research efforts, input from sales people and a service-driven input from a customer analysis. *Accessed* by support functions such as direct mail and telemarketing. *Needs* identified and developed by personal selling effort. *Solution* provided by personal selling effort. Positive buying decision *encouraged* by personal selling effort. In the case of A1 customers and possibly A2 customers, there is likely to be a team selling effort in conjunction with the service and support functions, as strong relationships are already being developed.

B customers: *Targeted* by corporate research efforts and a service-driven input for existing customers. *Accessed* by a shift towards less personal support functions such as direct response advertising and direct mail. *Need* identification and development, the provision of a *solution* and *encouraging* the customer to buy should focus on the most efficient selling systems. It is less appropriate to use a personal selling effort and this could be replaced by seminar/group selling or dedicated teleselling.

C customers: These should not be actively *targeted*. The exception to this is the desired long-term movement from category A1 to B1, through to C1. These customers will be targeted and supported through the provision of service levels which are likely to include technical support, product updates, customer care programmes, customer loyalty schemes and new product launch information. Inevitably, some members of this customer group will be *accessed* through some of the activities aimed at B customers, such as direct response advertising. The selling organisation must then decide whether or not it wishes to trade with such customers. The likelihood is that it will do so on the proviso that a minimal selling effort is required. *Need* identification and development, *solution* provision and *encouragement* to purchase will be loosely provided through reactive telesales activity and, say, mail order.

This exemplary framework serves to emphasise the different personal selling efforts which are required in relation to the three notional customer groups: A, B and C. Each organisation will need to develop its own framework and practices, based on the resources available and the requirements of customers in relation to the nature of the product(s). The key is that a high personal selling effort is aimed at A category customers, which reduces for B category customers, and so on through however many customer selling categories have been identified.

Tutorial activity B

For an organisation with which you are familiar, consider how many levels of customer selling categories are appropriate. Using TANSE as a framework, how would you differentiate between each category in terms of selling effort? Specifically identify the tools which could be used in this differentiation process.

Present these conclusions to your tutor in the form of summative notes.

16.4 Application of servicing resources

Servicing levels need to be appropriate to the volume of profitable sales which are being achieved in order to maintain existing levels, through the encouragement of relevant customer loyalty. 'Category 1' customers will receive the highest levels of service, reducing for 'category 2' customers, and so on through the levels.

Tutorial activity C

For an organisation with which you are familiar, consider how the current profitability of customers can be quantified, and therefore, how service levels can be targeted accordingly.

Discuss these conclusions with your tutor.

A model for servicing effort, based on the notional three-level system, is now considered:

Category 1: Relationship marketing This involves providing the highest levels of service possible. Personal service should be provided which is likely to include regular visits by sales people, reacting positively to individual customer feedback, product and organisational updates, information of new product launches, technical support as required, a comprehensive customer care programme and loyalty incentives. Additional considerations in this area may include hospitality, such as entertainment, activity days and seasonal gifts. In this way, the customers producing the highest level of profitable sales – that is the ones which are currently the most valuable to the organisation – are encouraged to remain loyal through exceptional service provision.

Category 2: Account management A personal service is provided on a reducing scale. The number of visits from sales people will decrease and will be replaced by, say, a telesales function. Customer feedback is more likely to be considered collectively rather than individually. New and existing product information is likely to be mailed and it is unlikely that organisational information will be provided unless it has a direct impact on the customer group. Customer care programmes and loyalty incentives are likely to remain but hospitality considerations will be minimal.

Categories B3 and A3: Sales support These customers currently produce a very low level of profitable sales volume but have potential for growth in this area. The requirement for independent service provision is minimal but a level of service should be provided relevant to supporting the selling effort which is being made. This is likely to involve technical support, customer care programmes, positive reaction to customer feedback, and provision of product and point-of-sale literature. In the case of B3 customers, sales follow-up calls in pursuit of repeat business may well be made by a telesales function, but with A3 customers this is likely to involve personal sales calls.

Category C3: Demarketing These are customers currently producing low volumes of profitable sales with limited scope for growth. Only a very limited servicing effort should exist and it is unlikely that any personal selling effort will be made. These customers should not be actively contacted by the organisation, and only a basic customer care programme should be offered which may include, say, limited telephone-based technical support. The lack of sales and service attention given to this customer group is likely to result in losing them to competitors. This has a double benefit to the organisation. First, the least profitable customers with the least potential are lost, which enables increased efforts to be directed at more valuable customers. Second, competitive organisations become burdened with low profitability customers.

Tutorial activity D

For an organisation with which you are familiar, consider how many customer servicing categories are appropriate. How would you differentiate between each category in terms of servicing effort? Specifically identify the tools which could be used in this differentiation process.

Present these conclusions to your tutor in the form of summative notes.

16.5 Operational flexibility

In Tutorial Activities A–D you were asked to consider ways in which customer groups could be quantified in relation to current profitability and the growth potential for future profitability. This activity provides the foundation for the centralised processes which can be used to identify and target customer groups. In turn, it would be the basis for the organisation's market, sales and service management strategies.

However, centralised processes are in danger of providing an inflexible approach to business, as they do not necessarily take account of local or regional variations and qualitative customer issues. For example, a customer providing moderate levels of profitable sales with limited growth potential (C2), may not warrant high levels of personal service or selling contact, in accordance with the centralised processes. On a local level, this same customer may be an excellent referral source for introducing new customers to the organisation and, therefore, it may be wise to provide them with higher levels of personal contact in order to cultivate the wider benefits of the relationship.

Although operation flexibility should be encouraged, there is a concern that some personnel will not truly think in terms of profitability. For example, a sales person may spend an undue amount of time with, say, a C2 customer for the wrong reasons, such as the hospitality they receive or the rapport which they share with the customer. In part, this is addressed by an organisation ensuring the principles, importance and benefits of the strategy are fully communicated and understood by all relevant personnel. Additionally, there must be a devolved management responsibility for ensuring individual actions are consistent with the organisational philosophy. Apart from training and communicating with managers to ensure their awareness and commitment is sufficiently strong, there is likely to be a need for localised management processes to be developed which enable individual activities to be controlled.

Tutorial activity E

For an organisation with which you are familiar, consider possible qualitative customer issues which may influence selling and servicing efforts. How could these be addressed in terms of localised management processes which both facilitate and control variation from organisational strategy?

Present these conclusions to your tutor in the form of a brief report.

16.6 Development of human resources

In Chapter 11, a general training process was considered and, although this remains valid in virtually all sales and management training situations, a more specific personal development process can be considered in relation to the customer-profile-based strategy in this chapter. Indeed, its successful implementation is dependent on well-trained, professionally aware and highly motivated personnel at all levels of selling and servicing.

This evolved process can be summarised by the mnemonic **IMPADE**:

Identification of skill and awareness requirements of the role
Management evaluation of current skill and awareness levels
Personal evaluation of current skill and awareness levels
Agreement of training needs for skills, product and organisational information
Delivery of training and provision of information
Evaluation of post-training performance.

Identification of skill and awareness requirements of the role

This is a management process which aims to consider each job type within the sales and service functions. Current practice of producing a job specification provides a suitable context, but the ideal person for the role should be profiled in terms of:

- What skills do they require to be totally successful in the role?
- What professional awareness must they have in order to deliver appropriate sales and service levels?
- If all these skills and professional awareness cannot be provided instantly, they should be sorted into an order of priority, including any aspects which must be regarded as absolutely essential.

Management evaluation of current skill and awareness levels

For each jobholder, the line manager needs to evaluate accurately and honestly the current levels of skill and professional awareness. This evaluation should be conducted in specific relation to the ideal levels previously identified. Given that managers are also jobholders, key skills which they must possess are:

- the ability to assess themselves objectively
- the ability to assess others objectively
- the ability to receive assessments from their own managers objectively.

Personal evaluation of current skill and awareness levels

It is not enough for people to be told of their personal development needs by their line managers. Every jobholder must identify for themselves the skills and professional awareness which they must have in order to excel in their roles. When this is achieved, a willingness to learn and improve personally will exist. This will ensure the individual is receptive to the training which is provided and will respond accordingly by applying new skills and knowledge in the practical environment. Key skills which all sales and customer service personnel must possess are:

- the ability to assess themselves objectively
- the ability to receive assessments from their own managers objectively.

Agreement of training needs and Delivery of training

Consultation between line manager and jobholder confirms the training needs which exist. These are likely to be prioritised and require planned action to be taken. The needs identified may include:

1 **Skills training:** on a local basis, in-house courses, general courses offered by external providers or bespoke courses offered to organisations by specialist training providers.
2 **Product training:** usually an in-house function provided by in-house courses, on a local basis, or through product literature and updates.
3 **Organisational training:** necessarily an in-house function provided by in-house courses and seminars, senior management communication, newsletters, in-house magazines and on a local basis.
4 **Background training:** usually provided through part-time attendance at university or college. This serves to reinforce an individual's professional awareness and appreciation, and will often be necessary for a promotional career path to be developed.

The skills required of a manager in achieving a genuine agreement to training needs and a positive response to addressing these needs revolves around excellence in:

- personal communication techniques
- motivational techniques.

Evaluation of post-training performance

The provision of training in itself is wasted unless it brings about an improvement in performance. Just as some customers may need to be demarketed, some sales or service personnel may not respond positively to their personal development needs and may need to be deselected or redeployed within the organisation.

Ethical note

In any situation where deselection or redeployment is being considered, due attention should be paid to the legal and moral responsibilities of the employer. However, the successful implementation of a selling and service based strategy requires that the right people are in the right jobs, suitably equipped with the appropriate skills, professionally aware and highly motivated.

Employers must find a balance between their immediate legal and moral responsibilities and their wider business management responsibilities.

Every effort should be made to fulfil an individual's personal development needs, and responsiveness to training should be monitored in relation to pace of receptability through the measurement of improved performance against agreed expectations. Further developmental needs can be identified, planned and delivered against revised expectations. Evaluating the success of training in this way by both the line manager and jobholder facilitates progress and rapidly improves performance in a motivating organisational environment.

16.7 Strategic alliances and partnerships

In a business environment where there are ever increasing demands for more efficiency and higher profitability, organisations have continuously to improve their strategies and operations. The issues discussed in this and the preceding chapter consider a new business philosophy based on maximising profits through the provision of optimum customer value.

The final consideration in this area is that of strategic alliances and partnerships; that is, complementary organisations working together on projects which facilitate efficient application of their joint resources, to provide mutual benefit in terms of increased opportunity and profitability. This concept is not new and has become increasingly common in the UK business environment over the past decade.

The reasons for building relationships which lead to strategic alliances and partnerships are based on the same principles as the philosophy put forward in this text. Therefore, in many situations, they can be considered an integral strategic element for organisations seeking to apply their resources efficiently in pursuit of maximising profitability.

Tutorial activity F

Think of a strategic alliance or partnership in the practical environment. How does it facilitate the efficient application of resources and, therefore, enable profit maximisation?

Discuss these conclusions with your tutor.

16.8 Summary

Building on the foundations of the preceding chapter, we have considered a model which facilitates the practical implementation of the principles. This model is based on profiling customers in terms of current profitability and the scope for future profitability. In turn, servicing and selling resources can be applied accordingly, in pursuit of profit maximisation through the provision of optimum customer value. That is, it makes good commercial sense to provide a level of selling and service effort which is directly related to the profit contribution made by each customer.

Strategically, this requires that customers are divided into broad group categories. In this chapter, a notional three-level dimension has been considered, although in practice the number of levels will vary according to individual organisational situations. Operationally, there is likely to be a need for more flexibility which accommodates local or regional variations, including individual customer considerations.

Strategic success and operational success depend on both high quality management processes and personnel who are professionally aware, suitably equipped with the right skills, and motivated to perform and deliver. These two areas are prerequisites of successful implementation and should provide the focus for senior management efforts. Additionally, senior managers should actively seek and evaluate opportunities for developing strategic alliances and partnerships which further enhance the efficient application of resources in pursuit of profit maximisation.

Essay question

In this and the preceding chapter, the author has developed what has been described as 'a new business philosophy'. This view is influenced by current practice in the US and growing trends in the UK business environment, driven by increasing pressures to attain maximum profitability.

In the form of an essay, compare and contrast the principles and practices of this 'new business philosophy' with current marketing philosophy. The length of your essay should be around 3000 words and you should conclude your piece with an evaluation of the merits and/or drawbacks of this alternative approach.

Further reading

Christopher, M., Payne, A. and Ballantyne, D. (1993), *Relationship Marketing*, Heinemann.

Cram, T. (1994), *Relationship Marketing*, Pitman Publishing.

Hinton, I. (1993), *Building Customer Loyalty*, Pitman Publishing.

Chapter 17

The role of information technology

Learning objectives

By the end of this chapter, you should :

- Appreciate the role of information technology in current selling practice

- Understand the main general applications of information technology

- Begin to appreciate the scope for future information technology applications and be encouraged to consider this in the context of their own organisations or ones with which they are familiar

- Appreciate the role of information technology as a management tool.

17.1 Introduction

Information technology has a major influence on the modern business environment. The pace of advancement in this area is phenomenal and used positively it encourages an environment of continuous opportunity. Against this, a denial or refusal of these advances and the benefits for the organisation in terms of increased efficiency and effectiveness will inevitably bring potential threats to the business.

In this chapter, we shall consider the main applications of information technology in direct relation to their positive impact on the sales force: specifically, how efficiency can be improved and, in turn, how profitability can be increased. Four broad areas are considered: telecommunications, storing and handling customer information, point-of-sale presentations and managing the sales force. Within each section, current practice is considered and the student is encouraged to evaluate critically the practical applications in terms of advantages and disadvantages for the sales person, sales manager and, most importantly, the customer.

Additionally, modern developments are considered and the student is encouraged to develop an appreciation for potential applications. Unlike other chapters in this book, the text of this chapter will be outdated by advancements in information technology in a very short space of time. Therefore, the overriding intention of this chapter is to encourage the student/practitioner to learn the benefits of and processes for managing information technology as a business tool.

17.2 Telecommunications

In the past, this area has primarily been concerned with tools such as the telephone and telex machines. In the past decade we have seen the growth of facsimile machines, mobile telephones, paging machines and point-to-point modem communications.

The telephone has long been established as a powerful tool for the sales person. The developments of the past decade have had a powerful impact on the working environment, particularly the selling environment. The remote field sales person can now be 'in touch' with branch/head offices and customers. Messages can be relayed, previously 'wasted time' can be utilised, information can be downloaded, and so on.

Tutorial activity A

The text states, 'Messages can be relayed, previously "wasted time" can be utilised, information can be downloaded . . .'. Consider practical situations in which the mentioned benefits enhance the efficiency of the field sales person.

Discuss these conclusions with your tutor.

Most recently, there has been the use of the much publicised 'information super-highway' which goes far beyond the previous point-to-point capabilities, significantly increasing the communication network. Indeed, some students will be using the 'super-highway' as a medium and/or resource for their studies.

Advanced tutorial activity B

The 'information super-highway' referred to in this text has been much publicised. There is currently intensive debate in the sales and marketing environment as to how businesses can best benefit from this enhanced communication network. Potential new business opportunities arise, together with enormous scope for increasing efficiency.

In a round table discussion, consider how new business opportunities may arise and the ways in which efficiency may be enhanced, particularly in relation to the sales force. Discuss these thoughts with your tutor, using any practical examples you can discover.

Extension: Undoubtedly, the next few years will see an enormous increase in the use of the 'super-highway' as a tool for sales and marketing applications. Beyond your studies/training, many of these developments are likely to have an enormous impact on your career and life in general. You are well advised continuously to appraise advancements and innovative applications and, therefore, to assess potential opportunities.

Perhaps the most powerful impact of advances in telecommunications has been the growth of teleworking. More and more workers are able to operate remotely from their organisational bases. In the case of field selling, many sales people have been working remotely for years. They are familiar with the benefits and disadvantages of performing in such an environment. However, the implications for businesses in general, and the wider scope of sales and marketing, are far greater. Typically there may be changes in management structures and systems, selling practices, the nature of customer information and contact, service delivery, and so on. It is important for managers within the sales and marketing environment not only to accept these and other changes brought on by advances in information technology but, to manage them positively so that they present opportunities as opposed to threats.

A practitioner's tale

"Opportunities come and opportunities go! I had made some good money out of selling and wanted to build my own business, make even more money and secure my future.

A good business starts with a good idea. I searched and searched for a good idea. I talked to many people in my attempt to find inspiration for a good opportunity. Among those I spoke to was a chap I shall refer to as Ken.

Ken was a successful sales manager with absolutely no desire to run his own business. But Ken had a vision and spent a good few hours passing on his wisdom to me. He told me that in a few years' time, lots of people would be working from home. He described how sales people would travel around with a mobile office on board their car; how virtually every household would have a PC; and how all these PCs would be connected together. In a nutshell, Ken told me that technological advances in communication were the key to the future and if I wanted a business idea, that was the area where I should be.

That was in 1989. Six years, a recession and more than a million pounds later, all I can say is, 'Thanks for the tip Ken!'."

17.3 Customer information: storage and handling

This is another area in which there has been tremendous growth in the past decade, being of particular significance to marketing in general, and as we are more specifically concerned with in this text, the selling function. Primarily, we are concerned with storing customer information on a database in such a way that it can be used to increase both efficiency and effectiveness.

In wider marketing terms, customer databases enable greater efficiency and accuracy in developing segmentation and targeting systems together with quantitative analysis for research purposes. That is, data can be searched to provide answers to numerical questions. For example, how many customers spent over £50 000?, how many customers purchased products X, Y, Z? and so on. Customers may be further broken down into categories of, say, industry types, or product usage, to provide a basis for segmenting and targeting both existing customers and potential ones.

The marketer working in an environment where the sales force enters all customer information on a database system can take this practical application a stage further. A so-called 'lead tracking system' provides powerful potential. For example, one can consider the effectiveness of advertising and promotional campaigns in very specific terms. Traditionally, this would have been measured primarily in terms of responses, whereas technological advances now enable these responses to be tracked throughout the selling process. In this way, responses can be measured in terms of the short- and long-term value which the organisation derives from, say, a particular advertisement or advertising medium; that is, which one(s) not only brought in the best responses but also resulted in closed sales (short-term) and repeat sales (long-term).

In the preceding narrative, lead tracking systems were considered in terms of measuring the effectiveness of promotional tools. For an organisation with which you are familiar, consider the range of promotional tools it uses for both existing and potential customers. In specific terms, how could a lead tracking system be used to measure:

(a) the effectiveness of promotional tools based on both short- and long-term considerations

(b) the efficient planning and application of resources?

Although databases provide a measure of the overall effectiveness of the sales force as a promotional tool, they also enable sales managers to measure the effectiveness of each individual sales person. Thus, the performance of a sales person can be measured at each stage of the selling process and also in relation to specific customer types. For example, an advertising campaign may have been effective in terms of responses/enquiries but only a few sales people are turning a high number of these into closed sales. In the field, the sales manager is able to identify problems requiring specific attention – usually ones which require a motivational or personal development solution.

To a large extent, the successful application of a customer database is dependent on the accuracy of information which is entered. When considering the sales force, there is a danger that inaccurate or subjective data will be input to the system. This is particularly likely if the system is implemented and viewed purely as a management tool. To overcome this, sales management must implement a new system, or indeed any situation of change, on the basis of the benefits which the sales people will derive from it.

Certainly, there are implied benefits to the sales person based on the marketing and sales management advantages which have already been considered. That is, more accurate segmentation, targeting and application of resources will have a knock-on effect for the sales force in terms of higher quality leads. Additionally, sales managers will be able to improve the performance of the sales force in terms of motivation and personal development. However, these benefits alone are unlikely to be sufficient in successfully implementing a major change to sales force practice. What explicit benefits can individual sales people expect to derive from a customer database?

There are several major benefits which can be considered. The sales person is provided with a micro-marketing capability and a personal productivity/efficiency tool resulting in the following:

- They are able to manage customer, prospect and suspect records.
- Personal mailings can be targeted and implemented efficiently, without the use of administrative support.

- Contact and follow-up calls can be managed to optimise the sales person's efficiency and effectiveness.
- Time management capability is enhanced.
- The sales person can target their own efforts in specific areas which are likely to provide the most profitable return.
- A higher level of customer care can be provided.

Group tutorial activity D

Consider each of the major benefits which a sales person can derive from using a customer database. For an organisation with which you are familiar, discuss in specific terms how these benefits may be achieved. Are these benefits sufficient to ensure sales people input complete and accurate information to the system?

Make a brief presentation to your tutor, explaining your findings and justifying your conclusion.

Advanced tutorial activity E

Gather information on a range of customer databases. In the context of an organisation with which you are familiar, evaluate the specific benefits which are provided by three of these systems. Compare and contrast them in terms of:

(a) value to the organisation/marketer
(b) value to sales management
(c) value to individual sales people within the sales force
(d) value to the customer.

Based on this evaluation, decide which is the most appropriate database system for the organisation, including a justification of the expenditure in relation to the overall value of the system.

Extension: Assume the role of sales manager and take your tutor or seminar group to be your sales team. Make a presentation to advise them of the impending implementation of the system you have selected, paying particular attention to the benefits which they will gain from it.

Note: You may like to include this presentation as part of planning and delivering a sales meeting (Practical Activity 1, Chapter 13).

17.4 Point-of-sale presentations

This area represents one of the most visible ways in which information technology has improved the effectiveness of the sales person. Traditionally, sales people have used presentation folders, product literature, overhead projector presentations, slide show presentations and video presentations. Although many of these tools remain in use to the present day, there have been enormous advances in recent years. Organisations adopting new methods of presenting their products and services at the point of sale have been able visibly to demonstrate increased levels of professionalism and, therefore, to provide customers with higher perceptions of value.

The past few years have seen the introduction of some generic presentational software packages. They can be used for personal presentations or projected for group presentations. Sales people are able to develop a set of core presentation 'slides' and amend, develop or add to these for tailoring a presentation to various audiences. Visually, this method is more powerful and stimulating than the traditional use of overhead projectors or slide show presentations.

Larger organisations may choose to develop their own presentational software rather than use a generic package. In this way, more specific corporate information may be included in the presentation, such as product literature presented electronically or the use of graphs and diagrams. Additionally, customer needs may be entered and the package may produce a suggested solution. This latter application has been adopted by, among others, the financial services industry where there is a high degree of technical analysis required in order to find a solution to the customer's situation.

Increasingly, sales people are being issued with laptop or notebook computers and mobile laser printers. Point-of-sale presentations are a common application of this technology, although additional advantages include:

- instant customer information on either a discrete database or, more frequently, one which connects to the main corporate database for both uploading and downloading customer information
- self-administrating sales people, including the ability to produce quotation software, and standard and individual correspondence
- remote training purposes, particularly product and corporate information and updates
- reporting and analysis of performance.

17.5 Managing the sales force

Information technology can also be applied as a very effective management tool. The use of spreadsheets is perhaps the most obvious application. Individual and collective performance can be analysed more efficiently, applying the principles of management control covered in Chapter 13. Additionally, spreadsheets enable planning and projecting sales force performance to be conducted more accurately and efficiently. We have already seen how customer information can be analysed and this too is a management consideration in the planning process.

Tutorial activity F

Using a spreadsheet package with which you are familiar, develop a sales force reporting form which incorporates a capability for both quantitative and qualitative analysis, as discussed in Chapter 13. Test this electronic form before presenting it to your tutor.

Extension: Build on the form and consider ways in which it can be further developed as a tool for projecting sales performance, say for up to three months in the future.

A recent and very exciting technological advance has been the introduction of *video conferencing*. For some time it has been predicted that the telephone will be improved to include visual capabilities, but video conferencing goes far beyond this basic concept. Simplistically, it involves the use of a personal computer with a built-in video camera, linked to another personal computer with similar software and technological capability, via a modem facility. The two parties can not only hear and see each other but also refer to various computer files during their exchange.

This presents enormous possibilities for the sales manager. For example, remote sales people can be managed more efficiently. Rather than the sales manager travelling, say, 50 miles for a meeting with a sales person, they can conduct the meeting from their home or office base. Moreover, they can refer to a spreadsheet analysis or product update during the meeting as though they were both sitting in the same room. Arguably, video conferencing will enable a single sales manager to manage a larger team than would have been practicable previously.

Video conferencing also has group communication facilities which further enhance its application as a management tool. For example, daily briefings could replace breakfast meetings and training could be conducted not only remotely but also perhaps outside of core selling time.

Further advancements and improvements in this area of information technology are likely to have a continuing impact on the sales force and the management of it; but what about the selling function itself? How long before sales calls are actually conducted using video conferencing facilities?

17.6 Summary

In this chapter, key aspects of information technology have been considered in relation to selling and sales management. Necessarily, coverage has been in outline, as there is a wide variety of applications relevant to individual selling and sales force situations.

The overriding objective of this chapter has been to encourage the student/practitioner to consider the range of applications with sufficient depth to stimulate further analysis of individual and corporate variants. The principle that information technology can increase both the efficiency and effectiveness of sales people and sales managers has been established and reinforced throughout the chapter.

Specifically, the broad areas of telecommunications, customer information, point-of-sale and sales force management applications have been considered. Inevitably, there will be a crossover between applications and, organisationally, systems need to be developed which enable optimum efficiency to be achieved; that is, applications which are complementary to each other and collectively produce an improvement on current systems and practices.

Essay question

Based on an organisation with which you are familiar, analyse its current use of information technology in direct relation to the sales force. What improvements could be made in order to increase the efficiency and effectiveness of sales force members? In writing this piece and making your suggestions, consider why these improvements have not been made already.

Further reading

Blattberg, R.C., Glazer, R. and Little, J.D.C. (eds) (1994), *The Marketing Information Revolution*, Harvard Business School Press.

Juer, M. (1996), *New Strategies for Marketing Information Technology*, Chapman & Hall, Chapter 17.

Price Waterhouse (1994), *Sales and Marketing Software Handbook*, Pitman Publishing.

Shaw, R. (1993), *Computer-aided Marketing and Selling*, Heinemann.

Chapter 18

International sales and marketing

Learning objectives

By the end of this chapter, you should :

- Understand the variants of international marketing as a contextual framework for the sales person

- Appreciate the business opportunities which open up with international markets

- Be aware of the main difficulties involved in entering and operating in international markets

- Appreciate the need for cultural empathy and be aware of how this is achieved

- Appreciate the role of sales people operating in international markets.

18.1 Introduction

Throughout this book, selling has been considered in the context of marketing-orientated organisations. The principle of marketing as a strategic management philosophy has been emphasised and its operational relationship with selling has been considered in depth.

When considering a trading situation which goes beyond national borders, the role of marketing becomes even more significant than with domestic operations. In domestic situations, sales people who do not have the benefit of working within a marketing-driven environment can still be effective and successful by adopting a micro-marketing role. However, it becomes increasingly difficult for sales people to remain effective in wider international markets without the influence and support of marketing.

A decision to enter and operate in international markets is a strategic one. The best method of doing so is also a major strategic decision. Personal selling is an operational consideration within such a strategy and, aside from the principles and practice of selling discussed throughout this text, there are additional skills and professional awareness which sales people and sales managers must take on board if they are to be successful in this field.

The following three sections of this chapter consider the wider marketing aspects of international business activity. The chapter then goes on to consider specific issues which are of relevance to sales people and sales managers.

18.2 Variants of international marketing

In the book 'Marketing: Principles and Practice'[1], there is an interesting summary of the five stages of international marketing. It is not to say that all organisations will follow all five stages; indeed it is unusual for an organisation starting at Stage 1 to progress to Stage 5. However, it does provide an overview of options available to the organisation in strategic terms, although, ultimately, the path selected will be dependent on many factors, most notably the resources available and the overseas market potential of the product/service.

Stage 1: Exporting/export sales

This is something of a sales-orientated approach to international trade. There is a dependency on personal selling which aims to win contracts for supplying the product/service overseas. It is the activity of sales people which identifies potential customers, either a major direct customer or agents/distributors who can generate reasonably large volumes of business. There is a tendency for export sales activity to satisfy short-term objectives, although, this said, it can be a very effective option for smaller organisations wishing to enter international markets. Additionally, short-term objectives are sometimes a valid option. For example, some UK organisations saw export sales activity as a method for surviving the recession of the early 1990s. In many cases this proved to be a valid and successful short-term objective.

Stage 2: Export marketing

This is a development from export sales activity. Operationally, there is marketing support for the personal selling function. This may include identification of potential customers, researching markets, advertising and other promotional activity, branding and managing products according to localised market needs, and co-ordination of product distribution. Again, direct customer sales are a possibility for major contracts but it is common to use overseas agents/distributors, although an increased investment in the application of marketing resources will dictate the need for increased commitment and motivation on behalf of these intermediaries.

Stage 3: International marketing operations

This can be viewed as a distinct progression from export marketing. There is likely to be a combination of exporting and overseas supply. That is, some capacity to produce the product locally is likely to exist. Personal selling is no longer supported by marketing activity; rather a far stronger marketing influence controls selling activity. There is likely to be less dependence on overseas independent agents/distributors, and these are likely to be replaced by strategic alliances, trading partnerships, traditional intermediary networks and fully structured channels of distribution.

Stage 4: Multinational marketing

Typically, this will involve setting up a subsidiary company in each major overseas market. The product will be produced and distributed by the subsidiary, including discrete sales and marketing activity. In this way, the needs of various overseas markets can be identified and specifically addressed. Once established, subsidiaries are likely to be self-supporting in many respects, with some profits being retained for reinvestment and surplus profits being repatriated to the parent company.

Stage 5: Global marketing

This involves marketing on a worldwide scale. A centrally co-ordinated marketing strategy targets broad customer groups globally. In many respects this is an extension of Stage3 but it is distinguished by a highly resourced strategy aimed at achieving very wide market appeal, typically dominating and leading markets in a large number of countries.

Tutorial activity A

For each of the five variants of international marketing discussed in this chapter, think of an example of a company which fits the author's description. Check these examples with your tutor to confirm your understanding.

18.3 Opportunities

In simple terms, the main opportunity presented by international marketing can be summed up by saying: more potential customers equals more sales and growth opportunity.

This principle is shown in Figure 18.1.

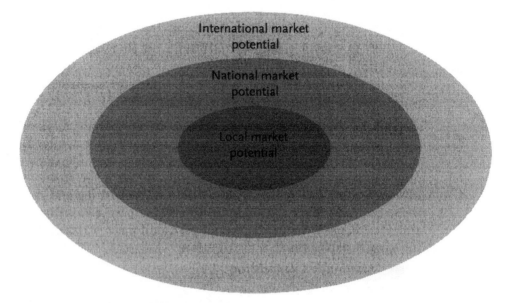

Fig. 18.1 *The basic opportunity presented by international marketing*

Whilst the objective of realising an increased number of customers may be an extremely valid reason for an organisation deciding to enter international markets, there are other, equally valid reasons for doing so:

Diversifying the market base

There may be several reasons for an organisation needing to widen its market base, apart from exploiting growth opportunities; for example, balancing home market fluctuations or instability, a saturated home market and a need to increase credibility, or customer perceptions as an 'international player'.

Competitor internationalisation

If major competitors are entering international markets, the failure of an organisation to follow may leave it disadvantaged in the long-term. A decision to move into overseas markets should not be based solely on competitor activity but it may provide the initial influence.

Key customer influences

If key customers are entering international markets, it may be wise to diversify with them. This is particularly true of service providers, as failure to follow key customers may result in losing them over the mid- to long-term. More positively, moving with key customers is likely to enhance trading relations, and the development of long-term strategic alliances may be a preferred outcome.

Economies of scale

Increased production is likely to lead to an organisation benefiting from economies of scale, both at home and overseas. Although this may be desirable and provide the organisation with a competitive advantage, the benefits of increased production must be carefully considered against the risks involved in overseas marketing, including the potentially high costs of entry, under-capitalisation and over exposure leading to a weakened position.

18.4 Difficulties

Although international markets present a number of opportunities, an organisation may be deterred from adopting an international strategy because of the number of difficulties involved. The usual risks of enterprise ventures are amplified by the international trading arena. Certainly, these additional difficulties need to be considered and addressed before an organisation proceeds with an international sales and marketing strategy. A major factor in overcoming many of these problems is to have the resources to be able to do so, including financial strength, expertise, management systems and operational flexibility. The main difficulties to be considered are:

Credit control and cashflow

This is a very large consideration for many organisations in their home market, but when an international dimension is added, the risks and difficulties increase. Letters of credit and bank guarantees go some way to reducing the problem, but when disputes arise, resolution is both costly and complicated.

Tariff barriers

This is a tax on products crossing an international boundary, used by governments to restrict imports. The *General Agreement on Tariffs and Trade (GATT)* was an international organisation set up to balance these tariffs across the world (now replaced by the World Trade Organisation (WTO)) but, nonetheless, tariffs do exist and present a major consideration for organisations seeking to trade internationally.

Non-tariff barriers

These are other forms of government action aimed at restricting the number of imports. For example, quotas, customs procedures, restrictive regulations and bureaucracy are all considerations. Careful analysis of non-tariff barriers is important as part of the strategic decision-making process.

Exchange rate fluctuations

This area represents a major consideration for organisations operating in international markets. A fluctuation may have either a positive or negative impact, but the difficulty is the uncertainty involved, making planning a precarious exercise, particularly with unstable economies.

Profit repatriation

Apart from the potential problems presented by exchange rate fluctuations, there may be further difficulties in repatriating profits. These may be due to taxation considerations or other monetary regulations.

Cultural variations

Culture covers a wide number of considerations, including language, religious and legislative differences. The full range of cultural differences is considered in the following section as we consider how organisations and individual sales people can achieve *cultural empathy* with their targeted market. At this stage, suffice it to say that achieving cultural empathy can be problematic and costly.

Political climate

Political issues are a major consideration in overseas trade. In some cases, political instability can decimate a market; for example, as in the case of the former Yugoslavia. On the other hand, political changes may present renewed opportunities; for example, the new democracies arising from the former Soviet Union or the recent changes in South Africa. However, it is not just the extremities of political issues with which we are concerned. In the 1980s, many overseas companies were concerned with the mandate put forward by the Labour party in the UK, which in turn led to a positive investment when the Conservative party was re-elected. Although political factors may present opportunities as well as threats to the organisation, the difficulty lies in assessing the situation, particularly in the context of long-term planning.

Tutorial activity B

For an organisation with which you are familiar, consider a country in which its product/service may be marketed. What are the main opportunities presented by this market and what are the specific difficulties which need to be considered?

Alternative: If you work for an organisation which already has an extensive international operation, analyse one market in which it operates, in terms of specific difficulties or risks which it must consider on an ongoing basis.

Present these considerations in note form to your tutor.

Advanced tutorial activity C

In the 1990s, many UK companies have identified new marketing opportunities in South Africa, China and Russia. Select one of these countries and in your tutor or seminar group discuss the range of products and services for which long-term opportunities exist.

Discuss these conclusions collectively with your tutor.

18.5 Cultural empathy

Achieving a state of rapport or empathy with customers is a primary requisite of effective sales and marketing activity. This very principle has been established throughout parts I and II of this book. When considering overseas markets, empathy takes on a new dimension, as cultural variations need to be understood and addressed.

Culture covers a number of areas and its composition is summarised in Figure 18.2.

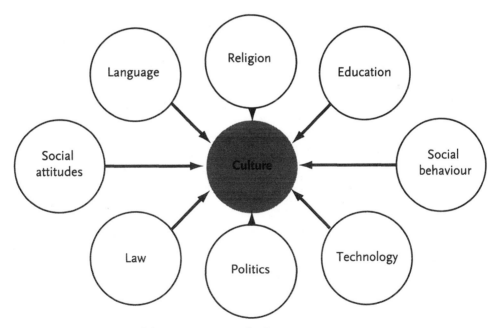

Fig. 18.2 *A summary of the composition of culture*

Language

This may seem to be an obvious consideration in addressing international markets, and yet, in the UK we tend to have an ignorant attitude to language.

Culturally we expect other countries to speak English as a second language, and, although many people do, we cannot assume it to be so. Many countries do use English as their main business language and, when this is the case, little adjustment is required, although a sales person will enhance their personal credibility if they make an attempt to learn a few phrases of the foreign tongue. When English is not the formal business language, every effort must be made to communicate in the main language. In many cases, this will involve employing sales people with appropriate fluency, or in cases where one-off large contracts or distribution deals are being negotiated, the use of an interpreter may suffice.

Religion

In many countries, religion is a major influence. Key considerations are prayer times, rituals, holidays, taboos, sacred values and philosophical systems. Failure to recognise and adapt to these issues is likely to cause offence and almost certainly reduce selling opportunities. On the other hand, a sales person who demonstrates an understanding and respect for a customer's religious values and customs is likely to enhance their personal credibility.

Education

The British educational system is held in high esteem by many second and third world countries. Indeed, wealthier people from these regions often send their children to be educated in the UK. However, when pitching communications activity at overseas markets, one cannot assume a basic level of education in the populous. This is more of a marketing consideration than a selling one but, nonetheless, achieving cultural empathy requires that communication is at the right intellectual level for the targeted audience.

Social attitudes

This is a wide area in itself and extends beyond purely religious influences. For example, what is the attitude towards women in society?, what is the attitude towards medicine and technology?, what is the attitude towards time, work and leisure? and so on. Sales people and marketers alike must be aware of the social attitudes of their targeted markets and adapt accordingly.

Social behaviour

Social attitudes revolve around the values and beliefs within society. Extending from this, social behaviour is the manifestation of these attitudes in terms of customs, rituals, living and working styles. Sales people in particular must appreciate the social behaviour within their targeted market and behave accordingly when visiting and transacting business overseas.

Law

We are concerned with several aspects here. First, an appreciation of international and local business law is essential. Failure in this area can be very costly. Second, one must appreciate regulatory and voluntary codes for business, such as advertising standards, technical quality standards, and so on. Additionally, sales people travelling overseas are advised to become familiar with the common law.

At the minor end of these considerations one may have to, say, pay unwanted speeding fines; but at the other end of the spectrum, failure to abide by local laws may result in imprisonment or deportation, a very serious consequence indeed.

Politics

Strategically, this has already been considered in Section 18.4 of this chapter. However, there is also a range of operational considerations for the sales person. Some cultures are very passionate about their politics. For example, black South Africans and Russians are understandably very passionate about their new democratic rights. Other countries are run by strict political regimes and people either conform or become political dissidents or exiles. For example, a trade party of major UK business leaders recently visited China and were welcomed on the basis of exploiting the large market potential but warned not interfere with the country's political issues, such as their human rights policy. These major examples serve to emphasise the type of political considerations which the sales person or marketer may encounter. The principle can be extended to a range of more minor political considerations in a wide number of countries and, indeed, local variations within each country. Additionally, one should consider the power and influence of politicians. In many countries, successful trading activity may be facilitated and simplified by building relationships or gaining endorsements from key politicians.

Technology

The technological state and capability is a key consideration when trading with many less-developed countries. What is the country's transportation infrastructure, communications capability, energy distribution, and so on? Such issues can play a major role in marketing campaigns and sales negotiations. Advances in worldwide technology have facilitated enormous growth in international marketing capability, but scope remains restricted in some countries. From a planning perspective, it may be appropriate to consider not only the current capability but also the future technological capability. Additionally, sales people and marketers operating in the technology industries may identify technological retardation as an opportunity to introduce their products to markets with enormous growth potential.

Advanced tutorial activity D

Select a non-European country, either of your choice or one selected by your tutor. Conduct a cultural analysis. That is, for each of the sub-headings in this section, what issues need to be considered and addressed by the sales person and/or marketer?

Formally present these conclusions to your tutor or seminar group.

Extension: At the direction of your tutor, prepare a set of summary notes to support your presentation and conclude your piece with an evaluation based on feedback given during your presentation.

The summary Figure 18.2 and subsequent discussion in this section present something of an alternative view of culture. Culture can be considered to be the whole aura of a country and, therefore, it is this whole range of influences which needs to be considered by the sales person/marketer. Students need to be aware of the more traditional approach to culture where it is considered purely in its social sense (e.g. religion, taboos). In the case of this more traditional perspective, the mnemonic **SLEPT** is often applied to the aspects of culture:

Social (and cultural)
Legal
Economic
Political
Technological (and natural).

Either model can be used when considering international sales and marketing. The important issue is to set and achieve an objective of reaching a state of rapport with the target audience, namely the customer groups within the population of targeted countries.

18.6 The role of the sales person and sales management

Earlier in this chapter the point was made that entry into international markets was likely to require a high degree of marketing involvement or, in considering export sales activity, a micro-marketing approach on behalf of the sales person. Considering the overall role of the sales person in international marketing activity, there are two levels with which we are concerned: the *basic level* where personal selling is utilised within the marketing mix, in the form of a sales force effort in the relevant country, and an *advanced level* where personal selling is used to set up and manage strategic relationships or negotiate major contracts.

Basic level

This will involve a discrete sales force structure based in the relevant country or region. Employees are likely to be drawn from the local workforce. In the case of the first two stages detailed in Section 18.2 of this chapter, they are likely to be employed by the distributor(s), and in the other three variants of international marketing, they are likely to be employed directly by the host organisation. Indeed, many sales people in the UK are employed by foreign organisations in this way. Therefore, the sales force structure and management is much the same as discussed in Part III of this book. Perhaps the only difference is that senior management may be working on secondment from the host organisation and, regardless of this, strategic direction will almost certainly be driven by the senior management of the mother company.

Advanced level

The alternative to employing a discrete sales force in each country is to set up a distribution network for marketing the organisation's product(s)/service(s).

Additionally, or instead of this, an organisation may choose to win contracts with major customers from a head office base. In both scenarios, senior sales people will be required to set up and negotiate the contracts. Such arrangements will be considered as strategic relationships or major account customers and will be managed in much the same way as discussed previously. The skills and awareness required of the sales person, or rather the sales manager, are likely to be at a very high level, as winning and managing business on an international basis is, arguably, the most challenging role that exists in the selling environment.

18.7 Summary

In this chapter we have seen how the role of marketing plays an intrinsic part in the international dimension of an organisation, certainly from a strategic perspective, but also operationally. Where an overall marketing operation does not exist, the sales person must take on a micro-marketing role, similar to the principle established in the first chapter of this book. Five variants of international marketing have been considered, the first of which is likely to relate to a sales orientation and the other four to a marketing orientation.

International markets present a number of opportunities, the most obvious of which is increased potential. Other influences or reasons for marketing overseas include diversifying the market base, competitor internationalisation, key customer influences, and economies of scale. In addition to the opportunities which arise, there are a number of difficulties which must be considered in order to arrive at a balanced decision regarding the viability of international marketing or, indeed, the extent to which an organisation should engage.

Operationally, much of an organisation's success in international markets will revolve around cultural empathy. The main components of culture and, therefore, the adaptations which sales people and marketers need to make have been considered. Finally, the roles of the sales person and sales management have been considered at two levels: a discrete sales force structure within each relevant country or region and a remote selling effort at an advanced level.

Essay question

In Section 18.6 of this chapter the author states, 'The skills and awareness required of the sales person, or rather the sales manager, are likely to be at a very high level, as winning and managing business on an international basis is, arguably, the most challenging role that exists in the selling environment.'

In the form of an essay, consider this argument in its entirety, including the use of the term 'sales manager' rather than 'sales person'. Conclude your piece with a justified confirmation or refutation of the author's comments.

Reference

1 Adcock, D., Bradfield, R., Halborg, A. and Ross, C. (1995), *Marketing: Principles and Practice* (2nd edn), Pitman Publishing, p. 376.

Further reading

Dillon, J. (1994), *Handbook of International Direct Marketing*, McGraw-Hill.

Paliwoda, S. (1994), *The Essence of International Marketing*, Prentice-Hall.

Phillips, C., Doole, I. and Lowe, R. (1994), *International Marketing Strategy (analysis, development and implementation)*, Routledge.

Chapter 19 # Direct marketing

Learning objectives

By the end of this chapter, you should :

- Understand what is meant by the term *direct marketing*

- Appreciate direct marketing as a growth area and the reasons for this

- Be aware of the main tools used in direct marketing

- Appreciate the duality between personal selling and direct marketing.

19.1 Introduction

A book which considers the many aspects of personal selling would not be complete without consideration of direct marketing. Indeed, there have been several references to it throughout the text, but its growth and impact on the role of the sales person require specific consideration.

In its purest form, direct marketing involves the promotion and distribution of products directly to the customer without use of channel intermediaries. It is in this context that we shall consider direct marketing.

However, before we do so, it is worth considering some of the misconceptions about direct marketing, such as *it is direct mail, it is mail order, it is direct response advertising*. These misconceptions are not surprising. If one were to read one of the many articles on direct marketing, these three aspects would be the most common considerations. On the other hand, if one were to consider *direct selling* journals and articles, the impression given is that direct marketing is a tool of direct selling. The reverse is in fact true, direct selling is a tool of direct marketing. Other tools include direct mail, mail order, direct response advertising, corporate advertising and physical distribution. These are all considered later in this chapter.

Above all, direct marketing is a strategy adopted by organisations based on the benefits which can be derived. In some cases, it is the sole distribution strategy adopted, and in other cases, it is used in addition to the use of intermediaries in a channel structure.

19.2 The growth of direct marketing

A growing number of organisations choose to adopt a direct marketing strategy.

Tutorial activity A

Before continuing with this text, consider why there has been a growth in direct marketing, including the potential advantages and disadvantages in general terms.

Compare your conclusions with the comments made by the author in the following narrative.

Reasons for growth

Arguably, the main reason for the growth in direct marketing is the advancement of *information technology*. Certainly, these advances have facilitated the growth of direct marketing, for example:

- Storing and analysing customer information has never been easier or more efficient. This is leading to more customer information than ever before and, also, it is more accurate than it has ever been. This has led to increased sophistication in segmenting and targeting customer groups.

- Enhanced communications capability has encouraged direct contact with customers. Media can be more accurately selected to reach a targeted audience. The 'information super-highway' discussed in Chapter 17 provides us with a good example of this. Additionally, customer feedback can be encouraged to flow more freely than ever before.

Technological advancement is not the only reason behind the growth of information technology. One can consider other reasons to be:

1 **Increased competition:** Organisations need to find ways of achieving a competitive advantage in order to remain profitable and successful. Direct marketing provides an ideal competitive advantage in many situations.

2 **Increased customer awareness:** As consumers and commercial end users become more aware, direct communications become more appropriate. They seek information about products and services which can often be provided more effectively by an organisation directly, rather than relying on an intermediary who offers a range of competitive products.

3 **Increased direct marketing skills:** Practitioners across the marketing arena have become more skilled in the application of direct marketing techniques. This is not the primary reason for the growth, but rather a positive development of it. However, increased skills acquired through education and training help to accelerate the growth and, indeed, the success of organisations adopting direct marketing strategies.

General advantages

Direct marketing enables an organisation to have control over its promotion and distribution operations, enabling activities to be co-ordinated in pursuit of maximum impact and optimum efficiency. Misuse of resources and effort is likely to be minimised. For example, the scenario where a promotional campaign is limited in its effectiveness because it is not fully supported by the channel intermediaries is replaced by increased effectiveness through internal communication and motivation of employees. Additionally, one can consider that it is easier to gain customer feedback, which in many cases will be more accurate, not only enabling more effective direct marketing in terms of promotion and distribution, but also improving the quality of other marketing mix decisions, such as product development and pricing.

General disadvantages

With all that has been said about direct marketing, one must be careful not to fall into the trap of thinking that direct marketing is always the right option. There are several valid reasons for an organisation electing to distribute its products via channel intermediaries. The cost of promoting and distributing directly may be too expensive. For example, although the trade discounts offered to intermediaries may be saved, the cost of employing a direct sales force or running an owned chain of retail outlets may exceed the cost of providing trade discounts. Additionally, one must consider whether sales revenue will increase as a result of marketing directly. In many cases, particularly when there is a broad customer base, direct marketing will only achieve limited market coverage and opportunities will be missed. In some industries, one should also consider the level of specialism, expertise and service offered by channel intermediaries and, necessarily, the cost to both the organisation and the customer in replacing or reducing them.

19.3 Tools of direct marketing

The introduction to this chapter considered the range of tools potentially available to the direct marketer. With the exception of personal selling, which will be discussed in the following section, the main tools of direct marketing are now considered.

Direct mail

This is one of the most prevalent tools of direct marketing. In domestic and commercial situations, we are all familiar with the volume of direct mail which is received and often termed 'junk mail'. Although some people do regard it as 'junk' and throw it away, many people do actually read it. The exercise of designing and writing a successful direct mail campaign is a highly skilful art and there are many aspects to consider. The basic promotional principle of **AIDA** remains valid, as does the need to develop empathy with the reader. The options and methods for achieving this are numerous; for example, should one or two pages of copy be used?, what involvement devices can be employed?, should the initial mailing be followed up by telephone or with a second mailing?, what incentives should be offered?, and so on. Indeed, such considerations go beyond the scope of this text and any students seeking a wider understanding or appreciation should consult a specialist text.

Tutorial activity **B**

Gather a collection of direct mailing literature from both domestic and commercial sources. Evaluate this material in terms of how **AIDA** and empathy with the targeted reader are achieved.

Select the item of direct mail which you feel provides the best example and justify this in a brief presentation to your tutor and/or seminar group.

The typical response rate of a good direct mail campaign is between two and five per cent. On the surface this may not seem very high but one should consider the minimal costs of direct mail in relation to the profit return on each sale. For example, a mailing to 1000 potential customers may incur a total cost of £500. If the profit return on each sale is, say, £50, a 1 per cent response will ensure the campaign breaks even. Anything beyond this can be regarded as profit, so a 5 per cent return will produce a profit of £2000, four times the cost of sale. An organisation may well consider this activity to be a desirable method of transacting business; alternatively, direct mail may be used as a component of a wider direct marketing effort used, say, to generate leads for the direct sales force.

Mail order

In many cases, mail order is intrinsically linked with direct response mailings and direct response advertising. However, it may also be a tool in its own right. Catalogue-based home shopping is a big business area in consumer marketing and the industrial marketing of consumable products. Home shopping has been extended in recent years to include wider media sources, such as television (home shopping channel and teletext service), promotional videos and, increasingly, the 'information super-highway'.

Direct response advertising

Again, this is intrinsically linked with some aspects of mail order but it also has its own place as a specific tool of direct marketing. Direct response advertising has many uses beyond those where it encourages a buying decision. For example, it may generate enquiries for more information which can be provided by direct mail or a sales person.

Tutorial activity C

Identify an example of direct response advertising from a public media source. What is the objective of the advertisement, i.e. what response is requested: an order, a request for more information? How does the advertisement achieve this objective in terms of AIDA and empathy with the reader?

Justify your conclusions in a brief presentation to your tutor and/or seminar group.

Extension: What is the targeted audience? Evaluate how the media source reaches the targeted audience, particularly with regard to how empathy is achieved, and include this in your presentation.

Corporate advertising and PR

These are wider marketing considerations. They will not be used as the main direct marketing tool but will often provide key support for the overall direct marketing effort. For example, enhanced name awareness and an appropriate image will often improve the effectiveness of mailings and sales force activity.

Physical distribution

Direct marketing often places an increased emphasis on the need for efficient physical distribution. Rather than bulk deliveries to intermediary warehouses or outlets, the product will now need to go directly to the customer. This may be achieved through an owned chain of retail outlets, an organisation's own transportation capabilities, or even the direct sales force, but more frequently a courier service will be used. When a courier service is used it becomes a key supplier to the organisation and must be selected and managed accordingly. For example, if the couriers make a mistake or provide a poor level of service, the customer will perceive it to be the fault of the host company rather than that of the couriers.

19.4 The dual role of selling

If we consider the physical distribution of the product discussed in the preceding section, selling may be regarded as taking on a triple role in direct marketing. This aside, personal selling takes on a very important dual role: first promoting the product and distributing it through closing sales and, second providing a medium for direct customer feedback. Arguably, the latter role may not be totally objective but, nonetheless, it provides an important and inexpensive tool for obtaining qualitative feedback, in addition to the quantitative data which can be obtained from the sales force statistics.

The term 'sales force' used here relates to the range of functions which may be used for personal selling activity on a direct basis, namely:

Field sales

This area of selling is used where personal, face-to-face selling is deemed appropriate, either working from incoming enquiries, leads generated by telemarketing activity or self-generated appointments. Operating a direct field sales force can be incredibly expensive, even when sales people are paid on a commission-only basis. A decision as to whether field sales is an appropriate tool should be considered carefully and, in the event that it is selected, it should be operated with optimum efficiency.

Telemarketing/sales support

Personal contact of this type can have several uses. It may be used to generate leads for field sales people or in support of response mailings and advertisements. Technically, one could argue that it is not true selling activity, as the sale is concluded through another medium. However, it can fulfil an important role in several aspects of the selling process, including customer follow-up and feedback.

Telesales

There are two types of direct telephone selling: outgoing and incoming. The former occurs where the telephone is used as a prospecting tool but also as the primary method for concluding the sale. For example, an outgoing telephone selling process may involve a letter of introduction, followed by a telephone approach to build rapport and establish needs, before a brochure is sent to the prospect and the sale concluded during a second call where benefits are highlighted and commitment is gained. This process is shown in Figure 19.1. Outgoing telephone selling is not only very difficult but also unlikely to be the most efficient use of resources if used in isolation. As a secondary activity to support a telemarketing role or to utilise workforce capacity for primarily incoming telephone selling, it is likely to be more appropriate.

| Letter of introduction | First call to build rapport and identify needs | Mail brochure | Second call to highlight benefits and close the sale |

Fig. 19.1 *A possible outgoing telephone selling process*

Incoming telephone selling activity is becoming increasingly common and in many cases will be a far more efficient tool of direct marketing. Here, enquiries are generated by other methods such as direct response mailings and advertising. The telesales function is then concerned with identifying needs, highlighting benefits and closing the sale. Among a wide number of organisations currently adopting this approach as a primary tool of their direct marketing strategy are a range of financial services companies, including household names such as 'Guardian Direct', 'First Direct', 'Direct Line'. Indeed, they have found it to be a very efficient and profitable method of operation.

Tutorial activity D

Develop a possible incoming telephone selling process, ideally for an organisation with which you are familiar. Represent this in diagrammatic and note form and discuss it with your tutor.

Retail selling

This occurs when an organisation has adopted a different approach to the direct marketing strategy by owning its own chain of retail outlets. In theory, the role of the retail sales person in this situation is much the same as for any other retail environment. However, the fact that the manufacturer and outlet are the same company takes us into a new realm of service provision, even beyond that which may be expected and perceived in exclusive distribution strategies. The retail sales people should be well trained and highly motivated to reflect the image which the organisation strives to achieve. A good example of this in practice is the car manufacturer 'Daewoo', which has gained a competitive advantage and won a market share by being innovative in its direct marketing strategy. One aspect of this is the high quality service and low pressure selling which it offers through its own retail outlets.

19.5 Summary

In this chapter, we have identified precisely what is meant by the term *direct marketing*. We have also clarified some common misconceptions of the terminology and identified that all of these are, in fact, tools of direct marketing. These tools have been considered in a reasonable amount of depth and a detailed account has been given of the dual role of personal selling as a tool for a variety of direct marketing strategies.

Over recent years, direct marketing has grown rapidly, and with continued advancements in technology and communication, increased competition and ever increasing levels of customer awareness, the growth looks set to continue. One could argue that the growth in direct marketing is fulfilling Levitt's prophecy, which was discussed in the first chapter of this book, in which case it would be a threat to the selling profession.

However, we have seen in this chapter how personal selling, albeit in a range of guises, has a valuable role to play in many direct marketing strategies. Rather than this presenting a threat to the selling profession, it provides an opportunity. It requires adaptation by sales people and an increased awareness of their role in the wider marketing strategy. The function of personal selling will vary in importance from one organisation to another. Undoubtedly, the selling function in many organisations will become more efficient and, as a result, there will be a justifiable demand for increased performance.

Sales people rising to these challenges, particularly in direct marketing but also in wider marketing strategies, will indeed ensure themselves of a professional career path which has a long-term future.

Essay question

In Section 19.4 of this chapter, the author stated, 'Operating a direct field sales force can be incredibly expensive . . . it should be operated with optimum efficiency.'

In the form of an essay, consider why operating a field sales force is so expensive and discuss general ways in which efficiency may be improved. It may be appropriate to write this piece in the context of a specific organisation which uses a direct field sales force or, alternatively, the piece can be written in general terms. Conclude your piece with an evaluation of why, given the difficulties, an organisation may well decide to continue with a direct field sales force effort.

Further reading

Bird, D. (1993), *Commonsense Direct Marketing* (3rd edn), Kogan Page.

Bird, D. (1994), *How to Write Sales Letters that Sell*, Kogan Page.

Fairlie, R. (1993), *Database Marketing and Direct Mail*, Kogan Page.

McCorkell, G. (1990), *Advertising that Pulls Response*, McGraw-Hill.

Ozimek, J. (1993), *Targeting for Success*, McGraw-Hill.

Vogele, S. (1992), *Handbook of Direct Mail*, Prentice-Hall.

Case study A: St. Austell Brewery Company Ltd.

St. Austell is a relatively small brewery company, operating in a localised regional market amidst competition from larger national competitors. Increasingly, the sales and distribution efforts of these larger competitors are becoming more sophisticated, and the trend for the industry as a whole is one of increased competition, tighter margins and shrinking profits.

Ian Blunt was appointed Sales Director of St. Austell in 1993 with the general brief of ensuring the continued well-being of the company by maintaining/increasing the volume of profitable sales. Three years on, the company is defying the national trend and continues to experience rapid, sustained growth. When asked about the organisation's success, Ian commented as follows:

> 'Our market place demands a very close working relationship with our customers. We need to know who our best customers are and which ones have the potential to become our best customers. To do this, our sales people need truly to understand the needs of our customers in order to apply the appropriate levels of selling and service effort . . . Much of our training focuses on developing excellent people skills and empowering sales people to build "relationship teams", consisting of the distribution function, internal staff (particularly marketing support) and, most importantly, the customer . . . Information technology has had a very positive impact on our business, enabling the sales person to be more professional and efficient.'

Task 1

Ian Blunt maintains that putting the customer first has been the key to his organisation's success. Consider how empowering the sales force with a micro-marketing responsibility enables St. Austell Brewery to succeed in a highly competitive market.

Task 2

Although information technology has had a positive impact on St. Austell Brewery, Ian Blunt is keen to point out that sales people must not be burdened with too much information, as this can have the reverse effect of creating inefficiency. Consider how information technology can cause inefficiency rather than the desired effect of improving efficiency.

Case study B: Professional Solutions for Sales and Marketing (PSSM) Ltd.

Background and current strategy/operations

Professional Solutions for Sales and Marketing (PSSM) Ltd. is a rapidly growing management and training consultancy, specialising in the areas of sales and marketing. It has a range of products to meet the needs of carefully targeted groups, including both corporate and private customers.

PSSM's core business is the design of management systems to support redirected corporate strategies and assisting the implementation of these systems through the design and delivery of bespoke in-house training courses. Historically, the company's efforts have been targeted at organisations with medium-sized sales forces (25 to 75 in numerical terms), as this was consistent with their resource capability and it was beneficial for these organisations to pay a reasonable premium for bespoke courses.

From these bespoke courses, a number of general courses have been developed for which there are two target markets: organisations with relatively small sales forces (less than 25 in numerical terms) and private individuals pursuing personal career development. It is not viable for either group to pay the premium for bespoke courses, but they benefit from acquiring transferable skills and knowledge, which can be adapted and applied in their own environments. These general courses are divided into four main product groups: Senior Management, Selling and Field Sales Management, Marketing Communications and Customer Care.

In itself, PSSM has been a marketing success story, successfully:

- segmenting and targeting customer groups
- developing products and services which are consistent with the needs of these customers
- accessing these groups with effective communication activity
- increasing revenue and profitability through the provision of a high quality service to customers.

The operational detail of these four strategic areas is now considered.

Segmenting and targeting customer groups

A customers = organisations with medium-sized sales forces
B customers = organisations with relatively small sales forces
C customers = private individuals pursuing sales, marketing and management careers.

Developing products and services which are consistent with the needs of these customers

A customers: Management consultancy, mainly related to the development of systems which support redirected corporate strategies, and the design and delivery of bespoke training courses to facilitate implementation of these systems. Generally, training courses are run on an in-house basis but provision is made for customers wishing their staff to be trained in a residential environment.

B customers: General courses provided either in-house or away from the business environment on a residential or single day seminar basis. An exclusively delivered course requires a minimum of eight staff attending or, alternatively, delegates may attend a publicly delivered programme. The courses are grouped into four categories: Senior Management, Selling and Sales Management, Marketing Communications and Customer Care.

C customers: General courses delivered through public programmes. The four course groupings and individual content is the same as for *B customers*.

Accessing customer groups with effective communication activity

A customers: A direct mail and telemarketing effort is used to generate leads for Business Consultants. The initial meeting is a free consultation designed to secure a retained consultancy and training contract. The Business Consultant is involved on a personal level with the customer before, during and after the service delivery. In this way, additional needs can be identified, developed and satisfied.

B customers: New customers are reached through direct response advertising and direct mail. A telesales team responds to these incoming enquiries and negotiates training contracts based on the business volume involved. It is unusual for a Business Consultant to visit these organisations, although a personal visit is occasionally deemed necessary for some larger contracts. Existing customer accounts are managed by the same telesales team, but this reverts to a direct mail approach if accounts are inactive for over one year.

C customers: New customers are targeted solely by direct response advertising and incoming enquiries are handled by the telesales team. Repeat purchasing within this group is relatively low and a system of quarterly direct mail activity in the first year and annually thereafter is used.

Increasing revenue and profitability through the provision of a high level of service to customers

A customers: Training notes and course delivery are personalised for each individual organisation. The effectiveness of the training is monitored by the Business Consultant in liaison with the senior management of each customer. Individual customer feedback is qualitatively considered. Additionally, PSSM produces a quarterly newsletter which is specifically sent to all existing customers in this targeted group.

B customers: Generic training notes are provided together with individual certificates for each delegate attending a course. Refreshments are complimentary and each course concludes with a feedback questionnaire; collectively these are quantitatively considered. Additionally, telesales staff liaise with the senior management of each customer to monitor the effectiveness of the training.

C customers: Again, generic training notes, individual certificates, complimentary refreshments and a feedback questionnaire are provided to all delegates attending the course. No further services are offered to this customer group other than the direct mail activity mentioned previously.

The scenario

The senior management of PSSM recognise the need to adapt to the changing requirements of the market and to review their own strategies in this context, consistent with their resource capabilities.

A period of outstanding growth has seen an enhanced resource capability. PSSM now feels it is able to attack the major corporate market; that is organisations which have a sales force in excess of 75 in numerical size. Once established as a customer group, this will become the new A category, with existing categories moving down the scale accordingly.

Two major professional institutes have recognised PSSM courses as being valid for Continuous Professional Training (CPT) hours. This enhances the value for individual delegates rather than the employing organisation.

Additionally, PSSM is in the process of becoming an accredited NVQ (National Vocational Qualification) training provider and many of its existing courses are consistent with the syllabus contents of current NVQ programmes. Potentially this provides additional value for individual delegates, although the real benefit is likely to be aimed at corporate customers.

Task 1

Critically evaluate the way in which PSSM currently segments and targets customers. Specifically consider the principle put forward in Chapter 16 of how selling and servicing resources are applied.

Task 2

Based on the changes which have been put forward in this scenario, devise, in outline, a new segmentation system for PSSM. In relation to this system, comment on how differentiated selling and servicing efforts can be targeted at each customer group, providing examples of the resources and tools which can be applied.

Task 3 (advanced)

Based on the changes which have been put forward in this scenario, consider new markets which may exist for PSSM and outline future strategic direction in relation to this.

Task 4 (advanced)

Based on the real outcome of Task 2 (see the case study solution in the Tutor's Guide), consider the organisation structure of PSSM, regardless of the size of the company. For example, should telesales and telemarketing be the same 'team'? Who should control the advertising? Who should control the Business Consultants and Trainers?

For each role you have identified within the structure for selling and servicing provision, build a profile of the ideal person for the job, based on your own perception of the organisation.

Part V

Supplementary learning material and resources

Study techniques

The first thing to establish when studying a marketing subject, such as selling or sales management, is that we are not dealing with an exact science. Historically, our education system in the UK has been focused on testing knowledge, typically through traditional GCSEs and A-Levels, assessed primarily by formal examination. It is not surprising that many students address these higher level, professional studies, with a similar attitude.

This is not the correct approach. Selling is more of an art and rarely offers an opportunity for indisputable facts to be applied. Rather, there are established and emerging principles which result in common practices. These norms are subject to variation, perhaps to accommodate industry, customer or product considerations, but moreover as individuals develop their skills in a quest continuously to improve performance. This factor extends to the management of the selling function and additional principles and practices enter the equation.

From a learning perspective, how should students approach the subjects handled in this text? To answer this question, students need to be grouped into two categories: those who are studying the subject as part of a wider course of academic/professional study and/or those who are developing a career in selling or sales management. Each group has different objectives: the former is concerned with achieving and demonstrating academic/professional awareness, whereas the latter needs to acquire and develop practical skills.

The structure of this book enables the objectives of both groups to be achieved. The accompanying Tutor's Guide provides tutors/trainers with a detailed analysis of how specific learning objectives are developed in relation to the needs of students and the level of study. However, tutors/trainers can only facilitate learning and it is students who must take ultimate responsibility. This starts with a desire to learn in the first instance backed up by a commitment to work hard in pursuit of one's goals. Assuming these two prerequisites exist, there are some specific considerations for each group of students which are outlined as follows.

Achieving and demonstrating academic/professional awareness

The narrative

Understanding the theme of the text is imperative. What does it mean? What is being implied? Where does it fit in with other topics? If one is unsure or has any queries during this process, it is vital that clarification is sought, either from one's tutor/trainer or, alternatively, by reading around the subject from the bibliographies provided.

Tip: Don't just acquire knowledge; understand its meaning and its place in relation to the wider subject area.

Tutorial activities

These support the learning and understanding which has been achieved through the narrative, either through reading and/or lectures. The activities presented in the text (together with any adaptations made by individual tutors), facilitate an enhancement of the learning experience. First, students are able to develop a more comprehensive appreciation of the topic and, second, both students and tutors are able to make an informal assessment of the learning which has taken place.

Tip: Once one has knowledge and understands it, this should be confirmed, developed and reinforced.

Essay questions

These enable the level of understanding to be formally assessed and correction/critique to be provided by tutorial feedback. However, essays are much more than tools for formal assessment. They provide a medium for students to express their ideas and make individual interpretations of what has been learnt. One should use relevant examples, cross reference the piece with other reading sources, and demonstrate a rational thought process in developing and expressing one's ideas.

Tip: A good approach to an essay is to:

- say what you are going to say (introduction)
- say it (core/argument)
- say what you have said (conclusion).

Case studies

These enable students to demonstrate their understanding and appreciation for the subject by encouraging them to apply what has been learnt in a practical scenario. This is where traditional education is left behind, as case studies do not have right or wrong answers. Admittedly, the Tutor's Guide contains the solutions which were actually applied in practice, but students are not required to match these solutions. It is far more important to demonstrate an appreciation for the problem(s) by providing a justified solution which would be valid in the scenario presented. Students may present a solution which is less, equally or more valid than the solution which was actually applied.

Tip: Develop and follow your instinct but justify your actions at every stage.

Acquiring and developing practical skills

The narrative

Before practical skills can be truly acquired and developed, one must first know which skills to develop and in what context they are to be used. Given that practice makes permanent rather than perfect, one must practise the right skills at the right time. The narrative provides the framework and direction on how and when skills should be applied.

Tutorial activities

Although these are more appropriate for academic and professional study, some will have value for practitioners as general transferable skills are developed (e.g. information technology, running discussions, making presentations).

Practical activities

These are specifically geared towards the development of practical and professional skills. Many refer to the role plays in this part of the book, whereas others may be achieved without these resources. For professional qualifications where skills are assessed, many of these exercises provide a framework for assessment. However, they have equal value if only an informal assessment is being made, be it tutor, peer group or self-evaluation.

Tip: Identify and maximise your strengths but also identify and minimise your weaknesses.

Tips for success/selling myths

These provide guidance for the developing practitioner. Some may appear to be a matter of common sense but one cannot assume this to be so. Others provide handy hints for practical application.

Practitioners' tales

A lively collection of anecdotes is given. Some provide alternative perspectives or analogies to support the narrative, whereas others will serve to inspire good practice. Selling is hard work, but for those who are successful, it also provides an enormous amount of fun. A good sales meeting, conference or training session requires its anecdotal tales, and the author extends this principle to the written form, providing added spice for professional and practical consumption.

Ethical notes

Sales people are generally governed by a code of ethics within their industry or organisation. Any such codes will also take account of relevant legislation and encourage good practice. This aside, there is ethical conduct which is appropriate for all sales people who seek to be truly professional. Disregard for these ethics serves to diminish the professional reputation of selling. The ethical notes made by the author in this book, above all, aim to encourage good practice.

Tip: Act professionally and aim for long-term success.

Role plays and simulated exercises

Contents of role plays and simulated exercises

1 Sales person: Telephone appointment making
- New customer – domestic (script for sales person and possible customer objections)
- New customer – commercial (script for sales person and possible customer objections)
- New customer – trade (script for sales person and possible customer objections).

2 Sales person: Need development
- Domestic sales situation – role scenario and briefings for sales person and customer
- Commercial sales situation – role scenario and briefings for sales person and customer
- Trade sales situation – role scenario and briefings for sales person and customer.

3 Sales person: Making the sale
- Domestic sales situation – follow-on briefings for sales person and customer
- Commercial sales situation – follow-on briefings for sales person and customer
- Trade sales situation – follow-on briefings for sales person and customer.

4 Sales person: Employment interview
- Trainee scenario – briefing for job applicant
- Changing industry scenario – briefing for job applicant
- Moving from selling to sales management scenario – briefing for job applicant.

5 Sales person: Group selling seminar
- Briefing for domestic selling scenario
- Briefing for commercial selling scenario (Role 1 and Role 2).

6 Sales manager: Recruitment interview

- Trainee scenario – briefing for sales manager
- Changing industry scenario – briefing for sales manager
- Moving from selling to sales management scenario – briefing for recruiting manager.

7 Sales manager: Weekly performance interview sequence

- The scenario
- Week 1 performance reporting form
- Week 2 performance reporting form
- Week 3 performance reporting form
- Week 4 performance reporting form.

8 Sales manager: Sales meeting

- The organisation
- The roles (managers and delegates).

1 Sales person: Telephone appointment making

New customer – domestic

Script for sales person

Good morning, Mr(s) Prospect. Mr(s) Prospect, my name is ...., calling from the XYZ financial planning group. Do you have a moment to speak?

I believe John Smith is a friend of yours and he recommended that I speak with you. I understand you are self-employed, is that correct?

I see. Mr(s) Prospect, I have a number of self-employed clients and I find that I am often able to provide them with considerable savings on their tax bill. I would very much like to meet with you to see if I can provide a similar service for you.

Are daytimes or evenings best for you?

Evenings. Well, next week I can make either a Tuesday or Thursday evening, which would you prefer?

Tuesday. Shall we say seven o'clock?

Mr(s) Prospect, I've written that in my diary – next Tuesday at 7.00 p.m. May I just confirm your address?

Thank you. I look forward to seeing you next Tuesday at seven then.

Possible objections and suggested ways of overcoming them

Objection 1: 'It's a bad time, I'm in the middle of my tea.'
Response: *I'm sorry to interrupt your meal, when would be a good time for me to call back?*

Objection 2: 'My accountant looks after all my tax affairs.'
Response: *I understand Mr(s) Prospect. Virtually all of my self-employed clients have retained the services of their accountants but find that I am still able to help them enormously. Would you prefer to come to my office or shall I come to your house?*

Objection 3: 'You just want to sell me a pension or some life assurance, don't you?'
Response: *Mr(s) Prospect, many of my best clients thought exactly the same when I first spoke to them but it really isn't the case. I offer a complete financial planning service and am merely suggesting a preliminary meeting. Is it best for us to meet during the day or in the evening?*

Objection 4: 'I can't afford to buy anything.'
Response: *And I'm not asking you to buy anything Mr(s) Prospect. Many of my clients find that I am actually able to save them money and I am merely suggesting a preliminary meeting to see if I can do the same for you. Would you prefer to come to my office or shall I come to your house?*

New customer – Commercial

Script for sales person

> Good morning, Mr(s) Prospect. Mr(s) Prospect, my name is............., calling from XYZ computers. Do you have a moment to speak?
>
> I believe John Smith of Eatalot Foods is a client of yours and he recommended that I speak with you. John said that you were considering upgrading some of your computer equipment in the near future, is that correct?
>
> I see. Mr(s) Prospect, our company has an excellent range of the most up-to-date equipment on the market, at very competitive prices. I would very much like to meet with you to establish exactly what you are looking for. What are best for you, mornings or afternoons?
>
> Mornings. Well, next week I can make either Tuesday or Thursday morning, which would you prefer?
>
> Tuesday. Shall we say ten o'clock?
>
> Mr(s) Prospect, I've written that in my diary – next Tuesday at 10.00 a.m. Where is the best place for me to park?
>
> Thank you. I look forward to seeing you next Tuesday at ten then.

Possible objections and suggested ways of overcoming them

Objection 1: 'No I don't have a moment to speak.'
Response: *When is the best time for me to call back?*

Objection 2: 'I don't need to meet with you, I've always bought my computer equipment from ABC company and I'm very happy with them.'
Response: *Mr(s) Prospect, ABC is a very good company and I'm sure you are happy with them, but as an astute business person, I'm sure you can also see the benefit of looking at some alternative options before you make your final decision. Now, what's best for you, mornings or afternoons?*

Objection 3: 'The best quote I've had so far is £4985 for a network of five PCs and a laser printer. Don't bother coming to see me unless you can beat that price.'

Response: *Mr(s) Prospect, many things are possible but I wouldn't dream of quoting a price until I had discussed your exact requirements in more detail with you. So, what's best for you, mornings or afternoons?*

Objection 4: 'Send me some literature and your price list and I'll give you a call if I'm interested.'

Response: *Mr(s) Prospect, I appreciate what you are asking but until I truly understand your requirements, I do not know what literature to send you. After we have met, I will be in a position to provide you with a full written proposal and the appropriate literature. Will it be best for us to meet in the mornings or afternoons?*

New customer – trade

Script for sales person

Good morning, Mr(s) Prospect. My name is ...., from FMCG Foods. Do you have a moment to speak?

We have a range of food products, some of which I believe would be an ideal line for you to carry. I would like to suggest a brief meeting to show some of these to you and see what you think. If we are looking at next week, would mornings or afternoons be better for you?

Mornings. Well, next week I can make Tuesday or Thursday, which would you prefer?

Tuesday. Shall we say ten o'clock?

Mr(s) Prospect, I've written that in my diary – next Tuesday at 10.00 a.m. Where is the best place for me to park?

Thank you. I look forward to seeing you next Tuesday at ten then.

Possible objections and suggested ways of overcoming them

Objection 1: 'No, it's a bad time. Give me your number and I'll call you back.'
Response: *Ordinarily that would be fine, Mr(s) Prospect, but I'm leaving the office shortly. When is the best time for me to call you this afternoon?*

Objection 2: 'Send me some literature and your price lists and I'll get back to you.'
Response: *I'm afraid I can't do that. You see, all our prices are individually negotiated and I really need to sit down with you and consider the whole package. I'll be able to bring some samples with me as well. I'm in your area on Tuesday and Thursday next week; which would be the best day for you?*

Objection 3: 'What promotional support are you providing?'
Response: *We have a comprehensive promotional strategy to support our product range. I'll be pleased to run through it with you when we meet. Do you prefer to meet with prospective suppliers in the mornings or afternoons?*

Objection 4: 'I'm looking for a 35 per cent discount on RRP, so don't bother to come unless you can match that.'
Response: *There are several possibilities, which is why all our prices are individually negotiated in relation to the complete package, such as order times, volumes and support. I really need to sit down with you and look at the wider picture. I'm in your area on Tuesday and Thursday next week; which would be the best day for you?*

2 Sales person: Need development

Domestic sales situation

Briefing for sales person

You represent XYZ Financial Planning Group and provide advice on a range of life assurance, pension and investment products. XYZ is a 'middle of the road' company and competes in all three product sectors on the basis of value rather than price. Investment performance in all product areas is good, particularly the pension fund, which is in the top ten in the country. Life assurance appears to be relatively expensive, although value can be substantially increased by referring to the USP; that is, any two from the following five options can be added to the core product, free of further charge:

- double accidental death benefit
- critical illness cover for 50 per cent of the sum insured
- premiums waived in the event of involuntary unemployment (for employed and self-employed people)
- an option for the sum insured to be increased by up to 100 per cent on any policy anniversary, without further medical evidence
- double the sum insured to be paid out in annual instalments (option applies in the event of death only).

Additionally, life assurance with the appropriate options can also be linked to a personal pension product.

The prospective customer you are about to meet with is Peter/Peta Brown and they were referred to you by John Smith. The reaction when you made the appointment was 'I can't really afford to spend any extra money, but if you think you can reduce my tax bill, then I'm all ears.' You are meeting the prospect at their house and you know they are self-employed and married. The tone of making the appointment was based on a business meeting and, therefore, their spouse is unlikely to be present.

Your task is to conduct a sales interview which identifies the needs – both hard and soft facts – of your prospective customer. You will need to develop a rapport, gain agreement to the needs, organise them into priority order and gain a commitment for a second appointment, ideally a commitment from them to buy if they are happy with the solution provided.

Briefing for customer

Your name is Peter/Peta Brown. You are 35 years old and you are a self-employed land agent. The nature of your work means that you receive relatively large fees but not on a regular monthly basis. However, you have a retained contract which provides a regular monthly income of £750 and over the last two years you have received an extra £5000 on roughly a quarterly basis.

Your regular outgoings, including mortgage, utilities, council tax and national insurance contributions, are £700 per month and this is covered by your monthly retainer. Your spouse's part-time income covers the family food costs and sundry expenditure, such as children's shoes. You have two children aged six and eight and your spouse is the same age as you.

From your quarterly fee income you provide for socialising, Christmas and birthdays, family holidays (two weeks in the summer and one week in the winter), vehicle maintenance and replacement and your taxation liability. You are disciplined in your approach to handling this money and currently have a surplus cashflow of £6000 in a building society account, accumulated over the past two years. However, £4000 of this is reserved for your next half-yearly tax payment.

You have a £60 000 repayment mortgage and a joint life assurance policy with your spouse to cover this sum. You have no plans to move house in the immediate future. Before becoming self-employed two years ago, you worked for an estate agent for ten years and have a frozen pension with them. Apart from this, you have no other retirement pension provision, although your accountant has suggested you should take out a personal pension plan. Your plans at present are to semi-retire in around twenty years' time when your children have passed through university, started their careers and your mortgage is paid off. You anticipate working on a casual, part-time basis to supplement your frozen pension. When you reach 65, you will probably retire completely as you become eligible for the state pension.

You can see the sense of backing up your frozen pension with a personal pension plan but to date have preferred to err on the side of caution from a cashflow perspective. You have not considered that you need any further life assurance. After all, if something happened to you, your spouse and children would have a house which is paid for and a part-time income. However, you are determined for your children to have every opportunity in life and see regular family holidays as important cultural and recreational experiences for them. You also see providing them with an opportunity to attend university as a vital part of your parental role.

The sales person you are about to meet with has suggested that they can save you money by reducing your tax bill, but you remember financial advisers from your days as an estate agent and believe there is an ulterior motive to their visit. That is, you expect them to try to sell you something. For you this is not a problem, as you are confident you can say no, if need be. However, deep down you know that you really should start up a personal pension plan and may well be prepared to do so at this meeting. In theory, you have £50 per month available, but you have earmarked a contribution of £30 per month to be on the safe side. You have not considered utilising any of your savings and have not considered there is a need for life assurance.

Receive the sales person with caution but hospitably. Aim to retain control of the meeting and let them convince you why you should contribute £30 per month to the personal pension plan they are offering. However, you are also required to respond to their questions, not volunteering information but providing it only when asked for. If a question is asked or information sought which is not explicit in this briefing, you are encouraged to 'ad lib' in the spirit of the role.

Commercial sales situation

Briefing for sales person

You represent a general commercial insurance brokerage. You have an appointment with the MD of a computer dealership whose commercial contents is up for renewal.

- You can provide contents insurance, including employers, public and professional liability cover, for £1300 per annum.
- You can provide fleet insurance for this customer for £1050 per annum.
- You can provide goods in transit insurance for this customer for £1000 per annum.

You can provide all three of these in a combined policy but do not have sufficient information with you to be able to provide a quotation. In the last twelve months your premiums have increased by an average of seven per cent compared to last year.

Conduct a sales interview which clearly identifies the needs and buying motivations of this prospective customer and gain a commitment in principle to buy from you, if you can provide an appropriate solution. You are not required to make a full sales presentation at this stage and the figures provided are only to give you an indication of your competitive capability.

Briefing for customer

You are the MD of a computer dealership. Your contents insurance, including public, employers and professional liability, is up for renewal. Your existing insurers have quoted a renewal cost of £1250, representing an increase of ten per cent on last year's premium. You feel the rate of increase is too high and have invited another insurance broker to quote before you decide whether to renew your existing policy or effect a new one.

Your fleet insurance is up for renewal in two months' time and a ten per cent increase would result in last year's premium of £1000 increasing to £1100. You are transporting more and more of your own orders and do not have any goods-in-transit insurance. You know you should have but, in the past, this has always been covered by the transport firm's carriage insurance. By delivering your own orders, you are saving around £1700 per annum.

You are interested in what this new broker has to say and will go ahead if the price is better. You will also go ahead if you can be persuaded by the benefits of dealing with them or the value added aspect of the arrangement they suggest to you.

Only disclose information, thoughts and feelings when the sales person asks you a relevant question; that is, do not volunteer information. If a question is asked or information sought which is not explicit in this briefing, you are encouraged to *ad lib* in the spirit of the role.

Trade sales situation

Briefing for sales person

You represent Eatalot PLC, a firm which produces prepared frozen meals. You have an appointment to meet with the senior buyer for a medium-sized retail chain (approximately 100 stores covering Central, Southern and South West England). Eatalot is a growing company and opening this account will be a key development in this growth, particularly given its potential for development as your product range expands. However, the company's growth has been based on sound business arrangements and you are not to win the account at any cost.

Eatalot's products are attractively packaged and offer the consumer good value for money in terms of meal sizes in relation to RRP. The range currently consists of twelve carefully targeted meals. Six are family sized and aimed at a typical family of four; four are meals-for-two, aimed at the professional working couple; and two are single servings aimed at the young single person.

Your products are also supported by carefully targeted end-user mailings (which include the names of major retailers where meals can be purchased) and limited period promotional offers. The latest promotional offer was a huge success. Each pack contained a coupon for the appropriate meal size, and when six coupons had been collected, a free promotional meal was provided. These promotional packs launched a new meal in each of the three size categories (taking the range from nine to twelve meals).

Eatalot usually makes a fortnightly delivery, with an order period one week in advance of delivery. The company uses computers for internal stock management and order processing but does not yet have the capability to communicate electronically with retailers. All customers work on an account basis of 30 days maximum, and this is paramount to Eatalot's cashflow. Strict credit control is exercised on customers who drift outside this arrangement and the company's sales people are required to highlight clearly this aspect for any account which is negotiated. Many sales people agree payment terms of 14 days to minimise the effect of late payment on the relationship.

Discounts are provided to retailers as follows:

- a commitment of up to 100 meals per fortnight – 25% discount on RRP
- a commitment of between 100 and 1000 meals per fortnight – 30% discount on RRP

- a commitment of over 1000 meals per fortnight – 35% discount on RRP.

You are taking some meal samples with you and initially need to convince the buyer of the quality and value offered by the products. Beyond this, you need to listen to their criteria for opening an account and agreeing to stock the product, being aware of the value they attach to each criterion in terms of priority and importance. Once their requirements have been fully established, you should gain a commitment from them to see you again with a view to negotiating a mutually beneficial arrangement.

Briefing for customer

You are the senior buyer for a medium-sized retail chain (approximately 100 stores) covering Central, Southern and South West England. You are meeting with a sales person from Eatalot PLC, having made it quite difficult for the sales person to make an appointment with you. This was a deliberate move as you believe it enhances your negotiating position. In fact, you are quite keen to stock Eatalot's products as they are rapidly gaining a reputation for offering the consumer good value for money. However, experience of negotiating a 'good deal' has told you that sales people should not be aware that you are keen to buy their product.

You have a set of clearly defined buying criteria, prioritised as follows:

- *First priority:* All organisations supplying you must transact business with you electronically. For organisations with adequate computer but not electronic communication capability, this represents a cost of £2000 to buy the necessary hardware and software and a further £500 for staff training. This is non-negotiable. Any organisation wishing to deal with you must have this electronic capability.
- *Second priority:* You like to have a weekly delivery with an order period three days in advance of delivery. You are generally unwilling to negotiate on this requirement.
- *Third priority:* You expect to receive 35 per cent trade discount on food products that you stock. Occasionally you have accepted less, but that has only been when the product is supported with national TV advertising. However, you have heard that Eatalot's promotional strategy is quite effective but you do not want to let them think that you know this. You really do feel that a relatively small company like Eatalot should be prepared to give you a 35 per cent discount.
- *Fourth priority:* You generally try to negotiate payment terms of 45 days but you do always pay on time. At a push you will go to 30 day payment terms but never any lower than this.
- *Fifth priority:* You would like to trial the products for one month in ten selected outlets. You anticipate a commitment to a minimum of ten meals per week in each location for the trial period and then extending this commitment to all outlets if the trial is successful. You expect to receive a 35

per cent discount before and after the trial and do not really want to negotiate on this point. However, you may consider waiving the need for electronic capability during the trial period but will not volunteer this point unless specifically asked.

Indeed, you are out to negotiate the best possible deal and intend to present all your criteria as non-negotiable. Do not offer a priority order unless the sales person specifically draws it from you with appropriate questions.

3 Sales person: Making the sale

Domestic sales situation

Briefing for sales person

The first appointment seemed to go very well. Peter/Peta agreed that they needed a pension plan and liked the idea of making a minimal monthly contribution and the ability to make lump sum contributions when cashflow permitted. They also liked the idea that you would keep in touch with them on a six-monthly basis to ensure that this happened.

The need for life assurance was a harder concept to develop. However, when they were placed in a position of 'What would happen if . . .?' and asked to consider the change in family lifestyle, the loss of the main breadwinner was powerfully emphasised. They now totally believe that life assurance on their own life is the most important need but have dismissed life assurance on the life of their spouse as a luxury, prioritising it below a personal pension plan. You do not fully agree with them but were in danger of damaging the sale if you pursued the matter at the first meeting. Instead you have decided to re-address it as a need on the next service call after they become a customer of yours.

In view of the power of your previous appointment, Peter/Peta has agreed to commit a regular £50 per month in providing a solution, rather than £30 which they initially volunteered. They were also particularly keen on the concept that pension contributions (and attached life assurance) would attract tax relief against profit figures submitted to the Inland Revenue, in effect reducing their tax liability in favour of their own pension fund. They were also comfortable with the pension fund investment performance of XYZ Financial Planning, consistently a top ten performer.

You have decided to offer the following solution in response to the needs which have been identified, the prioritisation and the buying motivations (life assurance figures can be adjusted on a pro-rata basis, if required):

- 20 year term assurance policy – £100 000 sum assured, monthly premium £30.
- Personal pension plan – £20 per month contribution (minimum gross premium) and flexible lump sum contribution option (minimum £500 in any one transaction).

In respect of the life assurance, you intend to link it with the pension plan in order to attract tax relief on the whole contribution, effectively reducing the real cost. You have only outlined the additional five options available and need to clarify which ones Peter/Peta wants during this meeting, as a way of reinforcing the sale.

Demonstrate how both 'hard' and 'soft' needs have been satisfied, highlighting appropriate features in the form of benefits. Start this meeting by recapping on the conclusion of the previous meeting and confirming that the situation has not changed.

Briefing for customer

You are about to meet the sales person from XYZ Financial Planning for the second time. You were impressed during the first meeting and felt that you were being listened to. Also, during the meeting you were convinced of the need for life assurance on your own life and now see this as your number one priority. However, you are not convinced there is a major need for your spouse's life to be covered. If you were to die, your wish is to ensure the family lifestyle (financially speaking) remains unaltered; that is, your children can still go to university, still go on regular overseas holidays and Christmas/birthdays remain well funded. This requires an income of around £10 000 per year and cover is required for approximately 20 years to ensure you can provide your children with a good start in life. You are a non-smoker, in good health, with no adverse family medical history – nonetheless, you still want to eliminate the risk.

With regard to a personal pension plan, you liked the idea of making low, regular monthly contributions and topping this up with lump sum contributions whenever cashflow allowed. You also liked the idea that the sales person would call on you a couple of times a year to remind you of the need to make a contribution. You genuinely felt that this sales person would look after you and they were not just out to make a quick buck; after all they refused to sell you a £30 per month pension plan when you initially said that was what you wanted. In the event, you agreed to commit £50 per month to a combined life assurance/pension plan and feel comfortable with this commitment. You also liked the idea that by contributing to a personal pension you would reduce tax payments to the Inland Revenue, although of course you understand that your net outgoings (from a cashflow perspective) would increase.

When you called your accountant to confirm the tax reductions which were suggested by the sales person, they recommended that you obtain a second opinion from an independent financial adviser. You duly agreed and one came to see you two days ago. On the negative side, you did not like them very much and didn't feel that you were important to them. For example, you felt that you could not rely on them to remind you to make lump sum contributions to your pension. However, on the positive side, you understand they are able to recommend from a full range of companies and accept that this may well give you a more competitive deal. They have offered you the following solution:

- £20 per month (gross) for a life assurance policy with £100 000 sum assured – 20 year term (no optional extras), linked to
- £30 per month (gross) into a personal pension plan with a top ten company and an option for voluntary lump sum contributions.

You would prefer to buy from the sales person from XYZ Financial Planning but will only do so if they can offer you a truly competitive deal. You are not entirely sure that £100 000 sum assured will produce a regular annual income of £10 000, but at this stage you are not prepared to commit any further contribution. You are working on the basis that it will do for now and can be upgraded in the future.

Commercial sales situation

Briefing for sales person

You have a second appointment with the MD of a computer dealership. The outcome of the first meeting was as follows:

1. The client agreed in principle to go ahead with the basic contents insurance at a cost of £1300 per annum, this being on the basis that the MD liked the idea of dealing with your company as your average premium increases were only seven per cent last year compared with a ten per cent increase from the company's existing broker. You are aware that this decision is one of principle, as the client was grossly unhappy with the level of increase, rather than overall cost, of their existing policy.

2. The client said they would probably go ahead with the goods-in-transit insurance at a cost of £1000 per annum because they need it. However, they did mention the proviso that they would obtain a quote from their existing insurance company.

3. The client said they would look at the fleet insurance when it became due for renewal (i.e. no immediate decision).

4. You mentioned the possibility of a combined policy and they said they would consider it. They were interested in the potential cost saving but concerned about the incompatibility of their existing renewal dates.

At this second meeting your objective is to make a sale. Ideally, this will be for the combined policy/complete package, but if this cannot be achieved, you should at least try to make a sale of one policy now and gain a commitment to invite you to quote for the fleet insurance policy in two months' time.

Briefing for customer

You are about to have a second meeting with a general commercial insurance broker. The outcome of the first meeting was as follows:

1. You agreed to go ahead with the basic contents insurance at a cost of £1300 per annum, this being a decision of principle as the new broker had only increased their rates by seven per cent in the past twelve months compared with a ten per cent increase for your existing policy. On reflection, you feel committing yourself to this policy was a little hasty, as it is still more expensive than the one offered by your existing insurance company. You were going to call the sales person and cancel the meeting but you had mislaid their card.

2 You said you would possibly go ahead with the goods-in-transit insurance at a cost of £1000 per annum but you said you would also obtain a quote from your existing insurers. Their quote is lower at £950 per annum and you intend to arrange this with them.

3 The new broker seemed to have a competitively priced fleet insurance policy and you may well buy this from them when your existing policy expires in two months' time.

You asked your existing insurers whether they offered a combined policy for all your insurance needs and they do not. The sales person from the new broker had mentioned that there may be cost savings by taking out a combined policy. Certainly you can see how it would save you time and aggravation every year by considering a single renewal rather than three separate ones.

Although you have an open mind on the prospect of taking out a combined policy, you do not have a lot of time to spare and aim to give the sales person only 15–20 minutes to come up with something better than you already have with your existing insurers. You are only really giving them any time at all because you feel guilty about not cancelling the meeting in advance.

Trade sales situation

Briefing for sales person

During the first meeting with the buyer, you identified the following buying criteria:

- *First priority:* If you are going to start a relationship with this retail chain, Eatalot will need to invest £2500 in developing an electronic capability. Your sales and marketing director has agreed to this expenditure but only for a minimum commitment to purchase in excess of 1000 meals per fortnight. He will not commit to this expenditure during a trial period and this is non-negotiable.

- *Second priority:* The retail chain requires weekly delivery with an order period three days in advance of delivery. Your sales and marketing director is happy with this arrangement when 1000 meals per fortnight are being purchased and there is electronic capability, but not during the trial period. Ideally, he would like you to negotiate normal delivery and order terms during the trial period but, alternatively, will accept weekly delivery with an order period one week in advance of delivery.

- *Third priority:* A 35 per cent trade discount is required which is fine after the trial period, as it is consistent with the organisation's discounting structure. However, during the trial period this goes outside the scope of the structure. At a push, the sales and marketing director has agreed to the exceptional discount arrangement during the trial period but would prefer you to negotiate a 30 per cent discount, if possible. He has suggested that you re-emphasise the benefits and effectiveness of Eatalot's promotional strategies based on carefully-targeted market segments.

- *Fourth priority:* The buyer was keen to agree 45 day payment terms and made a point of agreeing to pay promptly. Your finance director is unhappy with this arrangement and is insistent that strict 30 day payment terms be negotiated.
- *Fifth priority:* The buyer wants to trial the product in ten locations for a one-month period. You need either to talk them out of the need for a trial or to negotiate the best possible terms for the trial period based on the directions of Eatalot's senior management.

Your task is to negotiate an initial transaction and ongoing relationship based on the best possible terms you can achieve, within the remit agreed by your sales and marketing/finance directors.

Briefing for customer

You are about to have a second meeting with the sales person from Eatalot PLC. You have been impressed with their attitude and approach so far and are very keen to stock their product range. However, you remain keen to negotiate the best possible deal based on your clearly defined and prioritised buying criteria.

Only agree to the deal if it is acceptable to you.

4 Sales person: employment interview

Trainee sales person

Briefing for job applicant

You are 25 and desperate to develop a career in sales. In your early years you had a variety of jobs, which looks bad on your CV but arose because you were not satisfied with mundane, routine work. You have been active in your search for a career in sales and spent six months canvassing for a double-glazing company before taking your current position in a sales support role for an engineering firm.

You are excited at having been invited for an interview as a trainee sales executive with a local computer dealer. You are determined to impress and demonstrate how you can be a valuable asset to the company and are the best candidate for the job.

Experienced sales person moving from one industry to another

Briefing for job applicant

You have been direct selling in the insurance industry for four years. For some time now you have been looking to change your career. Although you have been relatively successful in the insurance industry, you feel your time in that sector is at an end, as you continually work long and unsociable hours, take a lot of rejection and your efforts to build client relationships are continuously being hampered by bad publicity for the industry and mediocre performance of your company's products.

You have been trying to find a sales representative position in the FMCG (fast-moving consumer goods) market, but so far, all your applications have been declined with not even the opportunity of an interview. This has made you somewhat disillusioned, but the last time you received a rejection letter, from Eatalot PLC, you called to find out why. To your surprise, the sales manager seemed very interested and has invited you to an interview.

You are excited and see this as your big chance to make a major career change. You intend to do everything you can to convince the sales manager that you have the qualities they are seeking.

Sales person applying for internal promotion to sales management

Briefing for job applicant

You have worked for Capital Equipment Ltd. for three years, selling directly to business end-users. This was your first 'real' position in sales, although previously you spent two years in a sales and marketing support role for a corporate training company.

Over the past twelve months, there has been a major overhaul of the sales force structure at Capital Equipment Ltd., as the company attempts to move from a sales orientation to a marketing one (a concept with which you are fully familiar through your previous employment and your professional studies). During this restructuring, your sales manager felt he 'lost out' and, as a result, has taken a position with a competitor.

You have a lot of respect for the outgoing manager, as he gave you your chance in selling and trained you in the role. Indeed, he has suggested you may be interested in moving with him to the competitor company and, although tempted, you have decided that Capital Equipment Ltd. is a better company, with better products and a better future.

Your sales performance over the three-year period is generally good. The first year saw you exceed your trainee targets by 15 per cent and in the second year you exceeded your target by 5 per cent, finishing thirtieth out of a sales force of 120. The last year has not been so successful. You are short of target by 10 per cent, although this is typical across the sales force. There has been a generally low morale caused by the restructuring (i.e. negative influences from those feeling threatened by the changes) and, in addition to this, you have been asked to act as mentor to two new sales people in your sales manager's area. Although you have enjoyed the field training/coaching and feel you have done a good job, this has served to detract from your selling duties.

You have applied for the sales management vacancy created by your manager's departure and feel you are ready to take on the challenge. The team currently stands at six (including yourself), two of which you have trained. Another two sales people are in their second year and not ready for sales management, but one team member has been with the company for two years longer than you and has also applied for the vacancy. Their development in selling has been less dramatic than yours, although their performance over the past twelve months has been better than yours, as they have reached their target. Additionally, two sales people within the company, one from another team in the area and another from an adjoining region, have applied for the position.

Your task is to demonstrate that you are the best person for the job and win promotion.

5 Sales person: Group selling seminar

Domestic selling scenario

You are an investment adviser working for a firm of 'Independent Financial Advisers'. The firm has organised a seminar to make people aware of the range of services which it offers, with a view to winning new clients. You have been asked to make one of four presentations during the hour-long seminar. The full seminar is titled, *'The Value Of Independent Advice'* and your section within this is titled 'The Investment Revolution'.

The audience is varied. Some have come from a direct response advertising campaign and others from a series of carefully targeted direct mailings. Broadly, there are four categories attending the seminar:

Group 1: Small business people, seeking to become more tax efficient

Group 2: Early retired people (aged 50–65), seeking to maximise their retirement incomes

Group 3: People who own between £2000 and £10 000 worth of shares in the privatised utilities

Group 4: People with a net worth in excess of £250 000 who are concerned about an inheritance tax liability.

The theme of the whole seminar is to convince people that taking independent financial advice is better than dealing with a financial adviser who can only sell one organisation's products. This theme needs to run through your presentation, although you also have some specific considerations:

- Your main targeted groups are Groups 2 and 3, although there may be some interest from members of Groups 1 and 4.
- Group 2 members need to be convinced that investing their retirement lump sums and savings is more desirable than depositing them in a bank or building society. The latter is generally considered safe and reliable, although you know that such options result in the long-term erosion of capital due to the effects of inflation. Also, fluctuating interest rates lead to a variable return from deposit-based savings. Against this, many will fear the risk factor involved in investing their money in stocks and shares, particularly given that there have been two well-publicised stock market 'crashes' in the past decade. However, the long-term trend is one of growth and these 'crashes' are merely blips in the overall picture. You are also aware that some products offer 'growth' and/or 'income' guarantees.
- Group 3 members are committed to the principle of share ownership but, so far, have been shown to develop their own portfolios of shares. In all likelihood, they have seen the privatised utilities as safe investments, although they will be aware of the risk elements. You know that the key to

good investment is to develop a balanced portfolio; that is, there will be some safe and reliable investments, combined with others which provide higher growth potential but which carry a greater degree of risk. Additionally, tax efficiency and the flexibility to transfer investments are generally key motivators for small investors.

- As you have access to the whole market place of investment providers, you can offer a service which advises clients on the most suitable portfolio, based on their own personal needs. Additionally, you have an investors' support department within the firm. This allows clients to have instant access to the performance of their portfolio and to instruct transfers of funds, as necessary. You normally require notice of around three working days to make a face-to-face meeting with clients, although you are available by telephone between 8.00 a.m. and 7.00 p.m.

Your task is to deliver a fifteen-minute seminar presentation which will encourage people to become clients of the firm. This presentation should avoid technical content and focus on satisfying the general needs of the main targeted groups, whilst also appealing to the whole audience.

Commercial selling scenario

Role 1

You are a sales executive for a computer software dealership. Your organisation carries a range of software packages which are suitable for small- and medium-sized enterprises (SMEs). Although bespoke changes can be made to the software, the consultancy costs of doing so generally preclude the smaller businesses. From the organisation's point of view, these smaller businesses are not sufficiently profitable to justify a dedicated personal selling effort.

It is these smaller business owners who are attending the seminar at which you are to give a presentation. They have been invited through a carefully-targeted direct mail campaign based on a software solution which will make their businesses more efficient and profitable. Your presentation will be followed by splitting the audience into three groups for a series of product demonstrations, before a colleague of yours addresses the whole group to encourage them to place orders to buy the product(s).

As the opening speaker, your job is to rouse the audience and develop a desire in them to view the products in action. To do this, you will need to create a state of rapport with the audience (perhaps empathising with the way they currently conduct business on a predominantly manual basis) before highlighting the key benefits which they will derive from this software. There are three main products:

- A full *accounting package* which covers VAT, PAYE, cashflow, profit and loss, balance sheet and management analysis. Although data entry is a key requirement, efficiency of human resources is likely to be increased by around 30 per cent.

- A *business planning package* which enables business owners to forecast trends, profitability and cashflow. Additionally, it provides a series of key prompts for owners to consider during their planning, such as product development, market size, competitive influences, USPs, promotional requirements and human resources. Although it places an initial burden on the owner to enter information and formulate their plans thoroughly, the benefits include a reduction in risk and substantially increased profitability. Experience with existing customers has shown that profitability increases by between 5 and 15 per cent.
- A *customer management and lead tracking package* which enables businesses to focus their efforts and resources in the most profitable areas. It shows which customers are the most profitable and which ones have the potential to become more profitable. Additionally, the system enables the business to identify precisely where each customer came from (e.g. advertising, referral etc.) and to analyse the effectiveness of each aspect of their marketing communications. It also provides qualitative customer information which enables appropriate levels of service to be offered, enhancing customer retention/ loyalty and increasing profitability. The data entry aspect of this package represents a fairly substantial increase in effort (around 10 per cent of time currently spent with customers). However, the results of this package, which was launched twelve months ago, have been quite phenomenal. Early feedback from existing customers has shown an average increase in profitability of 30 per cent.

You have fifteen minutes to achieve your objective.

Role 2

You are the second sales person in this seminar. The audience was well motivated by the first speaker and each delegate has now seen a demonstration of all three products. Your task now is to encourage them to take action to buy the product(s). To do this, you will need to demonstrate how valuable the products are in relation to price. Your organisation discourages personal selling visits to this customer group and, as such, treats any visits as consultancy work, charging £450 per day, which is the same as the cost for bespoke consultancy and training. The product costs are as follows:

- *Accounting package:* Initial cost is £2350 and updates are provided as and when there are taxation, legislative or procedural changes. This update service costs £120 per annum to subscribe to and is not optional. Additionally, a minimum of one day's training is recommended (although, as with all the products, a full manual is provided).
- *Business planning package:* Initial cost is £1850 and a minimum of one day's training is recommended.

- *Customer management and lead tracking package:* Initial cost is £3950 (this is largely due to the fact that research and development costs are still being recovered and in twelve months' time the price is likely to fall by about £1000) and a minimum of two days' training is recommended.

You are able to offer a special price of £7250 for anyone placing an order for all three packages at todays' seminar. This does not include the cost of training, and the subscription charges for the accounting package remain unaltered.

It is up to you whether you invite questions/objections from the audience. Your task is to persuade as many people as possible to place an order for the software *today*.

You have fifteen minutes to achieve your objective.

6 Sales Manager: Recruitment interview

Recruiting a trainee sales person

Briefing for sales manager

You are the sales manager of a rapidly growing computer dealership. You are charged with the job of building a dynamic, professional sales team. However, this objective has to be balanced with that of obtaining relatively instant results, as the resources made available to you from the overall marketing budget are intrinsically linked to incoming sales orders.

Any new appointment you make requires that the sales person is running profitably and independently within three months. This causes you something of a problem, as the lead time for sales is an average of six weeks. Therefore, your ideal recruit will come from within the industry and have a good sales track record. However, the package you can offer – maximum of £15k basic (£30k OTE) and company car – is low to attract this type of candidate.

The second option open to you is to appoint a junior or trainee sales person. By reducing the salary to £10k basic (£20k OTE) and company car after one month, you can increase the time required for them to become profitable to five months. However, your time is of a premium and you would need them to be virtually independent within three months.

You are about to interview a trainee candidate. They have some experience of canvassing for double glazing and currently work in a sales support role for a local engineering company. You fear they have insufficient experience for your requirements but you have decided to give them a chance of an interview as they seem pretty determined to make a career in selling, a quality which you admire.

Interview the candidate and make a recruitment decision.

Recruiting a sales person from a different industry

Briefing for sales manager

You are the regional sales manager (RSM) of Eatalot PLC, a company which produces a range of frozen foods and supplies directly to retailers. Due to an expansion of your sales force, you are looking to appoint a new representative to cover the Dorset area. The territory currently contains 60 accounts and the new representative needs to increase this to 100 within their first year. After this has been achieved, the role will become mainly an account management one with the emphasis on building relationships and increasing sales volume through the existing accounts rather than increasing the number of accounts.

You are faced with a recruiting dilemma!

Your job advertisement produced a large number of responses but relatively few applicants possessed the right level of experience – you had asked for a minimum of two years' FMCG (fast-moving consumer goods) sales experience. From the applications, you invited six candidates to interview. Having just completed the initial interviews, you have rejected four of them. The two you have shortlisted are both solid, reliable FMCG sales people with a track record of high quality account management. However, your reservation is that neither of them convinced you of their ability to open the new accounts, a key aspect of the first year.

You are just about to interview a seventh candidate. You declined this person's application initially but they called you to ask why and said that they were very keen on entering the FMCG market. After handling your objections professionally, they persuaded you to give them the chance of an interview. Their background is of four years direct selling in the insurance industry.

Your pre-interview thoughts are that this person may well have the ability and skills you are looking for to open new accounts (i.e. dynamic, determined, persuasive). However, your concern is that they will not be satisfied with the more stable and less dynamic role of pure account management which will be the case after the first year.

Interview the candidate and decide if they can solve your recruiting dilemma.

Promoting a sales person into a sales management role

Briefing for recruiting manager

You are a Regional Sales Manager (RSM) of Capital Equipment Ltd. A year ago, there was a major restructuring of the sales force as the company attempted to move from a sales orientation to a marketing one. Your record of innovative management, professional study and taking a positive attitude to change, resulted in you landing a key role in the restructuring programme. A rival for your position is the outgoing manager in this scenario. They lost out to you for the RSM post and were given a territory management role, managing a team of six.

The resentful manager played havoc with the team during the past twelve months and did not create a motivational environment. This affected performance and, three months ago, you gave them a final written warning (a fact which is not widely known among the sales force) and this prompted them to take a position with a minor competitor. You are relieved to be rid of them but are aware that they have been trying to poach some of the team members to take to the competitor company.

You believe in recruiting from within and feel that there is sufficient talent internally to be able to do so on this occasion. Your main selection criteria for a new sales manager are as follows:

- How will they go about remotivating the team?
- How will they react to change in the future?
- How committed are they to a marketing philosophy and, therefore, how able are they to take the company forward?
- Will they have the respect of other team members?
- It is a young team and so how good will they be at training/development?

You have interviewed three internal candidates already, the outcomes of which are as follows:

- **Candidate 1:** A member of the outgoing manager's team with a steady track record of over five years of selling for the company. He has not been a top performer but is reliable and consistent. You think he will be able to do a good job but wonder whether he will be inspirational to others and sufficiently positive about future changes. However, he is currently the best performer in the team, although this is more a result of others under-performing than exceptional performance on his behalf. On reflection, you do not feel he is right for the job but do not want to lose him from the team.
- **Candidate 2:** A sales person attached to a different team in your region. She has an excellent sales record and is currently ninth in the overall performance league table for the national sales force (excluding major and national accounts which are measured separately). As an inspirational and motivational influence, you feel she would be ideal. However, she is also very focused on her own performance and has not proved to be a team player in the past. You are concerned that she will not be sufficiently focused on team development and is likely to be somewhat intolerant of those who are not as talented as her. You have seen this work two ways in the past: either a top quality team results over the medium-term or the team becomes demotivated and under-performs. This candidate impresses you enormously but you feel she may be more appropriate to a major accounts selling role which would give her equal status to this position. You know that there is likely to be a major accounts position coming up in about three months and are 50/50 on whether to promote this person now or persuade her to wait for the next vacancy.
- **Candidate 3:** A sales person from outside the region. A consistently over-target performer over the past four years. He has impressed you in every aspect of his application but you have a couple of reservations. First, he has no local experience and this may affect some personal development capability in the short-term. Of more concern to you is his motivation for applying for the post. There are no vacancies in his current region and you feel that perhaps this is seen as a short-term option before transferring back again in the future. When you confronted him with this, he said he wanted to move to the area because of a personal relationship he was involved in – his current RSM was not aware of this motive, but this does not necessarily mean it is untrue. Nonetheless, you are left with doubts.

You are about to interview the fourth candidate. You feel they are a strong contender for the post. They are a popular member of the team and have, in effect, been responsible for developing the two latest recruits. Last year, they were thirtieth in the sales force league table (only their second year selling) and this year you had hoped they would progress to the top ten. However, performance has slipped and they are 10 per cent below target. In part, they have had mentoring responsibilities which have detracted from selling time but, also, they have been negatively affected by the outgoing sales manager. This concerns you, or rather you now wonder whether they will be able to remotivate the team. On the plus side, you believe they have a forward thinking mentality and have been impressed with their efforts to gain a professional qualification.

Interview the candidate and decide which of the four candidates you are going to appoint. Also, you will need to plan how to decline the other three applicants while retaining their motivation.

7 Sales Manager: Weekly performance interview sequence

The scenario

There are two active roles in this scenario: sales manager and sales person.

The business is involved in selling industrial hygiene products (capital equipment and consumables) to a range of commercial customers. Customers are categorised into three groups based on the number of employees. *Large* customers are handled by major account executives (not covered by the roles in this scenario). The *small-* and *medium-sized* customers are handled by territory sales people and a local telesales team for the whole branch. The organisation is keen to exert optimum effort in relation to customer profitability and, therefore, encourages the following practices:

- *New small customers:* These are targeted and approached by the telesales team who make appointments for the territory sales people. A single personal selling visit is then made. If the sales person is unsuccessful during this appointment, they have the option of pursuing the prospect themselves but are encouraged to utilise the telesales team for doing so.
- *Existing small customers:* These are managed by the telesales team, the primary focus of which is to continue supplying consumables. The territory sales person aims to visit twice a year or, if the telesales team identifies either an opportunity for selling additional/upgraded capital equipment or the threat of a customer being lost to a competitor, an exceptional visit can be made.
- *New medium-sized customers:* These are targeted and approached by territory sales people. Sales people usually require two visits: the first to identify requirements and the second to present a proposal.
- *Existing medium-sized customers:* Orders for consumables are handled by the telesales team but the account is developed by the territory sales person, making personal visits on a bi-monthly basis.

The territory sales person in this role play has two years' experience in the role and is a steady performer who generally hits (but not exceeds) overall sales targets. The sales manager has been in the role for three months and feels that the sales person is capable of more, even though performance to date has been on target.

A four-week sequence of reporting forms is provided. You are to conduct an end-of-week interview for each of the four weeks, which must be consistent with the figures provided, although some blank spaces in the forms allow scope for you to develop the role, as appropriate to the content of the preceding interviews.

Sales force reporting form as at end of Week 1

	Target this week	Actual this week	Target next week
NEW CUSTOMERS			
Small			
No. of first appointments	10	8	10
No. of second appointments	2	3	2
No. of sales	4	4	4
Closing ratio (total appointments : sales)	3:1	c.3:1	3:1
Sales revenue (£)	1000	1000	1000
Average order value (£)	250	250	250
Medium			
No. of calls	25	20	
No. of first appointments	5	4	
Closing ratio (calls : first appointments)	5:1	5:1	5:1
No. of second appointments	2	2	2
No. of sales	2	2	2
Closing ratio (second appointments : sales)	3.5:1	3:1	3.5:1
Sales revenue (£)	2000	2500	2000
Average order value (£)	1000	1250	1000
EXISTING CUSTOMERS			
Small			
No. of personal visits	10	8	10
Capital equipment sales revenue (£)	250	0	250
Consumables sales revenue (£)	750	750	750
Total sales revenue (£)	1000	750	1000
% difference on same period last quarter	0	− 25%	0
Medium			
No. of personal visits	10	8	0
Capital equipment sales revenue (£)	500	500	500
Consumables sales revenue (£)	2000	1750	2000
Total sales revenue (£)	2500	2250	2500
% difference on same period last quarter	0	− 10%	0
COMBINED ANALYSIS			
Total sales revenue this week (£)	6500	6500	6500
Commission earned @ 5% of revenue (£)	325	325	325
% Performance against target	N/A	100%	N/A

Sales force reporting form as at end of Week 2

	Target this week	Actual this week	Target next week
NEW CUSTOMERS			
Small			
No. of first appointments	10	7	
No. of second appointments	2	4	
No. of sales	4	4	4
Closing ratio (total appointments : sales)	3:1	c.3:1	
Sales revenue (£)	1000	800	1000
Average order value (£)	250	200	250
Medium			
No. of calls		25	25
No. of first appointments		5	5
Closing ratio (calls : first appointments)	5:1	5:1	5:1
No. of second appointments	2	2	2
No. of sales	2	1	2
Closing ratio (second appointments : sales)	3.5:1	7:1	3.5:1
Sales revenue (£)	2000	1250	2000
Average order value (£)	100	1250	1000
EXISTING CUSTOMERS			
Small			
No. of personal visits	10	12	
Capital equipment sales revenue (£)	250	500	
Consumables sales revenue (£)	750	750	750
Total sales revenue (£)	1000	1250	
% difference on same period last quarter	0	+ 25%	
Medium			
No. of personal visits	10	12	
Capital equipment sales revenue (£)	500	1000	
Consumables sales revenue (£)	2000	2000	2000
Total sales revenue (£)	2500	3000	
% difference on same period last quarter	0	+ 20%	
COMBINED ANALYSIS			
Total sales revenue this week (£)	6500	6300	
Commission earned @ 5% of revenue (£)	325	315	
% Performance against target	N/A	c.97%	N/A

Sales force reporting form as at end of Week 3

	Target this week	Actual this week	Target next week
NEW CUSTOMERS			
Small			
No. of first appointments		10	
No. of second appointments		1	
No. of sales	4	2	
Closing ratio (total appointments : sales)		5.5:1	
Sales revenue (£)		500	
Average order value (£)		250	
Medium			
No. of calls	25	25	
No. of first appointments	5	5	
Closing ratio (calls : first appointments)	5:1	5:1	5:1
No. of second appointments	2	2	
No. of sales	2	2	
Closing ratio (second appointments : sales)	3.5:1	3.5:1	3.5:1
Sales revenue (£)	2000	2500	
Average order value (£)	1000	1250	1250
EXISTING CUSTOMERS			
Small			
No. of personal visits		10	
Capital equipment sales revenue (£)		250	
Consumables sales revenue (£)		750	
Total sales revenue (£)		1000	
% difference on same period last quarter		0	
Medium			
No. of personal visits		14	
Capital equipment sales revenue (£)		1000	
Consumables sales revenue (£)		2500	
Total sales revenue (£)		3500	
% difference on same period last quarter		+40%	
COMBINED ANALYSIS			
Total sales revenue this week (£)	7500	8500	
Commission earned @ 5% of revenue (£)	375	425	
% Performance against target	N/A	N/A	

Sales force reporting form as at end of Week 4

	Target this week	Actual this week	Target next week
NEW CUSTOMERS			
Small			
No. of first appointments		8	
No. of second appointments		2	
No. of sales		2	
Closing ratio (total appointments : sales)		5:1	
Sales revenue (£)		500	
Average order value (£)		250	
Medium			
No. of calls		30	
No. of first appointments		6	
Closing ratio (calls : first appointments)	5:1	5:1	5:1
No. of second appointments		3	
No. of sales		3	
Closing ratio (second appointments : sales)	3.5:1	3:1	3.5:1
Sales revenue (£)		3750	
Average order value (£)	1250	1250	1250
EXISTING CUSTOMERS			
Small			
No. of personal visits		8	
Capital equipment sales revenue (£)		250	
Consumables sales revenue (£)		750	
Total sales revenue (£)		1000	
% difference on same period last quarter		0	
Medium			
No. of personal visits		15	
Capital equipment sales revenue (£)		1000	
Consumables sales revenue (£)		2500	
Total sales revenue (£)		3500	
% difference on same period last quarter		+40%	
COMBINED ANALYSIS			
Total sales revenue this week (£)	8500	8750	
Commission earned @ 5% of revenue (£)	425	437	
% Performance against target	N/A	c.103%	N/A

8 Sales manager: sales meeting

The organisation

Capital Direct Ltd. is a national chain of business equipment dealers, supplying commercial end-users. Its product portfolio includes a full range of photocopiers, laser printers and fax machines from a total of twelve manufacturers (a main manufacturer in each product sector and three supporting ones). At present, all products carry the manufacturer's badge.

Customers are wide ranging. They come from a variety of industry sectors and have differing requirements in terms of both product and order volumes. The sales force used to be divided by product type first and then into geographical areas. About twelve months ago, it was restructured and divided by customer type first and then geographical areas. As a result of this restructuring, there were some 'winners' and some 'losers'.

Some of the younger, aspiring sales people have been provided with a career path in selling as well as management, whereas some of the more senior sales people have lost status and find themselves with limited career opportunities. The very best sales people have found their status to be enhanced within the organisational framework, and the very best sales managers have been rewarded with larger areas of responsibility, through either team size or business volumes.

During the past twelve months, many of the disaffected sales people who lost status and career opportunity have left the company. This has caused disruption to the sales force and has negatively affected overall motivation. Some of the negative group still remain but, on the whole, are accepting their revised roles and turning in steady, reliable performance. A couple have turned full circle and are going out of their way to prove a point, producing ever increasing levels of business.

The current structure of the sales force is as follows:

- The country is split into four regions.
- Each region has a sales manager (RSM), all four reporting to a sales force manager who in turn, reports to a sales and marketing director.
- There are two national account managers (one for the North and one for the South), both reporting to the sales force manager.
- Each region has a Major Accounts Manager (MAM), reporting to the RSM.
- Also reporting to the RSM are three Area Sales Managers (ASMs), a senior administrator and a Marketing Support Manager (MSM).
- Each ASM runs a field sales team responsible for smaller/general customers, divided by geographical area. Team sizes range from six to ten, according to the dependency of the sales people and attrition factors.
- The MSM is responsible for an in-house team of three people. They support both pre- and post-selling activity, although because of the high sales force

turnover in the past year more time has been spent on post-selling activity (e.g. keeping customers happy) than on the field information and lead generation mechanism which the sales people have been calling for.

● The MAM is a senior sales person, pursuing a 'non-management' selling career. They have the respect of sales people and ASMs and are considered by the RSM as a key motivator within the region. They provide an example for all to follow.

The roles

Regional Sales Manager (RSM)

This is the main sales manager in this role play. The mood within the region has not been at its best for the past twelve months. As some of the more negative influences have been removed, there has been an enhanced level of motivation. On the whole, things are picking up and the level of sales is now increasing. The end of the financial year is only a month away. Although some sales force members have managed to hit target already, the majority will not do so and, therefore, the region will fall some way short of its target. The reasons for this have been accepted by the sales force manager but, at the last meeting of RSMs, he made it clear that under-performance would not be accepted during the coming year.

Your objectives at this sales meeting are to *'rally the troops', finish the year on a high and carry that level of motivation into the new financial year.* You have heard rumours that some sales people are planning on 'sandbagging' business in order to achieve a good start next year. You can understand this (indeed, you have been known to do it yourself in the past) but you have also learnt how it can provide a false sense of security and have a negative impact on the year as a whole. *You need to get this message across during the meeting.*

Sales figures for the region are up 5 per cent from last month but are still down 8 per cent on the same period last year and 12 per cent short of the target for the month. The year-to-date target for the region is 18 per cent down and the sales force members are generally disappointed with this performance. However, they have also been quick to point out the difficulties:

● The sales people leaving the company have not only been disruptive but many have gone to work for competitors and there has been the short-term 'stealing' of customers.

● Insufficient help has been provided, particularly by marketing support, but also by the wider marketing efforts of the company. Specifically, they feel that lead generation could be improved, customer information could be more readily available and a better corporate image should be portrayed.

● For some, it has taken time to become familiar with the full product range of the company. Although necessary, this has involved up to three, single day training courses which has led to less time with customers.

Additionally, some have claimed that it has taken them time to read up on product literature and become familiar with presenting/demonstrating the products.

The region's sales target for the new year represents a 2 per cent increase on last year. *You haven't decided whether to announce this during the meeting or leave it to be broken down to an individual level when you meet with everyone individually over the next three weeks.*

Area Sales Managers (ASMs)

There are three of you. You may be called to make a presentation on one of the following:

1 An announcement that the sales force will become fully computerised over the next twelve months. The full details are not yet available but, essentially, each sales person will have a laptop computer which will link up to the main one at head office. Initially, it will be used for point-of-sale purposes, with all product information being available for the sales person. The second half of the year will see the introduction of a customer database which will enable sales people to manage customer records and increase their efficiency and effectiveness. Some sales people will receive this news with caution; they may be 'technophobic', slow to accept change or fearful that there will be an increased administrative burden. *You need them to buy into the benefits and leave them motivated at the end of your presentation.*

2 An announcement that the main products in each category are to be 'badged' as the company's own brand. This will be supported by a centralised marketing campaign to introduce the brand name and develop a revitalised corporate image around this. *You are to promote this concept in a motivational environment.* However, news has leaked that one of these key manufacturers is planning on acquiring the company to create its own direct distribution channel. You have also heard these rumours but have been assured that the fact that three manufacturers are involved in supplying the 'badged' products, means there is no substance behind the rumour.

3 The major product training exercise of the past eleven months is at an end. During the coming year, any product changes will be advised by new product bulletins which will be transmitted in hard copy initially and then through the new computer system. Also, there will be more field training, with managers focusing their efforts on improving product presentations/demonstrations and the management of customer records. Again, this is consistent with the incoming computer system. Although there will be an increased focus on field training, *All* sales personnel will be required to attend a two-day, in-house training course to be trained in using the new system. *You are to present news of the field training programme over the next year, in a motivational environment.*

Marketing Support Manager (MSM)

Your role has been a difficult one over the past year as most of you and your teams' efforts have been spent reacting to customer demands. This has been brought on largely by the high turnover of staff, although the sales force has been blaming you for not producing more leads for them. You do not like appearing at these sales meetings as you often feel as though you are the scapegoat and spend most of your time on the defensive. The number of sales people leaving over the past couple of months has decreased and this stability has enabled you to release more capacity towards lead generation. This capacity will only allow for a limited internal service to be provided initially, but this should become more extensive as the months progress. The stages of internal service provision are as follows:

- *Immediately:* If sales people provide you with prospect information, you will send an appropriate mailing approach on their behalf. However, it will be their responsibility to follow up the mailing.
- *In three months:* You will have the capacity to provide a telemarketing follow-up to selected mailings. It is anticipated that sales people would prefer to follow up some of the mailings themselves.
- *In six months:* You will be able to gather some prospect information centrally and initiate a full mailing and telemarketing service. However, there will still be a requirement for sales people to gather prospect information locally.
- *In twelve months:* All prospect and customer information will be held on a central database and you will be able to access this information centrally to conduct mailings, update sales people and also to provide higher levels of customer service, as appropriate. This should also result in more business from existing customers, as well as making the prospecting efforts of sales people more efficient.

The RSM has encouraged you to be more positive during this presentation. The sales people must see that a clear effort is being made to help them and you should reinforce the benefits which will be derived from the computer system.

Major Accounts Manager (MAM)

Your selling expertise is respected by virtually all in the region. The RSM has asked you to tell one of your stories of success in the field. *You should focus on a selling tactic which you used and provide a moral to the story or a tip which can act to inspire the members of the meeting.*

Trainee sales person

You have just completed your monthly induction programme. This consisted of a two-week product, company and skills training course at head office, followed by two weeks shadowing your manager, during which time he introduced you to some customers in your territory, did some role plays with you, let you watch him prospecting/selling and spent some time discussing your targets and how you were going to achieve them. *The RSM has asked you to make a presentation to the meeting* (a ritual everyone has to go through, you were told!) *and discuss your experiences during the induction programme, your hopes and your fears for the future as you embark on your career with the company.*

Sales people

You may be attending the meeting purely in this capacity or you may be doubling up your role when other people are presenting. Either way, your participation has been implied throughout the briefing. You are to adopt the appropriate mood by asking relevant questions and making the right noises/statements, as required. Your active participation is crucial if this simulation is to be realistic.

Sources of information for the sales and marketing professional

Professional institutes and associations

The Institute of Sales & Marketing Management
Romeland House, Romeland Hill, St Albans AL3 4ET

Tel: 01727 812500

The Chartered Institute of Marketing
Moor Hall, Cookham, Maidenhead SL6 9QH

Tel: 01628 524922

The Institute of Direct Marketing
1 Park Road, Teddington, Middlesex TW11 0AR

Tel: 0181 977 5705

Direct Selling Association
29 Floral Street, London WC2E 9DP

Tel: 0171 497 1234

Institute of Sales Promotion
Arena House, 66/68 Pentonville Road, London N1 9HS

Tel: 0171 837 5340

Institute of Management
Cottingham Road, Corby, Northants NN17 1TT

Tel: 01536 204222

Institute of Public Relations
The Old Trading House, 15 Northburgh Street, London EC1V 0PR

Tel: 0171 253 5151

Prospect information (domestic consumer)

ACORN
CACI Ltd., London

Tel: 0171 602 6000

DEFINE
Infolink Decision Services Ltd., Croydon

Tel: 0181 686 7777

MOSAIC
CCN Group Ltd., Nottingham

Tel: 0115 934 4944

SUPERPROFILES
CDMS Marketing Services, London

Tel: 0171 495 4185

BEHAVIOURBANK
CMT Data Corporation Ltd., Teddington

Tel: 0181 977 8737

LIFESTYLE SURVEYS
ICD Marketing Services, London

Tel: 0171 251 2883

THE LIST REGISTER
London

Tel: 0171 407 5987

Prospect information (commercial business)

BUSINESS ACCUMIN
Dunn Humby Associates, London

Tel: 0181 994 2780

BUSINESS PROFILING
CCN Marketing, Nottingham

Tel: 0115 941 0888

SPICE
Mardev Ltd., London

Tel: 0171 411 2687

TDS
TDS Marketing Service Centre, High Wycombe

Tel: 01494 474647

THE LIST REGISTER
London

Tel: 0171 407 5987

THE BUSINESS DATABASE
Slough

Tel: 01753 583311

Government statistics

Central Statistical Office
Great George Street, London SW1P 3AQ

Tel: 0171 270 6363

Central Statistical Office Library
Government Buildings, Cardiff Road, Newport NP9 1XG

Tel: 01633 812973

Office of Population Censuses and Surveys
St. Catherine's House, 10 Kingsway, London WC2B 6JP

Tel: 0171 396 2208

Market reports

Economist Intelligence Unit
15 Regent Street, London W1A 1DW

Tel: 0171 830 1000

Euromonitor
87/88 Turnmill Street, London EC1M 5QU

Tel: 0171 251 8024

Key Note
72 Oldfield Road, Hampton, Middlesex TW12 2HQ

Tel: 0181 783 0755

Mintel International
18/19 Long Lane, London EC1A 9HE

Tel: 0171 606 4533

Annual publications of business information

Kompas – UK Directory
Kompas – Separate Directories for European Countries
Croner's Reference Book for Exporters
Hambro's Guide to Company Information
Kelly's Manufacturing and Merchants Year Book
Sales & Marketing Software Handbook
Stock Exchange Official Yearbook

Index